ASEAN
Economic Co-operation

Published by
Institute of Southeast Asian Studies
Heng Mui Keng Terrace
Pasir Panjang Road
Singapore 119596

Internet e-mail: publish@iseas.ac.sg
World Wide Web: http://www.iseas.ac.sg/pub.html

Cataloguing in Publication Data

ASEAN economic co-operation : transition and transformation / ASEAN Secretariat
1. ASEAN.
2. ASEAN countries--Economic integration.
3. ASEAN countries--Economic conditions.
4. ASEAN countries--Commerce.
5. ASEAN countries--Foreign economic relations.
I. ASEAN Secretariat.
HC441 A842 1997 sls96-98166

ISBN 981-3055-55-3

Typeset by International Typesetters Pte Ltd
Printed in Singapore by Chong Moh Offset Printing Pte Ltd

Foreword

The ASEAN Declaration of 8 August 1967 states that one of the aims of ASEAN is to accelerate economic growth in the region through joint endeavours in the spirit of equality and partnership in order to strengthen the foundation for a prosperous and peaceful community of Southeast Asian nations. In pursuit of that objective, ASEAN has over the years implemented various economic co-operation schemes.

While the progress of economic co-operation in ASEAN might have been slow in the early years of the Association's existence, the pace of such co-operation has significantly accelerated in the last few years. The turning point in ASEAN economic co-operation came at the Fourth ASEAN Summit in Singapore, 27–28 January 1992 when the Framework Agreement on Enhancing ASEAN Economic Co-operation was adopted. The most important initiative implemented within the Framework Agreement was the ASEAN Free Trade Area (AFTA).

Economic co-operation in ASEAN received a further boost in 1995 at the Fifth ASEAN Summit in Bangkok, 14–15 December 1995, when the Bangkok Declaration outlined an agenda for greater economic integration. This agenda is likely to generate further initiatives in new areas of ASEAN economic co-operation, specifically in services and investment.

Since the early years of ASEAN economic co-operation, which saw the implementation of the ASEAN Preferential Trading Arrangement and the Food Security Reserve for ASEAN in the late 1970s, economic co-operation in ASEAN has not only widened but also deepened. In an effort to take stock of ASEAN's progress in such co-operation, the ASEAN Secretariat has prepared this publication to put into perspective ASEAN's major achievements in various sectors of economic co-operation.

These achievements are a tribute to the founding fathers of ASEAN whose vision of a prosperous and peaceful community of Southeast Asian nations is now being realized through joint endeavours in various economic co-operation schemes. It is also a tribute to the present and all the past ASEAN economic ministers and senior economic officials who have spent countless hours charting the course of ASEAN economic co-operation.

Finally, the ASEAN Secretariat is pleased to acknowledge the assistance of Professor Florian Alburo in preparing this study and the United Nations Development Programme (UNDP) for funding this publication.

Dato' Ajit Singh
Secretary-General
Association of Southeast Asian Nations

Contents

List of Tables

List of Figures

1

Genesis and Growth of Economic Co-operation

I. Introduction

This chapter traces the evolution of economic co-operation among economies of the Association of Southeast Asian Nations (ASEAN) since the organization started more than twenty-five years ago. Economic co-operation grew from earlier co-operation arrangements with varying rationale, composition, and instrumentalities although there was already recognition of the mutual benefits from co-operation.

In the next section, ASEAN economies are described, using narrow macroeconomic and trade indicators that allow comparison among them. Specifically, a description of the environment under which co-operation grew and expanded over the years is discussed. A picture of the region would undoubtedly best describe the setting for common activities that were eventually pursued.

Section III gives details on the formation and organization of ASEAN from a variety of initiatives. This is not a digression into a historical account of many co-operation attempts from among ASEAN members and non-members but an argument to show that previous foundations (for example, political, social, security) were part of the fabric that fashioned ASEAN economic co-operation. The road to the region's organization has had many fits and starts. In the end, however, the lessons learned from previous arrangements proved invaluable in framing ASEAN's co-operation agenda.

Section IV focuses on the mechanisms for ASEAN economic co-operation. The evolution of the organizational hierarchy is explained from the First to the Fifth Summit. The evolution of the ASEAN Secretariat is likewise explained since, though inter-governmental, it dictated the pace of ASEAN economic co-operation activities. The increasing role of the ASEAN Secretariat, especially in the area of economic co-operation, takes cognizance of the parallel organizational changes at the senior official level. The section ends with an elaboration of the ASEAN Secretariat's specific functions in economic co-operation.

II. The ASEAN Economies

The countries that banded together in contemporary Asian history spanned from New Zealand to the Republic of Korea, from Thailand to Pakistan, though only the ASEAN grouping metamorphosed in substance and character in the last twenty-five years. From an original membership of five states, it expanded to seven in 1995 and is likely to increase to ten before the end of the century. From a plethora of *ad hoc* co-operation activities, it took bolder steps towards a more cohesive co-operation framework. From separate and individualized markets, it now plots a direction towards one single market.

The essence of ASEAN, however, in terms of its potential, lies within the member states that compose it. Its regional strength takes root in the economic strength of its members and its unbounded synergy (actual and potential) comes from the fundamental structure of each one.

Many areas of concern occupy the attention of ASEAN — political, social, and economic, among others. Still, the national political

BOX 1.1: ORIGINS OF ASEAN

As early as 1959, Malayan Prime Minister Tunku Abdul Rahman proposed the launching of an Association of Southeast Asia (ASA) which, apart from Maphilindo, was a predecessor of ASEAN. The Association had a brief life because of territorial and political disputes between member countries. Despite the common interest among ASEAN countries to contain the influence of communism, ASEAN was not set up primarily as a political-military alliance and therefore could not concretize co-operation in this field. Subsequent events made the founding of ASEAN almost prophetic. In July 1969, President Nixon proposed the withdrawal of U.S. military presence in Asia. This was simultaneous to the Soviet Union's suggestion to "set up a system of collective security in Asia" and the British Government's announcement of its military withdrawal east of the Suez Canal.

leadership of member countries may be concerned with other equally pressing problems, for example, poverty, urban agglomeration, the environment, and so forth. As important as these are to individual countries, however, for ASEAN as a region, macroeconomic and trade concerns appear to be the more critical issues. Thus, the members' underlying macroeconomic conditions and trade performance are what eventually sustain in ASEAN economic co-operation schemes.

Table 1.1 shows some basic data for the ASEAN economies. They depict the wide variation in physical size, population, and per capita gross national product (GNP) among these countries. In terms of purchasing-power-parity per capita gross domestic product (GDP), however, the variation diminishes. The data in Appendix A, which provide a larger array of information on individual ASEAN economic structures, suggest that most of the ASEAN countries are at the same level of development, produce the same product groups, and trade in the same industry categories.

Two aggregate indicators summarize the macroeconomic profile of ASEAN economies. Figure 1.1 traces the growth rate of real GDP in the last five years and the averages for the decade of the 1970s and 1980s. Notice that the average growth rate for four of the seven ASEAN countries was about the same (with a lower average for the Philippines). This is partly explained by the common external environment of ASEAN economies. These averages diverged in the 1980s and,

Table 1.1
Basic Data on ASEAN

Country	Area (sq. km.)	Population, 1993 (thousand)	Per Capita GNP, 1993 (US$)	Real GDP per Capita, 1992 (PPP US$)
Brunei	5,776	300	n.a.	20,589
Indonesia	1,906,240	187,200	732	2,950
Malaysia	332,456	19,000	3,156	7,790
Philippines	300,440	65,800	830	2,550
Singapore	618	2,900	19,314	18,330
Thailand	514,820	58,800	2,044	5,950
Vietnam	332,000	71,000	170	n.a.
ASEAN	3,392,350	405,000	26,246	58,159
Weighted average			1,086.92	3,824.05

Note: (a) Weighted average for per capita GNP does not include that of Brunei; (b) weighted average for real GDP per capita does not include that of Vietnam. n.a. = Not available.

Source: *Human Development Report, 1995*; *1995 Report on the APEC Regional Economy*.

since 1992, recovery is apparent for the seven countries except Brunei. Since then, the growth rates levelled off to what they were in the 1970s, with Singapore, Thailand, and Malaysia registering growth rates above their previous averages and, Indonesia, below. Notice, finally, that all members experienced similar swings (peaks and troughs) throughout the twenty-five years although the degree varies by country. For example, the Philippines had comparable swings but the net result was lower absolute average growth levels.

Figure 1.2 shows the inflation rates of the ASEAN countries for the same period. The averages for the 1970s and the 1980s vary across the five countries with Malaysia achieving the lowest, and Indonesia, the highest. Since the 1980s, average inflation rates went down relative to the 1970s and this seemed to hold through the 1990s. ASEAN countries likewise had comparable swings in their inflation rates. Figures 1.1 and 1.2 show the high growth rates of real GDP (with low inflation rates) exhibited by Singapore, Malaysia, and Thailand. On the other hand, the Philippines' low growth rates are associated with high inflation rates for the period. There are macroeconomic fundamentals

Figure 1.1
GDP Growth Rates of ASEAN Countries, 1988–94
(Percentages)

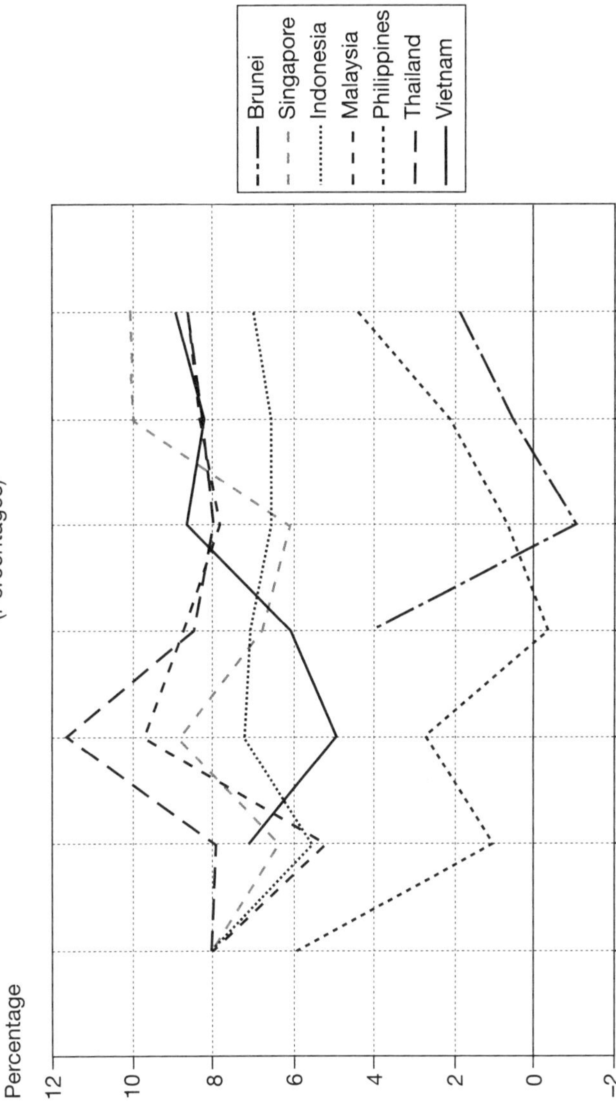

Note: Data for Brunei prior to 1991 are not available; data for Vietnam for the period 1971–80 are not available.
Source: Asian Development Bank and *1995 Report on the APEC Regional Economy.*

Figure 1.2
CPI of ASEAN Countries, 1988–94
(Percentages)

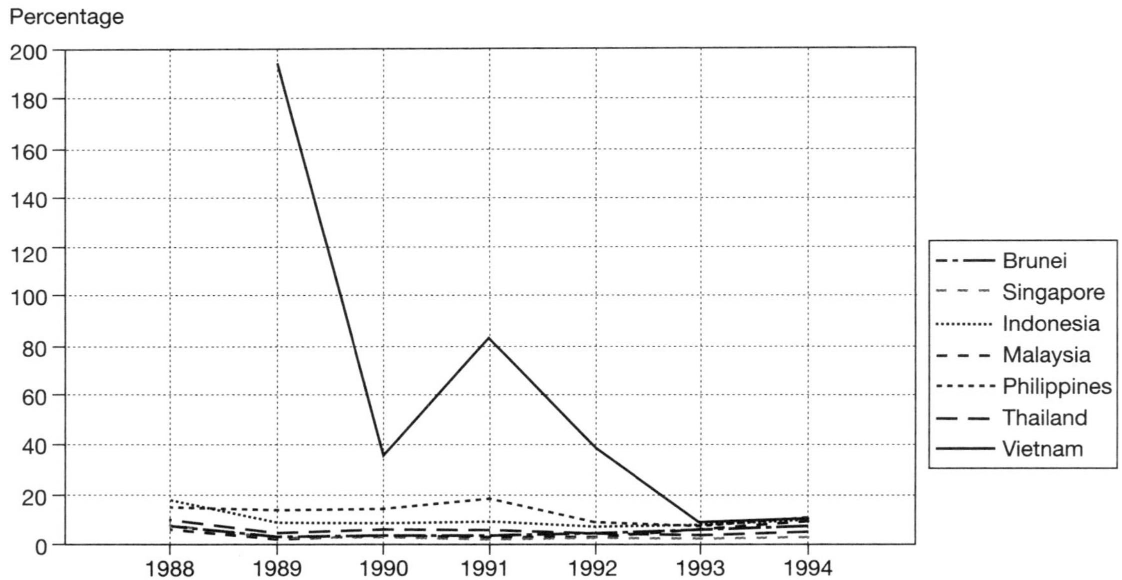

Note: Data for Brunei prior to 1990 are not available; data for Vietnam for the period 1971–80 are not available.
Source: Asian Development Bank and *1995 Report on the APEC Regional Economy*.

that lie behind these and they are national in character.

The aggregate profiles and performances of ASEAN countries are fairly respectable relative to other developing countries and regions. In fact, they are often considered spectacular. The inflation rates in ASEAN have not been unusually high, are quite stable, and reflect responsible economic management.

Of particular interest to ASEAN in the area of economic co-operation is industrial development. Figure 1.3 shows the share of industry in the GDP of the six ASEAN countries between 1970 and 1995 (projected). The average for the 1990s is almost 40 per cent, confirming a significant development of industries in the region. Over a span of twenty-five years, more notable shifts in the share of industry value-added can be seen in Indonesia and Thailand.

The second aggregate area of importance to ASEAN is its trade pattern. Table 1.2 shows the total trade ratios for ASEAN countries. Not only were these ratios consistently increasing but their magnitudes indicate that ASEAN economies are open. ASEAN's structure of exports shows an increasing amount in manufactures, although within them, there are differences among member countries.

Aggregate merchandise exports of ASEAN grew faster than the region's average growth of output, thus it is expected that the importance of trade will continue to increase over time. Figure 1.4 shows total ASEAN merchandise exports between 1988 and 1994 — from about US$100 billion to over US$200 billion. Although a major portion of export revenue is accounted for by Singapore, the gap of other ASEAN countries' exports narrowed considerably. For instance, Malaysia's exports in 1980 were 52 per cent of Singapore's exports. In 1994 this went up to 64 per cent. A similar pattern is evident for Thailand.

In a narrow sense, what matters is the share of ASEAN exports to ASEAN itself that, until the late 1980s, did not reach 10 per cent. However, more recent evidence indicates that, with the onset of the Common Effective Preferential Tariff (CEPT) scheme, the ratio may be rising rapidly. Viewed in a broader sense, the absolute value of intra-ASEAN trade similarly expanded at rates faster than domestic output growth. This supports the notion that ASEAN is further liberalizing.

Figure 1.3
ASEAN* Share in Value-Added in Industry, 1970–95
(Percentages)

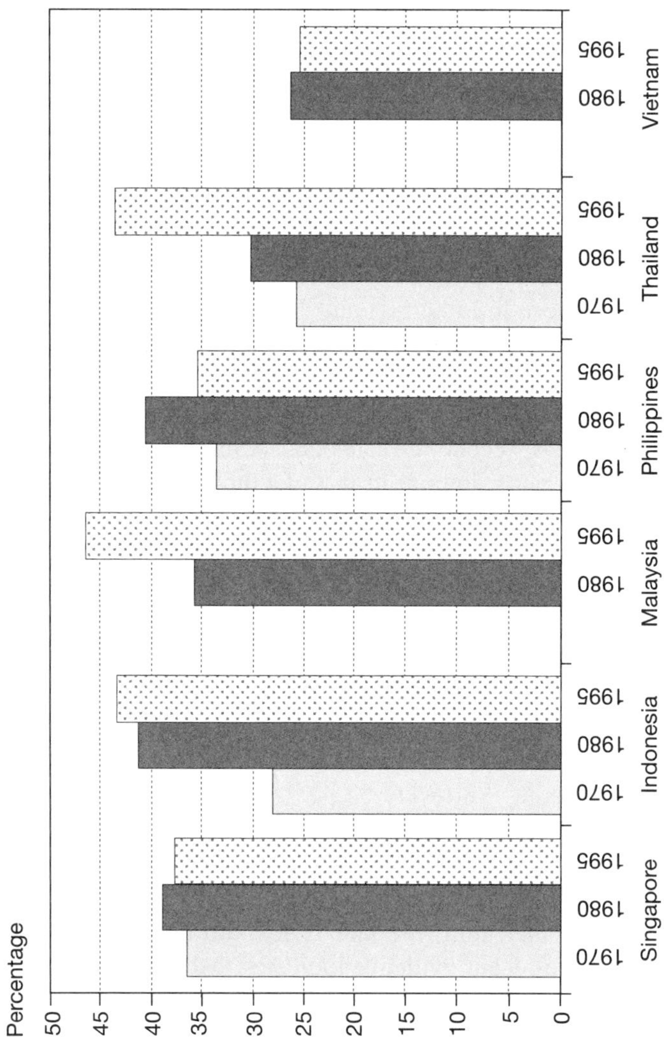

* Excluding Brunei.
Note: 1970 values for Malaysia and Vietnam are not available.
Source: Asian Development Bank.

Table 1.2
Trade Ratios[a] for ASEAN,[b] 1965–94

Country	1965	1970	1975	1980	1985	1990	1994
Indonesia	0.11	0.25	0.41	0.50	0.32	0.55[c]	0.43
Malaysia	0.96	0.74	0.87	0.86	0.93	1.43	1.73
Philippines	0.30	0.33	0.37	0.38	0.32	0.55	0.54
Singapore	2.20[d]	1.95	2.31	3.66	2.39	2.90	2.79
Thailand	0.32	0.31	0.37	0.45	0.41	0.61	0.81
Vietnam	0.12	n.a.	n.a.	n.a.	0.48	0.42	0.50[e]

[a] The sum of merchandise exports (f.o.b.) and merchandise imports (c.i.f.) as a ratio of GNP (all in current U.S. dollars).
[b] Except Brunei.
[c] The GNP is that of 1989.
[d] As a ratio of GDP.
[e] The figure is for 1993.
n.a. = Not available.

Source: Asian Development Bank, *Key Indicators of Developing Member Countries* (various issues).

The other side of the trade transaction is equally important. Merchandise imports do not only measure some other countries' exports but their increasing values imply a more direct form of outward orientation that is not mercantilist. In fact, one distinction of ASEAN from some newly industrializing economies (NIEs) is the matching expansion of imports with exports. Figure 1.5 shows the amount of ASEAN's merchandise imports from 1988 to 1994. The value of imports increased from close to US$100 billion in 1988 to US$250 billion in 1994 or 2.5 times within six years. In recent years, import penetration in ASEAN grew faster than overall growth and even faster than merchandise exports.

Comparison between Figures 1.4 and 1.5 reveals that ASEAN has had a negative trade balance with the rest of the world. This negative trade balance holds true within ASEAN itself although there are differences in the magnitude of trade imbalances of each member. This implies that vigorous exchange of goods are taking place within ASEAN.

Foreign trade is important to ASEAN both as a "vent for surplus" and as a "source of need". It does not indicate an inclination for trade

Figure 1.4
ASEAN* Merchandise Exports, 1988–94
(US$ million)

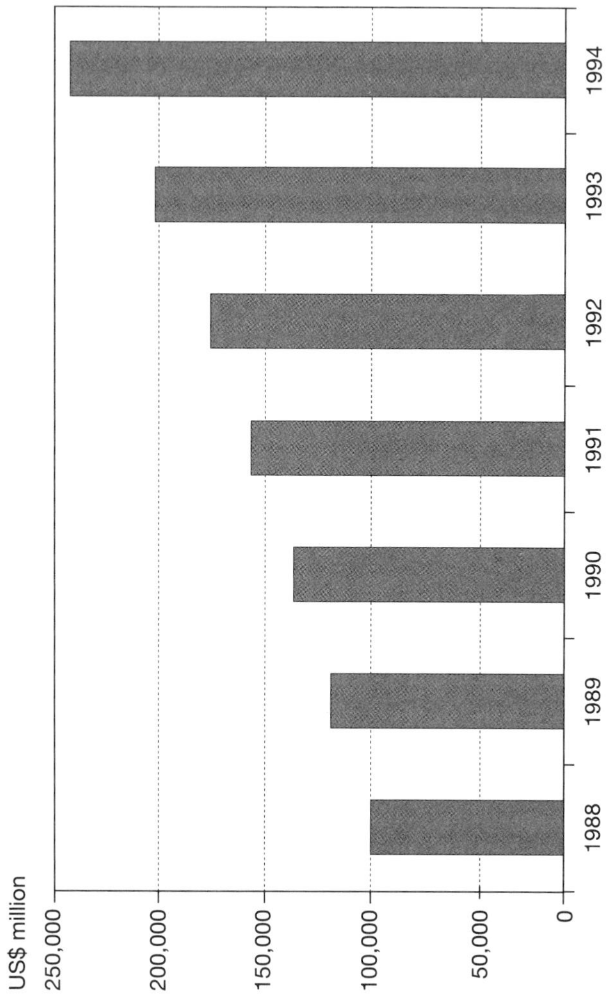

* Excluding Brunei.
Source: Asian Development Bank.

Figure 1.5
ASEAN* Merchandise Imports, 1988–94
(US$ million)

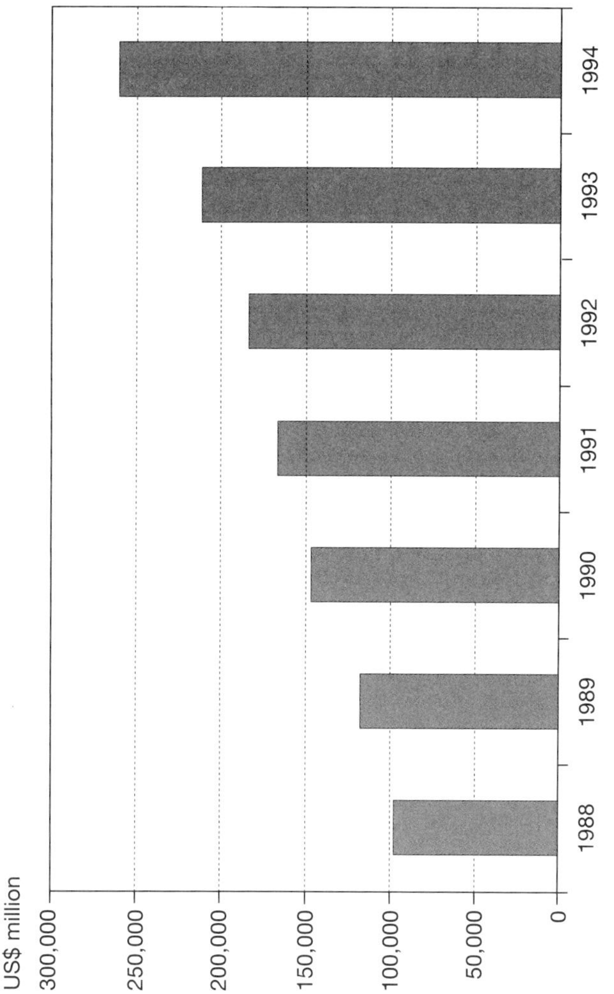

* Excluding Brunei.
Source: Asian Development Bank.

accumulation or neo-mercantilism. Indeed, trade seems to be a venue for mutual exchange of goods, a means for structural transformation and improvement of the overall well-being of the region even if trade patterns differ between countries across time (that is, for some countries, exports may exceed imports and vice versa for others).

The macroeconomic and trade sectors are ASEAN's windows to the global economy. Sustained macroeconomic performance in the long haul among ASEAN countries (with some short-run disturbances) reflects strong underlying economic fundamentals. These facilitated ASEAN's continued interdependence with the rest of the world, and within ASEAN, greater interdependence among member countries. In particular, the healthy and robust economies of ASEAN freed member countries from macroeconomic constraints in pursuing trade policies. A 6.8 per cent average GDP growth rate for ASEAN in 1994 is not only healthy but sufficiently robust to benefit from external relations.

A relatively low and stable inflation regime in ASEAN, compared with other developing countries' regimes (and even some developed economies), supports regional trade. High inflation rates quickly erode a country's competitiveness in international markets, distort domestic resource allocation, and necessitate further macroeconomic adjustments. The ability of individual members to contain inflation and achieve sustained economic growth are important parameters to promote economic co-operation, and increase trade among each other and with its global partners.

As a group committed to enhancing free trade among themselves, the two factors mentioned above are what makes ASEAN's economic performance admirable. The internal market of the region is larger than the European Union and is estimated at over 405 million, representing 7.4 per cent of the world's population. Figure 1.6 shows the 1994 mid-year population of the ASEAN countries. More than half is accounted for by Indonesia, followed by Vietnam, the Philippines, Thailand, Malaysia, Singapore, and Brunei, in that order. With the wide variance in population density among ASEAN countries (that is, with Indonesia having the largest population base, and Brunei and Singapore, the smallest), the market is expectedly uneven. Yet when one takes into account the amount of per capita income (that is, GNP), an

Figure 1.6
1994 Mid-Year Population of ASEAN Countries
(Million)

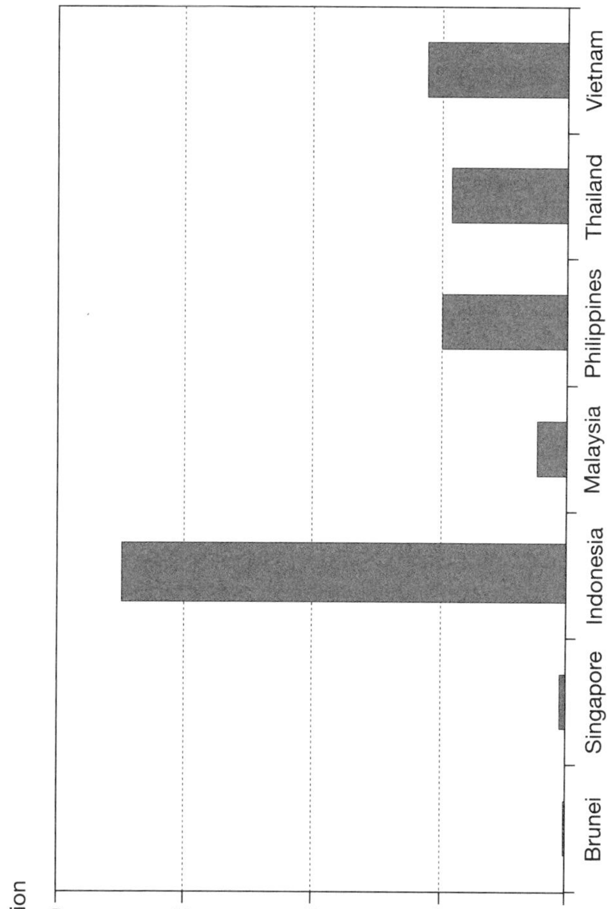

Note: The 1993 figure was used for Brunei.
Source: Asian Development Bank and *1995 Report on the APEC Regional Economy*.

inverse relationship exists among these economies. This implies that markets for manufactures may naturally be segregated. On the other hand, the potential may be large given the dynamic growth of the region.

Though trade expansion and stable inflation regimes are not the only aggregate factors that matter to ASEAN, in economic terms they appear to be crucial to attain a whole market. These also suggest a role for economic co-operation in terms of exploring regional market potentials and mapping out collective policies that best attain ASEAN goals. Other dimensions that bear on a regional market include relative incentives, priority sectors, taxation, and so forth. One way of examining these is to construct comparative tables across ASEAN. This is now possible with the use of a common menu-driven data base available on the Internet (see Box 1.2).

BOX 1.2: ASEAN ESTABLISHES THE ASEANWEB

The ASEANWEB was launched at the Fifth Summit in Bangkok held in December 1995. The principal objective of the ASEANWEB is to disseminate information on ASEAN as a region, general information on each ASEAN member country, and trade and investment information useful to the business community and the general public.

The ASEANWEB is an Internet-based information system with two components, namely, the ASEAN Secretariat HomePage and the HomePage of each ASEAN member country. The ASEAN Secretariat HomePage carries general information on the history and background of the Association, economic and political co-operation activities, and a summary of investment/industrial policies, trade opportunities, statistics, and business directories of each member country.

Detailed country information can be found in the HomePage of each member country that is linked to the ASEAN Secretariat HomePage. The information contained in the member countries' HomePage includes policies (for example, investment/industry/trade, incentives/taxation); trade and investment opportunities (for example, priority industries/sectors, trade fairs/exhibitions/conventions/seminars); statistics (for example, demographic, economic/social indicators, intra- and extra-ASEAN trade, and investment flows); and directories (for example, industries/sectors, government organizational structure, other WEB sites).

Users will be able to access the ASEANWEB at "WWW.ASEAN.OR.ID".

III. The Formation and Organization of ASEAN

Regional co-operation among ASEAN countries went through three tumultuous stages since 1945.[1] The first phase, which lasted from the end of World War II till the mid-1950s, was mainly dominated by the ideology prevailing in both the United States and Britain on the nature and type of regional association for Southeast Asia. Within the region, political realities and traditional colonial ties constrained the organization of an integrated Asia. Malaya, the Borneo territories, and Singapore were still British colonies while Laos and Cambodia until 1954 remained under the leadership of France. Meanwhile, the Philippines and Thailand looked towards the United States rather than to Southeast Asia while Burma sought guidance from India and even Britain. Indonesia, on the other hand, seemed uninvolved in the region. Not surprisingly, this was the setting that saw the formation of the Economic Commission for Asia and the Far East (ECAFE) and the Colombo Plan, which were both largely dependent upon the two superpowers.

In a Manila conference in September 1954, the Southeast Asia Treaty Organization (SEATO) was formally launched with the influence of the United States.[2] In the conference, participating nations such as Britain, France, Australia, New Zealand, Pakistan, the Philippines, and Thailand signed the Southeast Asia Collective Defense Treaty (the Manila Treaty). Though only the Philippines, Thailand, and Pakistan were signatories to the treaty, "the general area of Southeast Asia" was designated as the "treaty area" and separate protocol extended the provisions to include Indochina. The treaty called for collective action in the event of an armed attack on any Southeast Asian country. Subsequent events, however, made it clear that the United States took the Manila Treaty to mean providing collective defence only against communist aggression. In the end, SEATO proved to be more of an anti-communist military alliance than a true regional organization. It eventually lost ground amidst lack of commitment from member countries and increasing criticisms by the Soviet Union, other communist countries, and many non-communist Southeast Asian countries that were not signatories to the treaty.

After SEATO, various attempts to institutionalize co-operation among Southeast Asian countries took many forms. ECAFE and the Colombo Plan, for example, continued till the mid-1960s. Others included the launching of the Association of Southeast Asia (ASA), the Asian and Pacific Council (ASPAC), and Maphilindo. Though all three did not evolve into significant regional organizations, other regional organizations established during this period lent credence to co-operation in Southeast Asia. These are the Asian Development Bank (ADB), Asian Institute for Economic Development and Planning (AIEDP), Asian Industrial Development Council (AIDC), and the Asian Institute of Technology (AIT).

The second phase was heralded by the launching of the Association of Southeast Asia in 1961 at the proposal of Malayan Prime Minister Tunku Abdul Rahman.[3] The association had a brief life owing to the dispute between the newly formed Federation of Malaysia (that included Malaya, Sarawak, and Sabah) and the Philippines, that by virtue of its long-standing claim to Sabah, refused to recognize the enlarged federation. Two years later, in 1963, Malaya, the Philippines, and Indonesia formed another association called "Maphilindo". A month after its establishment, the formation of an enlarged Federation of Malaysia also caused a rift among members, with both the Philippines and Indonesia refusing to recognize the federation. Soon afterwards, Indonesian President Soekarno launched a guerrilla war against Malaysia that lasted until 1967. This proved to be one of the most serious barriers to regional co-operation.

In 1966, South Korean President Park Chung-Hee organized the Asian and Pacific Council. Designed to be a multi-regional organization for non-communist nations of the Western Pacific, its main purpose was to organize "free countries in the region to form a 'second front' for U.S. military action in Vietnam".[4] Implicitly, it also aimed to assist member countries, namely, Malaysia, New Zealand, Japan, Australia, Taiwan, the Philippines, South Korea, Thailand, and South Vietnam, deal with external aggression and to provide a framework for future co-operation efforts.

Political developments in the late 1960s, including the preoccupation with securing national borders against communism and the desire to contain the rise of communist influence internally, led countries such as Malaysia, the Philippines, and Thailand to maintain their membership in the ASA and ASPAC. Singapore and Indonesia, on the other hand, proclaimed a non-aligned foreign policy (see Box 1.1). The wide range of ideologies held by members that, at the outset, should have been resolved, was reflected in the desire of members to make ASPAC "non-military, non-ideological, and not anti-communist". This despite a common pronouncement of their "determination to preserve their integrity and sovereignty in the face of external threats". All told, with the end of the Vietnam War in sight and as Japan, the United States, and other non-communist nations began to normalize ties with the People's Republic of China, ASPAC went into oblivion and was dissolved in 1973.

In August 1967, the inception of ASEAN marked the third phase of institutional co-operation among Southeast Asian countries. The Vietnam War and the U.S involvement in it and the "Great Proletarian Cultural Revolution in China" was the backdrop of the founding of ASEAN. Before ASEAN was formally launched, however, Japan initiated the formation of the Ministerial Conference for Economic Development in Southeast Asia (MCEDSEA) and gave strong support to the ADB and the Southeast Asian Ministers of Education Organization (SEAMEO).[5]

The Bangkok Declaration specified that ASEAN's objective is to

> accelerate the economic growth, social progress and cultural development in the region through joint endeavour and partnership to strengthen the foundation for a prosperous and equal community of Southeast Asian nations.[6]

Conceived as a collective venue for action by senior government and political leaders, it also envisioned ASEAN as a forum for private business and community-level interactions. Though the Declaration hinted at co-operative efforts at the regional level, the majority of the aims in the Declaration were related to the development needs of founding members. Moreover, despite the belief that regional co-operation would contribute to the economic growth of their respective economies, members stopped short of committing to full economic integration. The same level of reservation applied to military issues as ASEAN was not conceived as a military alliance.

Shortly after the formation of ASEAN, various issues related to national sovereignty and integrity of individual countries had to be dealt with before any significant strides in intra-regional co-operation could be achieved. In its first nine years, progress in co-operative endeavours, both for promoting intra-ASEAN trade and industrial co-operation, was slow and halted by many political tensions among member countries. The squabble of the Philippines and Malaysia over Sabah resurfaced while Indonesia and Singapore were at odds over the execution of two Indonesian marines in Singapore. These tensions dampened economic relations between ASEAN countries. From 1970 to 1975, intra-ASEAN trade, as a percentage of total ASEAN trade, actually declined from 15.5 to 12.6 per cent. As a proportion of total foreign trade of each of the five member countries, intra-ASEAN trade was hardly significant.[7]

To its credit, nonetheless, ASEAN since the early 1970s had instituted a system of bilateral relations with developed countries, collectively called as "dialogue partners". The system covered a wide range of issues that not only strengthened the bargaining position of all members *vis-à-vis* other regional players but also enhanced the organization's clout and prestige among non-ASEAN countries. In 1972, a Special Co-ordination Committee for ASEAN Nations (SCCAN) was organized to negotiate with the European Community (EC).[8] Shortly thereafter, the ASEAN-Geneva Committee was formed. Both strengthened ASEAN's position at the Multilateral Trade Negotiations under the General Agreement on Tariffs and Trade (GATT). Succeeding efforts proved fruitful in obtaining favourable terms with Japan on synthetic rubber, and with Australia on the provision of economic assistance to ASEAN.

By the end of 1968, ASEAN was well on its way to instituting regional co-operative efforts. Various committees on food production and supply, civil air transport, air traffic services, shipping, meteorology, and commerce and industry were set up and a seven-day no-visa scheme for ASEAN nationals was put in place. In the 1971 Manila conference of ASEAN foreign ministers, an ASEAN common market and a payment union for economic co-operation were proposed. Soon afterwards, an agreement in principle was made to include the promotion of peace and security within the region. One defence arrangement was the formation of ANZUK, composed of Australia, Malaysia, New Zealand, Singapore, and the United Kingdom. Another was the maintenance of U.S. military bases in the Philippines and Thailand. Meanwhile, Indonesia continued to receive military aid from the United States. By April 1973, at the sixth ASEAN Foreign Ministers Meeting held at Pattaya, Thailand, the range and scope of issues and the arrangements formed reached new heights of regional co-operation.

While political co-operation was not an expressed goal in the Bangkok Declaration, indications of such efforts were apparent at the *ad hoc* or ministerial level. In an *ad hoc* meeting in Kuala Lumpur, for example, ASEAN foreign ministers called for the establishment of a Zone of Peace, Freedom, and Neutrality in Southeast Asia (ZOPFAN). This was the modified version of a Malaysian proposal to ensure the neutrality of Southeast Asia as guaranteed by the United States, Russia, and China. In a later version, the guarantors were called upon to recognize and respect the ZOPFAN arrangement for Southeast Asia. Subsequent informal ministerial meetings held in July 1972 and February 1973 discussed the possible settlement of the Indochinese conflict and the implications of the Paris Peace Treaty on Southeast Asia. These efforts signal the readiness of ASEAN as a regional organization to tackle peace and security issues that can evolve into political arrangements.

The results of the 1976 Bali Summit reflected the determination of member countries to project ASEAN as a purposeful group intent on fostering regional co-operation. Three important documents were signed in the Summit, namely, the Treaty of Amity and Co-operation in Southeast Asia, the Declaration of ASEAN Concord, and the Agreement for the Establishment of the ASEAN Secretariat. These documents established the framework for ASEAN co-operation and interstate relations, foundations that were to guide intra-ASEAN activities henceforth. More specific areas of co-operative efforts were delineated and, for the first time, political co-operation was expressly recognized as an ASEAN objective. Of interest is the provision in the Treaty that exhorts member countries "to maintain regular contacts and consultations with one another on international and regional matters to co-ordinate views, actions and policies". Moreover, to settle disputes, parties were encouraged to resort to mechanisms provided by the Treaty and to refrain from threat or use of force. The Declaration of ASEAN Concord lends further support to ASEAN as a political organization by exhorting member states to improve the ASEAN machinery and use it to "promote the harmonization of views, co-ordinate positions and whenever possible, take common actions".

By the late 1980s, developments among ASEAN's neighbourhood posed even greater challenges to the ability of ASEAN as an organization. Of particular interest to ASEAN is the perceived strategic importance of the Asia-Pacific region and the interplay of political interests in the region. Moreover, the Kampuchean conflict and the increased involvement of the Soviet Union and other Eastern European countries in the global economy were poignant issues. On the economic front, ASEAN faced a combination of indicative and conflicting realities. China's four modernization programmes, Japan's rise as a financial superpower, and the unrivalled success of the NIEs, namely, Singapore, Taiwan, Korea, and Hong Kong, were set against the recession in most developed countries. On the other hand, many developing countries were hard hit by rising trade imbalances, low commodity prices for exports, and international debt problems. These made it imperative for ASEAN to review its co-operative mechanisms and replot its economic, political, and social action agenda to ensure more effective ASEAN collaboration.

There is a consensus that the survival of ASEAN as a cohesive working organization depends in large part on member countries' greater understanding of ASEAN ideals, a stronger sense of belonging and identifying with the goals and objectives of ASEAN, and wider participation of ASEAN nationals in ASEAN affairs. Using regional resources, both physical and human, for example, can translate into collaborative efforts to develop a stream of industries that increase the market share of ASEAN and benefit individual ASEAN countries. Complementary measures also include enhancing markets and promoting market openness.

In the January 1992 Fourth ASEAN Summit meeting in Singapore, member countries, faced with the emergence of stronger integrated trading blocs, such as the EC and the North American Free Trade Agreement (NAFTA), supported the establishment of an ASEAN Free Trade Area (AFTA). A few months earlier, ASEAN economic ministers laid the groundwork for the free trade area concept by putting the CEPT scheme in place.

A structured reorganization of the ASEAN Secretariat in recent years strengthened and upgraded the capabilities, authority, and stature of ASEAN as a truly representative regional organization. At the helm of ASEAN's five economic committees is an inter-governmental group, the Senior Economic Officials Meeting (SEOM), which supervises ASEAN's five economic committees. Support and recognition from member countries also allowed the Secretariat, now headed by the Secretary-General, to move swiftly in co-ordinating policy decisions and implementing programme agendas.

Finally, as ASEAN approaches the twenty-first century, the challenge remains for it to evolve into an organization that can develop a legal framework to support intra-regional and extra-ASEAN relations to include economic, political, social, cultural, and technological exchanges among member countries. Though it must continually adapt to the stream of regional and international influences that impinge on it, it is unlikely that the founding principles recognized in the 1967 Declaration will be set aside.

IV. Mechanisms for ASEAN Co-operation

The formal creation of ASEAN ushered in concrete institutional mechanisms for co-operation in fields ranging from culture to science, industry, and agriculture.

Figure 1.7 is the structure of ASEAN depicting the "ASEAN Declaration" made at the First ASEAN Ministerial Meeting in 1967 in Bangkok. The figure incorporates most of the changes that took place between the 1967 meeting and the Bali Summit of 1977. The annual Foreign Ministers Meeting is the highest decision-making body. The work of ASEAN, however, rests on the Standing Committee, chaired by the host country foreign minister and with resident ASEAN ambassadors as members. The Standing Committee meets several times a year to deliberate on matters acted upon at the Annual Meeting, the venue of which rotates among ASEAN capitals, while the Standing Committee supervises special and *ad hoc* committees (nine of these are shown in Figure 1.7). Three special committees (that is, Co-ordinating Committee of ASEAN Nations, ASEAN-Brussels Committees, and

Figure 1.7
Organizational Structure of ASEAN Before the Bali Summit (February 1976)

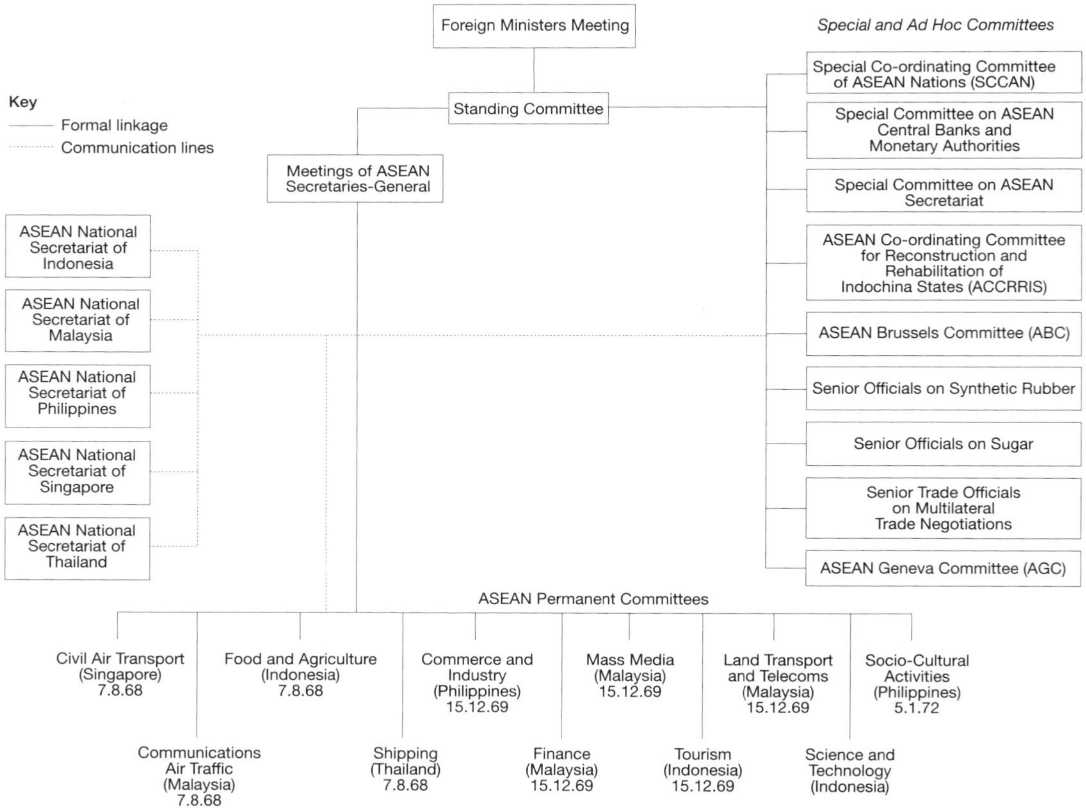

Source: Adapted from ASEAN Secretariat, *Ten Years ASEAN* (Jakarta, April 1978).

ASEAN-Geneva Committee) take care of external relations while the rest are vehicles for co-operation in other areas internal to ASEAN.

Given the rotational basis of the Standing Committee and the infrequent Foreign Ministers Meeting, the continuity of ASEAN's work was actually carried out by the committee of senior foreign ministry officials (at the Permanent Secretary or equivalent level) at the Senior Officials Meeting (SOM). Though belatedly created in 1971, it is now a permanent committee in ASEAN.

In the period between the Bangkok Declaration and the Bali Summit, ASEAN had eleven permanent committees as shown in Figure 1.7. Different ASEAN countries were original sites of these (the site rotating every two or three years). The Standing Committee co-ordinated with at least twenty ASEAN permanent, special, and *ad hoc* committees.

The original structure of ASEAN mixed sectoral and commodity-based concerns in organizing co-operation activities. For example, the ASEAN Permanent Committee on Food and Agriculture encompassed sugar and synthetic rubber although there were separate *ad hoc* organizations for both commodities. However, the Permanent Committee (that was later organized) could have absorbed the work on sugar and synthetic rubber. The same was true for the ASEAN-Brussels and ASEAN-Geneva Committees, whose work could have been absorbed by the ASEAN Permanent Committee on Commerce and Industry.

The ASEAN structure had at least two similar mechanisms for economic co-operation at the same time. However, there is no reason why the work of the special committee (for example, pursuing a specific collective task such as negotiating with Japan for reduced production of synthetic rubber) could not be undertaken by the general permanent committees. Moreover, it was likely that officials were on similar committees, for according to the Bangkok Declaration, the machinery that shall be established should include "*ad hoc* committees and permanent committees of specialists and officials on specific subjects".

With the Bali Summit in 1976, several changes took place in ASEAN's structure and machinery for co-operation. The meeting of ASEAN economic ministers (AEM) was added to the Foreign Ministers Meeting. Other ministerial meetings involving the ASEAN Ministers of Energy Education, Environment, Health, Information, Labour, Science and Technology, and Social Welfare, though *ad hoc*, became the third scale in the structure. Committees were reorganized into five economic and three non-economic ones. The ASEAN Secretariat was also created with a Secretary-General as Head. Also, Heads of ASEAN National Secretariat were renamed Directors-General.

Figure 1.8 presents the post-Bali ASEAN institutional structure, which differs from Figure 1.7 in many respects. For one, the AEM, now an institution in ASEAN, directly controls the five economic committees to ensure that special attention is given to economic matters. Second, the ASEAN Secretariat reports to the Standing Committee, which in turn supervises three non-economic committees and seven committees with dialogue countries and international organizations. The original twenty committees handled by the Standing Committee was reduced to ten although there are now sub-committees, working groups, and *ad hoc* committees.

Matters that relate to co-operation in trade and tourism are discussed in the Committee on Trade and Tourism (COTT), which is chaired by Singapore. On the other hand, the Philippines chairs the Committee on Industry, Minerals, and Energy (COIME), the committee responsible for co-operation in industry, minerals, and energy. For finance and banking, Thailand is in charge, while Indonesia chairs the committee that oversees co-operation in forestry, agriculture, and fisheries. Finally, Malaysia is responsible for co-operation in the area of transport and communications. Between these committees and the AEM is the SEOM that sets the agenda for the AEM (which is usually chaired by the host country).

The mechanisms for economic co-operation appear to be confined to these five committees. However, when third countries are involved, either in terms of resource needs or collective policy stance, the matter is coursed through the ASEAN committees with dialogue countries. An ASEAN collective view regarding the Generalized System of Preferences (GSP) with the United States could very well be tabled in the COTT and/or the ASEAN-U.S. Committee. Joint ASEAN projects requiring resources from the United Nations Development Programme (UNDP) may be coursed through the ASEAN-UNDP Committee.

Figure 1.8
ASEAN Institutional Structure, 1983

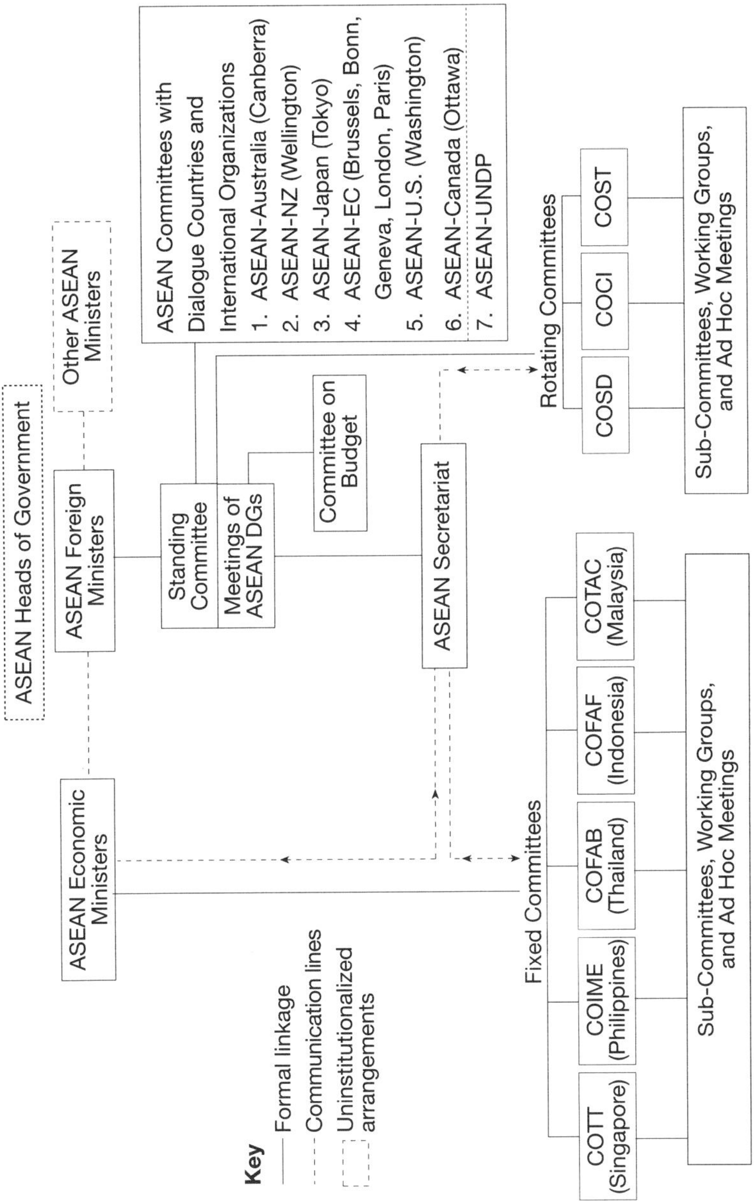

The sectoral or commodity bases of the co-operation mechanisms of Figure 1.7 were replaced by the more general coverage of the economic committees. The convening of the meetings of other ASEAN ministers (that need not report to the AMM or the AEM) continues to preserve the possible overlap among these committees. Each of these may have their own Senior Officials Meeting even if other ministers' meetings are not institutionalized. Figure 1.8 notes communication lines among the ministers and through the ASEAN Secretariat that presumably reduce potential overlaps.

It is in the numerous subsidiary bodies of the ASEAN committees that specific sectors or commodities are formally integrated. Figure 1.9 identifies these bodies for the five economic committees under the AEM. The Committee on Food, Agriculture, and Forestry (COFAF) does not really branch out into commodities but nevertheless organizes groups and sub-committees into grain, horticulture, and livestock. The COIME, on the other hand, has sixteen expert groups that covers ASEAN Industrial Projects and other specific industries (for example, automotive, motorcycle, and so forth). In all, there are forty-five subsidiary bodies indicated in Figure 1.9. In the case of the COFAF, there is both a co-ordinating group and a working group on Fisheries under the Sub-Committee on Food Handling. Both the COFAF and the COIME are ASEAN committees that have various sub-organizations that either go into specific products or distinct sub-sectors. The other three committees do not have a large number of subsidiary bodies.

The three non-economic ASEAN committees also have subsidiary bodies but these are not shown in Figure 1.9. A total of twenty bodies is in the three ASEAN non-economic committees. In total, some sixty-five subsidiary bodies formally belong to ASEAN mechanisms for co-operation. Apart from these, numerous *ad hoc* bodies tackle specific issues. When the other committees are added up, the number of organizational units exceeds eighty-five (combining Figures 1.8 and 1.9). This number is a multiple of the eleven bodies created in the pre-Bali ASEAN Summit. These bodies regularly meet to consider various options for co-operation.

The establishment of the Secretariat added another structure into ASEAN but from Figure 1.8, the Secretariat was at the disposal of the

Figure 1.9
Subsidiary Bodies of the ASEAN Committees

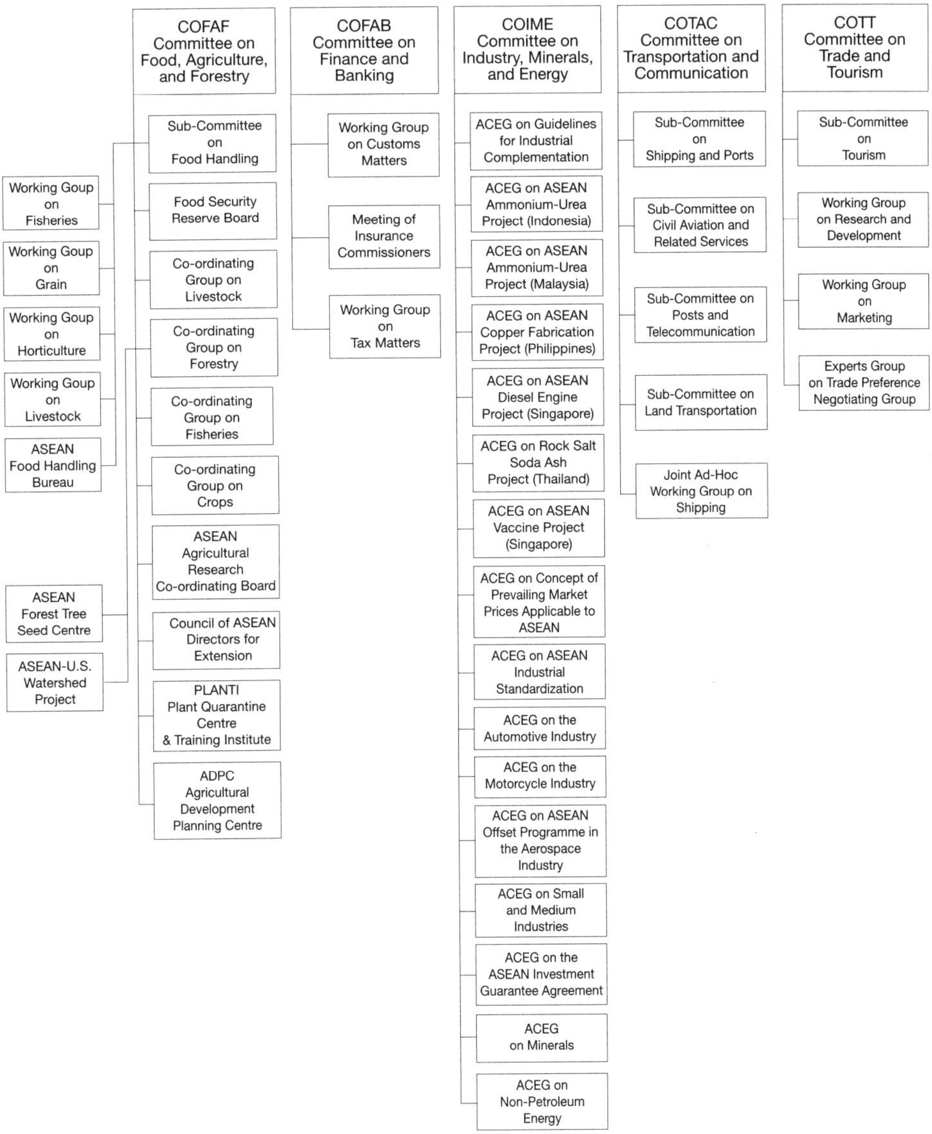

* ACEG: ASEAN COIME Experts Group

Standing Committee. In fact, the Secretary-General of the Secretariat was the "Secretary" of the ASEAN Ministerial Meetings, and was to be informed of all activities of the ASEAN committees and other bodies (note communication lines in Figure 1.8). Where the Secretariat staff participated in ASEAN meetings, it became the Secretary. Still, there was little by way of substantive participation by the Secretariat on co-operation activities. The ASEAN Secretariat then was commonly perceived as a "glorified post office". This was despite the seeming flexibility in the functions of the Deputy Secretary-General and the three Bureau Directors (who were all under the supervision of the Secretary-General) for more substantive work than in the case of the Secretary-General.

The Bali Declaration provided for a continuing review of the ASEAN organization. However, the five economic committees became permanent arrangements as member countries could not agree on the chairmanship of the committees. Even as the Manila Declaration reiterated the continued improvement of the ASEAN organizational structure, it was not until the Fourth ASEAN Summit that concrete organizational changes took place in ASEAN.

Figure 1.10 brings together various changes in ASEAN, among others, the strengthening of the ASEAN Secretariat, institutionalization of the meeting of ASEAN Heads of Government, explicit recognition of Senior Officials Meetings, and abolition of the five economic committees. The lines of both authority and communications, however, remained basically the same.

The ASEAN Secretary-General is now a prominent feature of the organization, being a member of various meetings at different levels — from Heads of Government to Senior Officials Meetings. This is based on a 1992 decision to give greater power to the Secretary-General (that is, from a Secretary-General of the ASEAN Secretariat to the ASEAN Secretary-General, with the rank of minister). In Figure 1.10, a distinction is made between the ASEAN Secretary-General as a political figure and as Head of the ASEAN Secretariat. In the former, the Secretary-General is a spokesperson for the regional organization.

The explicit delineation of the SEOM mandates its takeover of the five economic committees in terms of co-operation activities while the ASEAN Secretariat provides technical services to the SEOM. The

Figure 1.10
New Organizational Structure of ASEAN, 1995

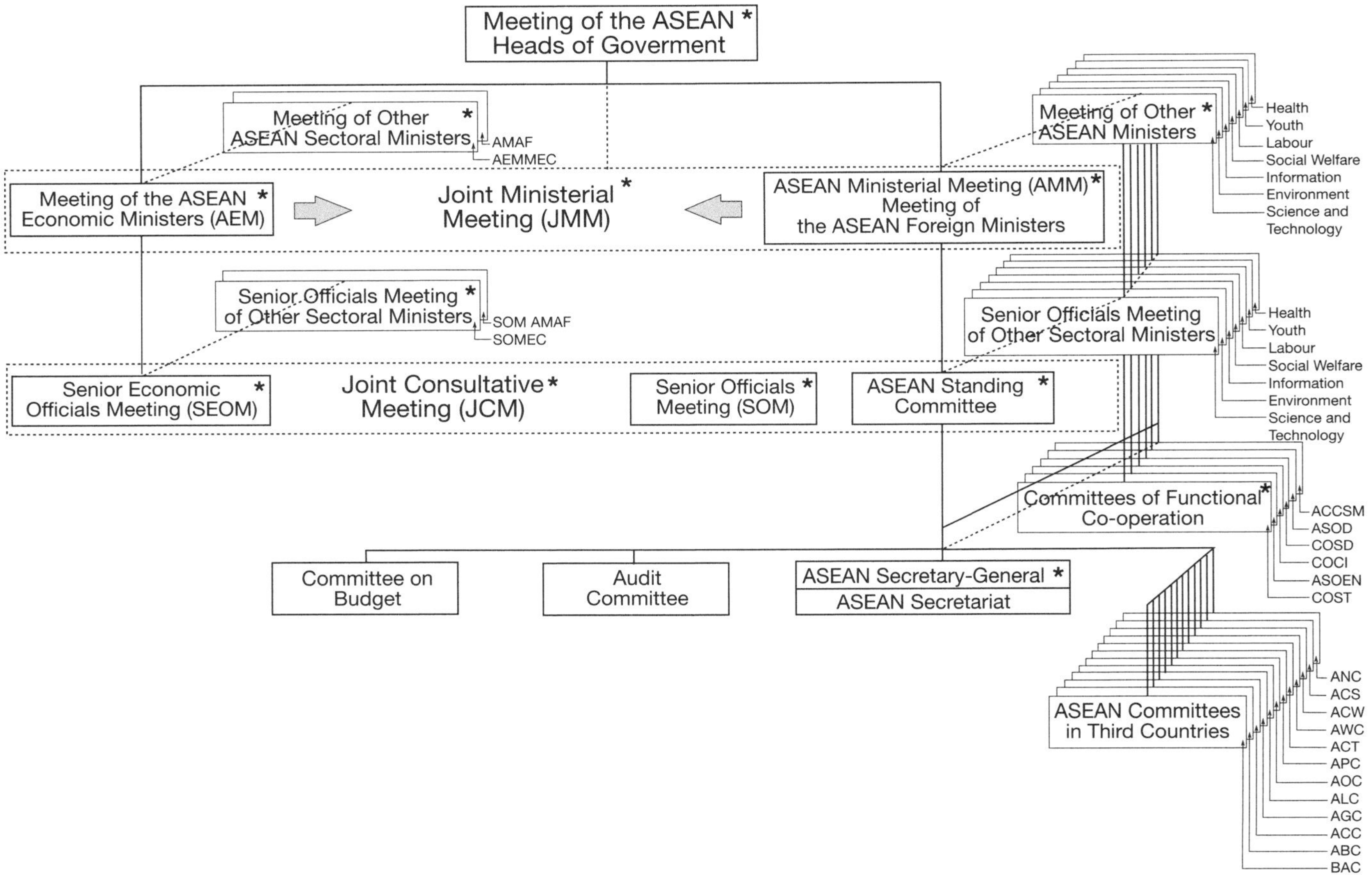

Meeting of Other ASEAN Sectoral Ministers is institutionalized and would in part take over the sectoral aspects of the work of the five committees. The number of economic co-operation meetings falls into two categories: the AEM/SEOM and sectoral ministries (see Box 1.3).

The six non-economic committees that were either newly created or reorganized from the previous structure now fall directly under the Meeting of Other ASEAN Sectoral Ministers. These are in science and technology, social development, culture and information, drug matters, the environment, and the civil service.

The Standing Committee oversees the ASEAN Secretariat and two groups of committees dealing with dialogue partners and the ASEAN Committee in third countries. Currently, there are ASEAN committees in Bonn, Brussels, Canberra, Geneva, London, Ottawa, Paris, Seoul, Tokyo, Washington, and Wellington.

Apart from the institutionalization of the meeting of the ASEAN Heads of Government, a new layer was added into ASEAN. This is the Joint Ministerial Meeting (JMM), which combines the meetings of the AEM and the ASEAN foreign ministers. This formally consolidates co-operation agreements between the two ministerial meetings.

The new structure, as indicated in Figures 1.8 and 1.9, eliminated the cumbersome layers and bodies (at least for economic co-operation). Under this set-up, the SEOM is directly responsible for all economic matters formerly split into several committees. The ASEAN Secretariat assists the SEOM in spelling out economic co-operation issues.

The reverse occurred in non-economic committees. The number expanded from three (in the post-Bali Declaration) to six as shown in Figure 1.10. There is no fixed specification of other bodies, working groups, or sub-committees covering these committees. Although two of the six are meetings of senior officials (on drug matters and the environment), this does not imply that other meetings (of experts or related bodies) on related matters cannot take place.

As described earlier, ASEAN had several mechanisms for co-operation. What seems to be lacking, however, is a regional focus to these so that they are not merely a summation of individual country interests. True enough, the lack of regional focus in ASEAN co-operation mechanisms did not appear urgent and necessary until threats to a global order slowly surfaced later on. Nowhere is this more appar-

BOX 1.3: ASEAN POLICY ORGANS AND INSTITUTIONAL STRUCTURE

The ASEAN Summit: The Heads of Government meet at the ASEAN Summit, the highest forum for ASEAN co-operation. Summit meetings are held once every three years and are hosted on a rotating basis according to the alphabetical order of member countries. There have been four ASEAN Summits to date, the most recent being the one held at Bangkok on 14–15 December 1995. The next Summit will be held in Vietnam in 1998.

The ASEAN Ministerial Meeting (AMM): After the ASEAN Summit, the AMM is the next highest decision-making body. The AMM, which is composed of ASEAN foreign ministers, is organized at least once a year and covers the political, diplomatic, social, and cultural areas. Non-ASEAN countries can be invited to attend the AMM as observers. Vietnam and Laos were observers at the 26th AMM in July 1993.

Post-Ministerial Conference (PMC): Immediately following the AMM, a PMC is held, where ASEAN foreign ministers meet their counterparts from the dialogue partner countries.

Senior Officials Meeting (SOM): The SOM is made up of permanent secretaries of ministries of foreign affairs from the respective ASEAN member countries and is held three or four times a year. The SOM serves as a preparatory organ for the AMM.

ASEAN Economic Ministers (AEM): The AEM meets at least once a year to discuss ASEAN economic co-operation.

Senior Economic Officials Meeting (SEOM): The SEOM is composed of high-ranking economic officials who meet every three months in Jakarta at the ASEAN Secretariat. Under the AEM, the SEOM oversees all aspects of economic co-operation (policy and programme formulation, monitoring and evaluation, and so forth) in the fields of trade and tourism, industry, mineral and energy, finance and banking, food and agriculture, and transport and communications. The SEOM's most important function is to prepare for the AEM.

ent than in economic issues. The next chapter traces several of these.

Between 1967 and 1992, ASEAN adopted two organizational modes into its co-operation mechanisms. Their evolution, in sequence, resulted in a number of observations. First, there were overlaps in the functions of different committees, be they permanent, special, or *ad hoc*. (Earlier, it was noted that the old ASEAN tended to be commodity- or sector-specific and had a narrow view.) Second, the institutionalization of the AEM clearly recognized the importance of economic matters to ASEAN. Specific economic committees became the AEM's instruments. Third, the establishment of the ASEAN Secretariat displayed ASEAN's commitment to a regional entity even if the Secretariat was strengthened only after the 1992 reorganization.

The Fourth ASEAN Summit provided a stronger mandate to the ASEAN Secretariat as a mechanism for economic co-operation. For instance, the Bureau of Economic Co-operation (BEC), one of the four bureaus of ASEAN as shown in Figure 1.11, handles co-operation activities. The BEC's functions include (a) the planning, co-ordination, and monitoring of economic co-operation activities in ASEAN, (b) the co-ordination and servicing of meetings of ASEAN bodies dealing with economic co-operation, and (c) the initiation, implementation, and monitoring of plans of actions and programmes for regional co-operation. The BEC is also responsible for co-ordinating with the private sector through the ASEAN Chambers of Commerce and Industry (ASEAN-CCI).

The BEC services six *ad hoc*, interim, or consultative groups or committees covering different fields of co-operation, as shown in Figure 1.12. Though the substantive collation and consolidation of economic co-operation activities fall under the SEOM, the Secretariat's role (through the BEC) is crucial because it is responsible for the integration of the results of ASEAN meetings and various agreements. The Secretariat's strategic position in the ASEAN organization also allows it to shape the direction of economic co-operation towards clear regional objectives.

The Fifth ASEAN Summit in Bangkok in 1995 formalized the new economic initiatives set out after the Fourth ASEAN Summit but did not propose any amendments in the mechanisms for economic co-operation.

The episodes that ASEAN went through for more than twenty-five years enriched the range and quality of economic co-operation in ASEAN. The transition of these mechanisms no doubt augurs well for succeeding ASEAN economic co-operation and integration arrangements (see Box 1.4 for a summary of ASEAN's institutional structure).

Figure 1.11
ASEAN Secretariat

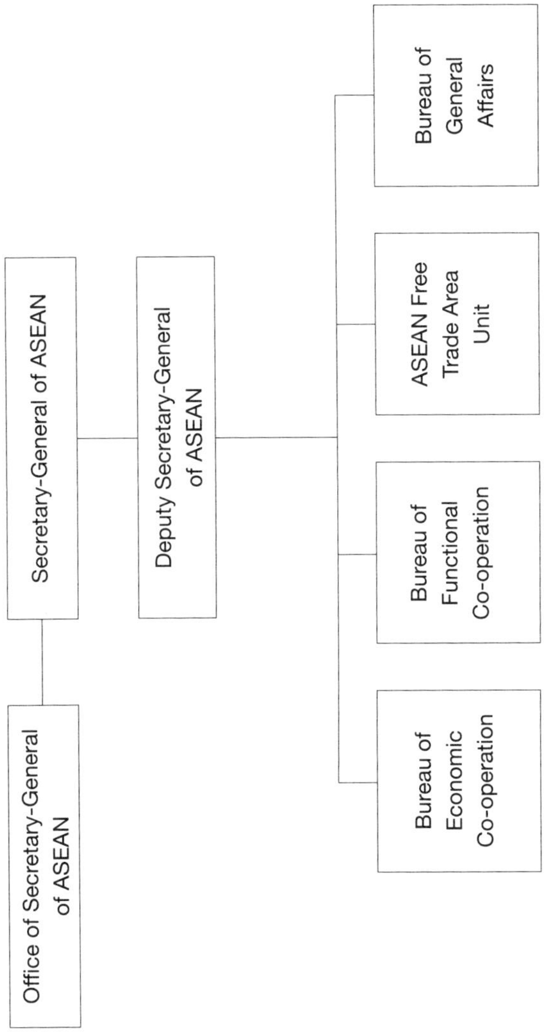

Figure 1.12
The Machinery of ASEAN Economic Co-operation

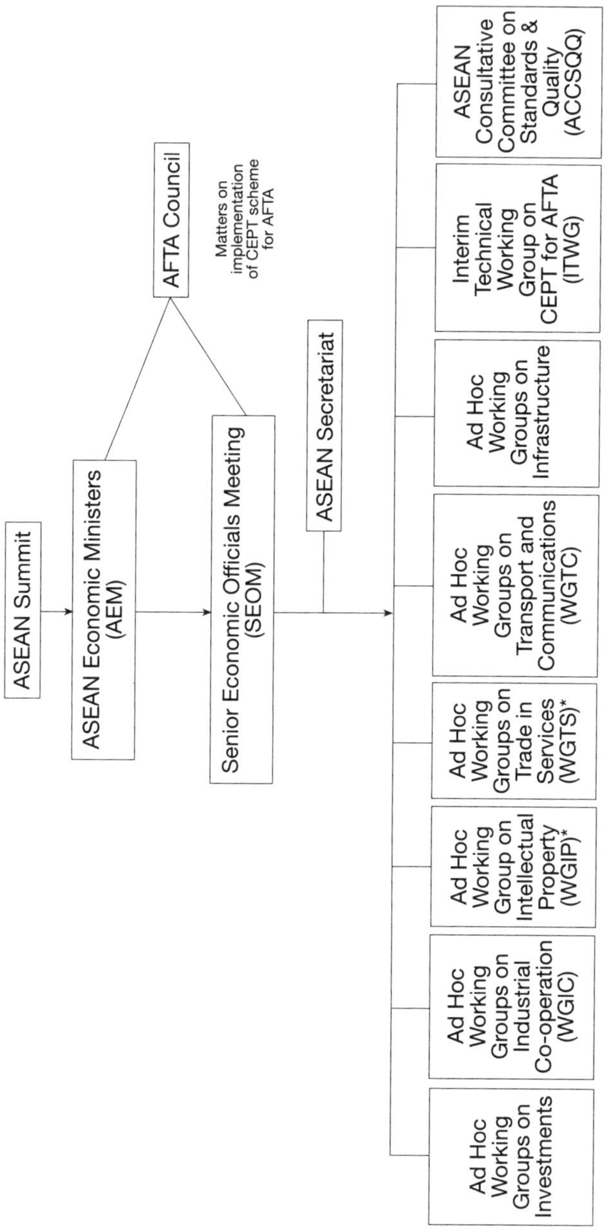

* Dissolved.

BOX 1.4: ASEAN MEETINGS ON ECONOMIC CO-OPERATION

The number of annual official ASEAN meetings on economic co-operation is seventy-seven. This number includes meetings that are considered informal and preparatory. For instance, while the AEM formally meets only once a year, they also meet once a year informally. The SEOM likewise has two preparatory and one informal meeting. The table below lists the various meetings.

A. ASEAN Economic Ministers/Senior Economic Officials Meeting:	
1. Ministerial:	
ASEAN economic ministers	2
AFTA Council	2
2. Senior officials: senior economic officials	7
3. Co-ordinating committees:	
CEPT implementation for AFTA	4
Services (+ 7 negotiating groups)	4
4. Working groups:	
Tariff nomenclature	2
Customs procedures	2
Joint SEOM-SOM-AMAF	2
SEOM-ASEAN Federation of Textile Industries	2
WG-World Trade Organization Ministers' Conference	2
Accession	4
Standards and quality (ACCSQ)	2
Industrial co-operation	4
Investment co-operation and promotion	4
Intellectual property	3
Sub-total	46
B. Sectoral ministers	
1. Agriculture (ministerial + SOM + WG)	17
2. Transport and Communications (ministerial + SOM + WG)	5
3. Energy (ministerial + SOM + WG)	4
4. Tourism (ministerial + SOM + WG)	2
5. Finance (ministerial + SOM + WG)	3
Sub-total	31
Total	77

NOTES

1. Peter Lyon, in K.S. Sandhu et al. (1992).
2. Norman D. Palmer, in ibid.
3. Ibid.
4. Ibid.
5. Yoshiyuki Hagiwara (1973), in K.S. Sandhu et al. (1992).
6. Ibid.
7. Khaw Guat Hoon (1984), in K.S. Sandhu et al. (1992).
8. The European Community (EC) later became known as the European Union (EU) with the ratification of the Maastricht Treaty in November 1993. The two names are used interchangeably in this book.

2

Review and Assessment of Economic Co-operation

I. Introduction

This chapter proposes to undertake a review and assessment of economic co-operation in a number of specific areas. While there is no direct causality that can be attributed to the dynamic economic performance of the ASEAN economies to economic co-operation in the last twenty-five years, it cannot be denied that the relative peace and stability in the region, and the increasing interactions among ASEAN states (officials, businesses, citizens) greatly enhanced the process and character of growth.

There is a large body of literature that reviews and assesses ASEAN economic co-operation at various stages.[1] Both official and unofficial assessments were made by, among others, external (non-ASEAN) scholars who have followed the regional co-operation. Rather than provide details of economic co-operation (for example, specific agreements, dates and topics of meetings, and so forth), this chapter presents the transitions and transformations in economic co-operation that took place over two decades. The assessments made are in terms of their totalities and broad significance. Thus, there may be differences in the manner in which some details are highlighted. As earlier described, the machineries and modalities for co-operation in the past were dramatically changed following agreements at the Fourth ASEAN Summit in Singapore in 1992.

ASEAN officials reviewed and assessed co-operation efforts in the past twenty-five years as part of the dissolution process of the five economic committees and in preparation for a transition. A careful reading of these official (but unpublished) reviews indicate several salient points. For one, significant accomplishments were made in various areas. These range from regular ministerial meetings and dialogues to specific agreements (for example, coverage of tariff concessions, ASEAN Industrial Joint Ventures (AIJV) approvals, quantities of food security reserves, creation of *ad hoc* committees, and so forth). Another is the completion of many collaborative studies and understandings among all ASEAN states collectively or a sub-group of them (the 6 – *x* principle). These range from simple declarations to concrete policy directives (for example, the use of ASEAN currencies for the settlement of trade payments, brand-to-brand complementation, the Singapore-Johor-Riau agreements, and so forth). Also, ASEAN solidarity was exhibited in various external fora, ranging from the ratification of international conventions to trade negotiations. The ASEAN-Geneva Committee, for example, contributed greatly to a broad ASEAN presence in various negotiating groups in the recently concluded Uruguay Round of Multilateral Trade Negotiations. The initiation of development discussions with dialogue partners also strengthened ASEAN's voice in dealings with bilateral donor countries.

On the other hand, there is no external concluding assessment of ASEAN economic co-operation in the post-Fourth ASEAN Summit despite the many reviews of past co-operation efforts in a number of sectors. From among ASEAN and non-ASEAN scholars and observers, at least three pervasive views can be discerned. First, judgements range from weak results and modest output to dismal records. Of course, these depend critically on the kind of economic co-operation being examined. Industrial co-operation, for instance, is viewed as disappointing while the record in transport co-operation is dismal and lacks urgency.[2] On the other hand, trade co-operation is punctuated by nominal agreements that mimicked progress rather than reflect forthright efforts.[3]

Second, the economic performance of ASEAN economies since the organization started is dubbed impressive, if not spectacular. Observers take great care in their pronouncements about the causal influence of ASEAN in this respect. Yet there is acceptance of the fact that ASEAN's conscious efforts at the conference table to achieve relative peace and stability in the region have resulted in the region's ability to concentrate on substantial economic matters.

The economic progress achieved by member states since 1970 appears to be a result of unilateral economic reforms and policies. Each member recognized early on that progress hinged on a predictable economic environment and sufficient public resources for infrastructure, resources that would have been earmarked for non-economic activities under less stable, less peaceful, and more hostile conditions.

With internal threats set aside, ASEAN was poised to take advantage of global restructuring in the late 1970s and mid-1980s. In particular, the currency realignments following the Plaza Accord helped, in large measure, the export boom of most ASEAN members and reaffirmed the importance of trade to these economies.

A final salient point of the reviews of ASEAN is the conclusion that ASEAN stands at a crossroads of its existence. Though this may be unique to a particular sector or area of co-operation, what permeates across them is the wide scope for regional co-operation that will enhance ASEAN's overall progress. This transitional prospect is even articulated in co-operation areas considered dismal in the past.

One reason put forward for the slow pace of ASEAN co-operation is the lack of a regional perspective. For example, in transport and communications, ASEAN would benefit from training programmes and practices that are regional rather than national in focus (for example, training programmes for seafarers and container terminal operations are good test cases).[4] Beyond this, there are arguments for common standards to be used and adopted in ASEAN — from a standard unit of account for intra-ASEAN contracts, standardized energy statistics to harmonized tariff codes.

Another reason indicating that ASEAN is at its crossroads is that a change of focus in existing co-operation could generate greater positive impact on the region. For example, shifting industrial co-operation from the development of large-scale enterprises to small enterprises will entail less resources and more immediate benefits to the vast number of ASEAN entrepreneurs.[5] On the other hand, co-operation activities in human resource development (HRD) will be more relevant if, as inputs to an ASEAN programme, the focus of current HRD schemes is elevated from national to regional rather than merely summing up national HRD priorities.

There is also a point made with regard to ASEAN adopting common policies in certain areas to strengthen co-operation. This, however, appears to be a contentious point in regional discussions. There will always be differences in the distribution of benefits from a common regional policy and compensatory mechanisms for adjustment problems may not be automatic, as in the case of a proposal for a common agricultural policy in ASEAN. What needs to be realized, though, is that ASEAN states exhibit a lot of complementarity even in a sector (for example, agriculture) that is perceived to be common (thus competitive) among members. Thus, a clear understanding of where comparative advantages lie in each country appears to be the first hurdle that member countries must pass before a common agricultural policy is defined.[6]

In sum, the observation that ASEAN stands at a crossroads gives a generous benefit of doubt to regional co-operation and an admission that member countries gain more from co-operation than individual efforts. The assessments are fortunately not short of directions, in general and specific terms, for ASEAN co-operation.

After the Fourth Summit in 1992, crucial changes in the structure and modalities of economic co-operation were made, and were further reinforced, along with additional co-operation arrangements at the Fifth Summit in 1995. Six specific areas of economic co-operation and the accompanying threshold changes are examined in this chapter. The review on intra-ASEAN trade focuses on the instruments of co-operation used to promote trade while ASEAN's industrial development is reviewed along the lines of growing competitiveness and complementarities among ASEAN industries. In transport, communications, and tourism co-operation, the review focuses on the manner in which ASEAN is interconnected. In banking and finance, financial integration is examined. In food, agriculture, and forestry, the original objectives of co-operation are reviewed in the light of recent changes. Finally, for minerals and energy, the review dwells on further enhancement of co-operation.

The composition of ASEAN expanded throughout the period of its economic co-operation. From an original group of five members, ASEAN expanded to six with the inclusion of Brunei in 1984. At the Fifth ASEAN Summit, Vietnam was formally admitted as the seventh member. With these compositional changes in mind, the future direction of economic co-operation is treated in the next chapter and reviewed in a larger context.

ASEAN economies have always been open economies relying on trade to support their growth and dynamism. Of the original five, only Indonesia had a low export/GDP ratio prior to the formation of ASEAN. Subsequently, all ASEAN economies registered high trade ratios. Table 2.1 notes the export/GDP ratios for the five original members between 1965 and 1992 (prior to the Fourth ASEAN Summit).

Table 2.1
Export-GDP Ratios, 1965–92
(Percentages)

Country	1965	1975	1990	1992
Indonesia	5	23.3	26	26.5
Malaysia	42	41.2	79	72.8[a]
Philippines	17	14.5	28	18.5
Singapore	123	95.3	190	130.7
Thailand	16	n.a.	29.2	27.3
Brunei	n.a.	93.1[b]	61.6	60.6
Vietnam	n.a.	n.a.	n.a.	n.a.

n.a. = Not available.
[a] 1991.
[b] 1981.

Source: International Monetary Fund, *International Financial Statistics* (various issues); World Bank, *World Development Report* (various issues); Industry Canada.

The degree of ASEAN economic openness was less towards each other and more to traditional markets such as the United States, Japan, and the EC. Table 2.2 shows the percentage of ASEAN exports and imports going to, or coming from, the three traditional markets and ASEAN. The figures for ASEAN ranged from less than 10 per cent for the Philippines to 29 per cent for Malaysia (in terms of exports), and from 9.5 per cent for Indonesia to 44.1 per cent for Brunei (in terms of imports). More recently, ASEAN is becoming more important as a market for its own exports although in imports, Japan is still the more important source. These numbers, however, are biased by the weight of Singapore trade, with about 30 to 40 per cent of ASEAN exports and imports accounted for by Singapore. Excluding Singapore, previous es-

Table 2.2
ASEAN: Direction of Trade, 1993
(Percentages)

Country	USA	Japan	EC	ASEAN, 1970	ASEAN, 1993
Export					
Brunei	1.2	54.2	17.8	83.2	19.2
Indonesia	14.2	30.3	14.4	21.1	13.4
Malaysia	20.3	13	14.5	25.4	28.2
Philippines	38.3	16.3	16.8	1.2	7.1
Singapore	20.3	7.5	14	29.4	23.9
Thailand	21.6	17	17	14.9	16.3
Vietnam	n.a.	32.3	19.6	n.a.	17.6
ASEAN	19.9	15.7	15	21.4[a]	20.2
Import					
Brunei	20.2	5.4	27.1	49.4	38.3
Indonesia	11.5	22	19.9	7.6	9.3
Malaysia	16.9	27.5	11.6	22.5	20
Philippines	19.8	22.8	10.3	5.2	10.9
Singapore	16.3	21.8	11.5	26.7	21.8
Thailand	11.7	30.3	14.9	3.2	12.1
Vietnam	0.1	13.1	11.1	n.a.	29.4
ASEAN	14.9	24.4	13.3	16.3[a]	17.5

Note: Data for Brunei are estimates (by the ASEAN Secretariat).
[a] Excluding Vietnam.

Source: International Monetary Fund, *Direction of Trade Statistics* (various issues).

timates of intra-ASEAN trade ranged from 3 to 5 per cent.

The trade structure of the original members also changed significantly between 1965 and 1990. From a heavy dominance of fuels, metals, and primary commodity exports, manufactures, machinery, and transport equipment now comprise the larger component of exports. As industrialization proceeded in ASEAN, a corresponding shift in imports from foods and fuel to machinery, transport equipment, and other manufactured goods also occurred. These shifts imply a wider market base for intra-ASEAN trade in higher value-added products.

II. Economic Co-operation

A. Intra-ASEAN Trade: From PTA to AFTA

In the early years of ASEAN, the magnitude of intra-ASEAN trade was neither large nor significant. Estimates between 1967 and the early 1970s were between 12 and 15 per cent of total trade with much of these accounted for by trade between Indonesia and Singapore. A trade average among ASEAN countries of about 10 per cent did not speak well of the importance of ASEAN to ASEAN as members obviously traded more with non-ASEAN countries than among themselves.[7]

Thus, one of the earliest manifestations of ASEAN co-operation was the promotion of increased intra-ASEAN trade. The principal instrument for carrying this out was the signing of the Preferential Trading Arrangement (PTA) in 1977. As the lowest form of economic integration, the PTA provided for tariff preferences for trade among ASEAN states. The margins of preferences (MOP) started at 10 per cent.

ASEAN co-operation efforts concentrated in the MOP. However, it also put in place long-term quantity contracts, preferential terms for financing imports, preferential imports by government agencies, and liberalization of non-tariff barriers.

Apart from the *levels* of MOP, the PTA covered a limited *scope* in manufactures trade. Furthermore, this was not across the board and was dependent on items offered by individual countries within the non-agricultural sector.

Eligibility for the MOP was based on ASEAN content or rules-of-origin. To avail of the margins, goods had to be either wholly produced in ASEAN or its non-ASEAN content not more than 50 per cent in value and the final stage of manufacture had to take place in ASEAN. Goods that satisfied this requirement were issued Form C certificates.

The level, scope, and eligibility for the MOP under the PTA created their own problems in the process of implementation. First, the levels of margins were too low to have any significant impact on raising intra-ASEAN imports. Most import elasticity estimates were also low if not inelastic. For instance, when the MOPs started, a 10 per cent across-the-board tariff cut would have raised imports in the Philippines by only 2.5 per cent, in Thailand by 0.6 per cent, and overall intra-ASEAN trade by less than 2 per cent.[8] Three other factors compounded this empirically based weakness. One was the low level of utilization by traders, either because of lack of interest or information. In 1982, for example, the ratio of PTA trade to total trade was estimated at about 0.4 per cent.[9] Another was the cumbersome bureaucracy involved in availing of the MOPs. For many traders, the paper work involved in getting a low MOP was not worth the effort. Finally, the wide variation in existing tariff levels across ASEAN made reciprocal exchanges appear inequitable. A country with a high tariff base would perceive a 10 per cent cut to be large compared with a partner country whose tariff base rate is low.

The scope of the MOP under the PTA was even more problematic. It began with a product-by-product approach to tariff reduction wherein a decision had to be made for each MOP granted to a specific product. This had two undesirable results. One was the granting of preferences to products not traded among ASEAN states. The other was the creation of new product extracts in the classification codes for essentially the same good (the new extract, for example, would be for a product with a different colour, or fewer items in a pack). These results gave the impression that substantial progress was being made in trade liberalization.

A second aspect in the scope of MOP is the choice of products considered "sensitive" (that is, exempted from liberalization within ASEAN). Since most member economies are competitive rather than complementary, it was natural to expect each to protect similar industries or products. As a consequence, there was a limited set of products for harmonized liberalization.

Although there were minor difficulties in determining eligibility, there were doubts about products reaching an ASEAN content of 60 per cent by value. Thus, though the possible trans-shipment of goods via countries with low tariff rates was considered, the content, even on an ASEAN cumulative basis of 60 per cent, was still perceived as relatively high.

As the PTA progressed through time, these weaknesses were recognized and policy pronouncements were made to improve the mechanisms. In 1980 the product-by-product scheme was substituted with an across-the-board approach where preferences would automatically be given (subject to eligibility) to items below a certain import-value ceiling. The import ceilings increased from an initial US$50,000 to US$10 million, then to US$20 million and finally, without a ceiling (that is, open-ended). The levels of MOP were raised in several stages. At the AEM meeting in 1981, the minimum MOP was raised to between 20 and 25 per cent. This was further raised to a maximum of 50 per cent at the next AEM.

The comprehensive coverage of the MOP would have triggered substantial intra-ASEAN trade were it not for the fact that (while ceilings were raised), ASEAN countries were free to define a sensitive list of products for which the MOPs did not apply. The extensive national exclusion lists effectively negated the PTA and were collectively viewed as an obstacle to intra-ASEAN trade.

To reduce the number of items in the sensitive lists, some general criteria were considered by ASEAN officials, among them: (a) products that were being promoted, (b) items with revenue or employment significance, and (c) products controlled to safeguard national interests. Because these criteria were not subjected to further (quantifiable) specifications, they did not help in paring down the list to increase the effectiveness of the PTA.

The solution was to have the exclusion list limited to a certain proportion of liberalized items, with each country determining its list. In 1984, ASEAN officials agreed in principle to a list not exceeding 10 to 15 per cent of liberalized items. However, as a base for sensitivity, there is a difference in trade impact when one uses trade values or list of items.

Five years into the PTA, the amount of intra-ASEAN trade had not increased significantly. Changes in the mechanisms for MOP were made in discrete steps culminating in a maximum MOP rate of 50 per cent. Such marginal changes over a long period of time prevented the possible interacting and cumulative effects of the different measures aimed at correcting the general weaknesses of the PTA. In addition, some of them (for example, consideration of the criteria for the exclusion list) never got beyond the discussion stage.

With the PTA well into its tenth year, new ways were considered by ASEAN, in preparation for the Third ASEAN Summit in the Philippines, to raise intra-ASEAN trade. Both ASEAN officials and the private sector, led by the ASEAN-CCI, formulated schemes to improve the PTA. The ASEAN-CCI report by the Group of Fourteen (see Chapter 4) put forward concrete suggestions to further improve intra-ASEAN trade.[10]

The 1987 measures adopted at the Third ASEAN Summit were not radical departures from the PTA concept and remained cautious towards free trade in ASEAN.[11] In an effort to promote intra-ASEAN trade, for instance, the Summit adopted an "Enhanced PTA Programme" supplemented by other non-tariff commitments, such as increasing the MOP maximum to 50 per cent. The exclusion list was also set to no more than 10 per cent of traded items and 50 per cent of the value of intra-ASEAN trade.

The supplement to the MOP was perhaps the more important aspect of the trade measures. The agreement to use a standard intra-ASEAN trade classification scheme in determining exclusion lists essentially normalized what were once disparate lists. The imposition of further trade barriers was brought to a standstill and there was a rollback of non-tariff barriers.

It must be noted that the Third ASEAN Summit took place during the early part of the Uruguay Round of Multilateral Trade Negotiations. The PTA was in force at a time when there was a great deal of uncertainty in the world trading environment, with the power blocs taking insurance against a GATT breakdown. The United States, for example, accelerated agreements for the North American Free Trade Agreement (NAFTA) while the European Union held on to a "Maastricht Treaty". These developments urged ASEAN to consider a bolder move that departs from its usual cautious trade liberalization stance.

Amidst difficulties with the 1987 Enhanced PTA Programme, ASEAN started a framework for AFTA and couched it as a CEPT scheme. The ultimate objective was to achieve tariff rates for intra-ASEAN trade at 0 to 5 per cent (in an AFTA environment) while maintaining other supplemental measures of the 1987 PTA Programme.

At the Fourth ASEAN Summit in Singapore in 1992, the Heads of Government of member countries approved the CEPT scheme and identified fifteen product groups. Moreover, the Summit agreed to a timetable of fifteen years to achieve the goal of the CEPT scheme. Free trade in ASEAN was envisioned for 2008, starting in 1993. Figure 2.1 shows the CEPT rates as approved at the Summit. It has a fast (the fifteen product groups) and normal track. In the fast track, free trade will be achieved in ten years for items with rates below 20 per cent, while those with rates above 20 per cent will be completed by 2003. In the normal track, the rates for products with tariffs of more than 20 per cent were to be reduced in three stages, namely, 20 per cent by 2001, 15 per cent by 2003, 10 per cent by 2005, and free trade (0 to 5 per cent) by 2008. For products with tariff rates of less than 20 per cent, reductions were to be completed by 2003.

In the original agreement, the coverage of the CEPT scheme included all manufactures, processed agricultural products, and capital goods at the Harmonized System (HS-Code) 6-digit level, excluding agricultural products. In addition, members could maintain exclusion lists at the HS 8/9-digit levels.

With the conclusion of the Uruguay Round in 1994, which had larger tariff cuts (for developed countries) and a shorter time frame for global liberalization (though not towards global free trade), ASEAN economic ministers decided to accelerate AFTA in ten years instead of the original fifteen-year timetable. This meant the fast track was to be completed in seven instead of the original ten years. In concrete terms, the normal track was to be completed by 2003 in two steps through (a) reduction in tariff rates in excess of 20 per cent to 20 per cent by January 1998, and (b) reduction from 20 per cent to 0–5 per cent by January 2003. In the fast track, two steps were called for, namely, (a) tariffs in excess of 20 per cent were to be reduced to 0–5 per cent by January 2000, and (b) tariffs below 20 per cent were to be reduced to 0–5 per cent by 1998 (see Box 2.1).

Figure 2.1(a)
Average CEPT Rates, Original Programme (1994–2008)

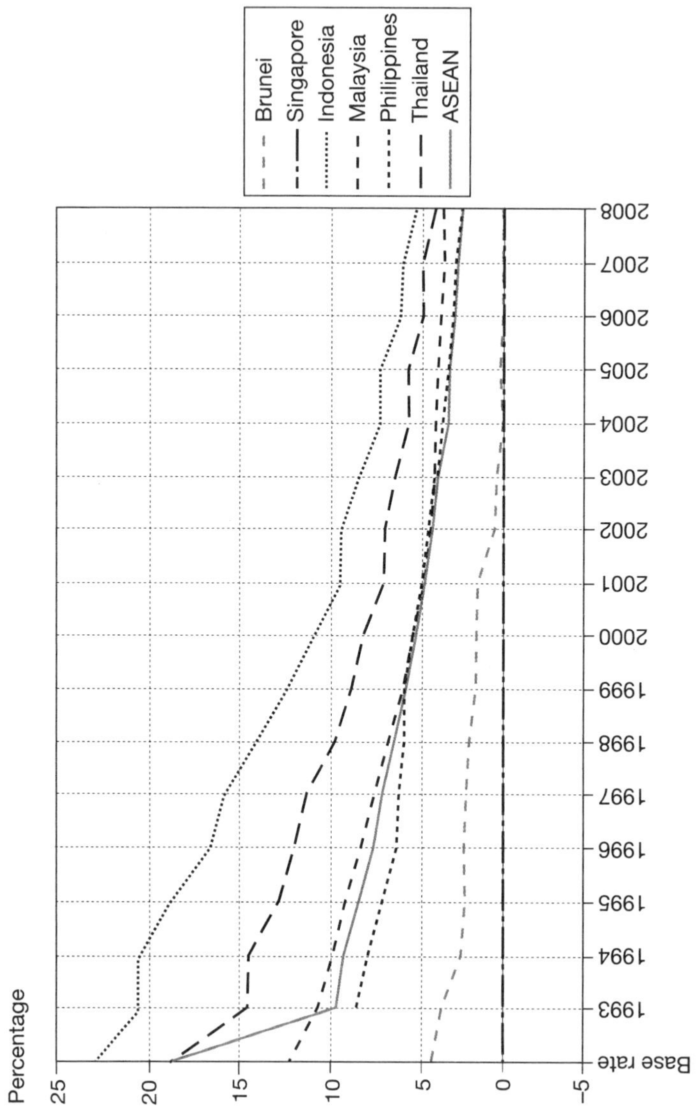

Source: ASEAN Secretariat

Figure 2.1(b)
Average CEPT Rates, Accelerated Programme (1996–2003)

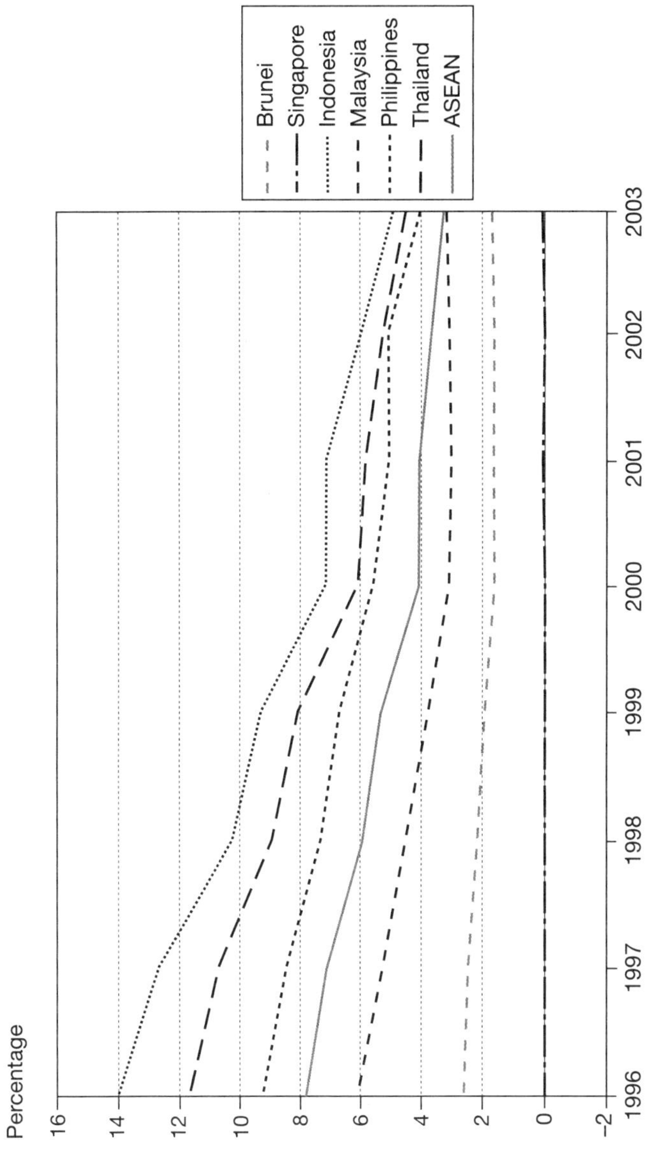

Source: ASEAN Secretariat

BOX 2.1: URUGUAY ROUND AND ASEAN

ASEAN stands to gain from the successful completion of the Uruguay Round in several ways. Firstly, the elimination of quotas on "textiles and clothing" over a period of ten years will benefit ASEAN since Indonesia and Thailand are among the world's major textiles and clothing exporters. Secondly, since ASEAN exports relatively more industrial products than other developing countries, the tariff reductions on such products will make it easier for potential newly industrializing economies such as Malaysia and Thailand to achieve NIE status within a decade or less. ASEAN countries can expect to export more to developed countries where tariffs will fall substantially by the year 2000.

One study shows that Indonesia's exports may increase by 11 per cent following the complete implementation of the Uruguay Round.

In short, the coming decade is likely to be a period of prosperity for ASEAN as exports become as buoyant as in the first three years of the 1990s.

Thirdly, ASEAN is estimated to reap a fair share of the estimated US$475 billion increase in the level of world merchandise trade. Those trade benefits will even be larger than those derived from the ASEAN Free Trade Area (AFTA). More importantly, those benefits will reinforce those from AFTA while free trade in the sub-region will make ASEAN countries more competitive at the global level.

In other words, far from making AFTA irrelevant, the new global trade agreement will vindicate ASEAN's vision of accelerating its timetable for the implementation of AFTA.

Finally, in the area of agriculture, the new GATT agreement will reduce tariffs on tropical products and lower U.S. and EC support for their agricultural sectors. The new agreement will also ensure a marginal opening of Japanese and Korean markets for agricultural imports. Thus, the liberalization of trade in agriculture will be advantageous to major agricultural exporters in ASEAN, such as Thailand. However, consumers will also benefit although farmers may be hurt in the medium term.

On the negative side, ASEAN can expect to face strong challenges from MNCs of developed countries, which may have a competitive edge in the services sector, especially financial, telecommunication, and information services. ASEAN countries that have a weak services sector such as Indonesia will face tremendous pressures from MNCs of developed countries.

ASEAN countries can also expect to make higher payments for services and royalty payments as rules relating to the protection of intellectual property rights are strengthened. The upward harmonization of intellectual property standards will mean significant immediate costs to ASEAN.

Although the agreement on trade-related investment measures (TRIMS) may have long-term beneficial effects on investment in ASEAN, it implies immediate changes in the existing regimes of ASEAN countries. ASEAN countries that have not done so may have to start considering making these changes sooner rather than later.

In addition, ASEAN countries may also face new forms of protectionism in the post–Uruguay Round era. In the final settlements to the Uruguay Round agreement, developed countries tried to include labour and other social clauses to trade relationships.

On balance, however, there are net gains for ASEAN from the new global agreement on trade. In order to maximize these gains, ASEAN should take new initiatives to resolve outstanding issues and difficulties in accelerating the progress of AFTA.

More concrete steps were taken on supplementary measures. While the number of tariff lines in the Temporary Exclusion List was minimized (7.5 per cent of total tariff lines), it was agreed that these would be transferred to the Inclusion List between 1996 and 2000 (with a yearly instalment of at least 20 per cent). Members agreed to include unprocessed agricultural products in the CEPT scheme and a shorter list of "sensitive" agricultural products. Trade in services was also added into the CEPT scheme but a framework for co-operation is yet to be completed. Other steps include harmonization of standards, reciprocal recognition of tests and product certification, and harmonization of tariff nomenclature beyond the HS 6-digit level.

Efforts to increase intra-ASEAN trade have come a long way. Fifteen years of PTA fostered mutual familiarity among ASEAN governments and officials although significant regional trade has yet to occur. If, however, the CEPT scheme in AFTA (which requires fifteen years) runs on schedule, followed by AFTA's fast track timetable of ten years, the mechanisms for greater intra-ASEAN trade will have been in place in twenty-five years.

A transition was made from the PTA to AFTA as a vehicle for intra-ASEAN trade. The first fifteen years were marked by attention to detail, product negotiations, and general intervention in trade flows. In contrast, the way towards the CEPT scheme, and especially in the aftermath of the Fourth ASEAN Summit, is a broader approach to liberalization, a focus on long-term scenarios, and an appreciation of mutual benefits. The next decade is viewed as encompassing comprehensiveness in trade transactions as free trade is achieved in ASEAN. Already, the estimates of the trade values covered by the CEPT scheme within ASEAN is above 85 per cent, about the same as ASEAN's trade with non-ASEAN countries (see Table 2.3).

The events that shaped co-operation in intra-ASEAN trade were cumulative — from the first stage of preferential trading to the final stage of a free trade area. While the ideal magnitudes of regional trade may be long in coming, there is no doubt that the roots of greater intra-ASEAN trade were firmly established from the PTA to the CEPT scheme.

Table 2.3
Share of Trade Values Covered by the CEPT, 1994
(As a percentage of intra-ASEAN exports)

Country	Share (%)	Exports to ASEAN (million US$)	Total Exports (billion US$)
Brunei	99.4	467.52	3.4
Indonesia	89.2	5,787.97	38.6
Malaysia[a]	86.9	15,002.15	56.1
Philippines	83.1	1,425.12	13.4
Singapore	88.4	28,806.68	93.4
Thailand	46.8	7,991.37	44.6
Vietnam	n.a.	794.70	3.4[b]
Total	—	60,275.52	—

[a] Fourth quarter exports to Thailand and Vietnam are not included for Malaysia.
[b] Data from the Asian Development Bank.
n.a. = Not available.

Source: ASEAN Secretariat.

B. ASEAN Industrial Development: Competitiveness and Complementarities

The industrial structure in ASEAN was fairly entrenched even prior to the creation of ASEAN. Among the original five members, the early stages of industrial development were driven by import-substitution in varying degrees. As some members broke away from import-substitution to export-promotion at different points in their economic history, the industrial base served as the impetus to increase trade in manufactured goods.

Table 2.4 presents the industry share of GDP for the original five ASEAN economies between 1970 and 1995 (projected). Except for the Philippines (and marginally for Singapore), ASEAN showed the increased importance of industry with an average share of 41.3 per cent. This manifests the establishment of an industrial foundation in the region.

The industrial sector is led by manufacturing, contributing 70 per cent or more to the industry's total value-added. For a few members (for example, Indonesia and Malaysia), mining and utilities are the leading sectors. Within manufacturing, major industries include food,

Table 2.4
Share of Industry in GDP, 1970–95
(Percentages)

Country	1970	1980	1993	1995[a]
Brunei	n.a.	81	48	n.a.
Indonesia	28	41.3	42	43.4
Malaysia	n.a.	35.8	44	46.3
Philippines	33.7	40.5	34	35.5
Singapore	36.4	38.8	37	37.6
Thailand	25.7	30.1	41	43.5
Vietnam	n.a.	26.3	28	25.3

[a] Projected data.
n.a. = Not available.

Source: Asian Development Bank.

beverages, and tobacco, textiles, wearing apparel, chemical, plastic and rubber products, and petroleum products.

Table 2.5 depicts the value-added growth rate of ASEAN industry as being higher in the 1970s than in the 1980s. This was the scenario for all members as they experienced a sharp fall in growth rates, and the Philippines, in particular, suffered a negative annual decline while other members experienced a sharp fall in growth rates. Recovery for some is noticeable only in the early 1990s.

Since the development of industry in the ASEAN member states cannot be separated from developments in intra-and extra-ASEAN trade, ASEAN also paid attention to co-operation in industry. The COIME, for example, until its dissolution, was an ASEAN committee responsible for industrial co-operation.

The broad philosophy of ASEAN co-operation in industry can be traced to the original Kansu Report that proposed industrial projects based on resource-pooling and market-sharing. An underlying idea was that upstream projects would be allocated to the (original) five ASEAN states based on factor endowments and comparative advantage. ASEAN states would commit to absorb the supply capacities of the plants on the basis of some pre-determined prices that ensured viability.[12]

This market-support system meant each member would "guarantee" a market for each other's industrial output, through both equity

Table 2.5
Growth Rates of Value-Added in Industry, 1971–94
(Percentages)

Country	1971–80	1981–90	1991	1992	1993	1994
Indonesia	11.3	5.9	10.4	5.6	7.3	9.5
Malaysia	9.6	7.4	11.2	8.9	10	11.4
Philippines	8.2	–0.8	–3.6	–0.5	1.6	6.1
Singapore	8.1	5.2	7.8	5.4	9.3	12.8
Thailand	12.1	10.4	12.5	10	10.8	12
Vietnam	n.a.	6.5	8.3	13.5	12.8	13.6
ASEAN[a]	9.9	5.6	1.6	1.1	1.4	1.9

[a] Excluding Brunei and Vietnam,1991–94 weighted by population.
n.a. = Not available.

Source: Asian Development Bank.

participation and tariff preferences. Though the project's viability was always central to decision-making, market support required some range of profitability rates (that is, 8 to 20 per cent), and pricing consistent with prevailing world prices (before tariff preferences).

There was also some implied exclusivity in production facilities within ASEAN wherever the project is located. This means that only one country would be the production source for all of ASEAN. Though there could be non-ASEAN sources, commitment to the market support system suggested some kind of a guaranteed market.

In the process of promoting ASEAN industrial development, three modalities of co-operation were pursued since 1977. These are the ASEAN Industrial Project (AIP), ASEAN Industrial Complementation (AIC), and ASEAN Industrial Joint Venture (AIJV).

The original five ASEAN states had individual industrial projects, namely: (a) fertilizer in Indonesia, (b) urea in Malaysia, (c) super phosphate in the Philippines, (d) diesel engine in Singapore, and (e) rock salt–soda ash in Thailand. Although the Basic Agreement on the AIP was finalized only in 1980, it was not until 1984 that Indonesia's fertilizer project began commercial operation.

There were setbacks to operating other AIPs due to conflicts between national and regional projects. For example, Singapore eventually abandoned its diesel project because its commercially viable output would have competed with Indonesia's national diesel engine production. With half of the ASEAN market coming from Indonesia, Singapore had to identify another AIP (a hepa-B vaccine plant). When Indonesia announced that it wanted to put up a soda ash plant as a national project, there was an implied conflict with Thailand's AIP despite Indonesia's assurance that it would purchase its committed demand of soda ash from Thailand. On the other hand, the Philippines wavered in its AIP from super phosphate, integrated pulp and paper, to copper fabrication.

Despite the initial enthusiasm for it, AIPs encountered several problems in implementation. Apart from the inherent conflicts in pursuing an "ASEAN-exclusive" plant *vis-à-vis* national projects, AIPs were caught in the bureaucracy that handed out approvals and sanctioned agreements, in particular, those agencies that determined pricing and commercial viability.[13] By the time these were resolved, new market conditions had emerged and feasibility results were subject to another round of reviews. In addition, because of the magnitude of the projects, financing options required extended negotiations (despite the facilitation of then Prime Minister Fukuda that channelled soft loans from Japan). When some understanding was finally reached in financing (including ASEAN equity, loan rates, and so forth), the costs of the project had escalated, thus necessitating a recast of financing arrangements.

Perhaps the more serious problem was the implied apprehension about the philosophy of the AIP itself. There were at least three manifestations of this. First, member countries needed to provide some protection in terms of tariff preferences for the allocated project. Although it was clear that the pricing of AIP outputs would be competitive, the provision of floor and ceiling prices to maintain profitability remained contentious. Second, there was an implication that member countries limit their industrial choices by virtue of a chosen project for each. By promoting an ASEAN industry, they denied themselves of industrial alternatives. Third, the binding element of market guarantee for a specific AIP also cast some doubts on the concept of the AIP. All these meant some ambiguity to the commitment of member countries to forge ASEAN industrial co-operation.

Despite these apprehensions, the visibility of the AIP gave impetus to the identification of other industrial projects and its allocation to member countries subsequent to the first set. At least three member states, Malaysia, Singapore, and Thailand, urged for a review of the concept given its range of problems, conceptual and practical, that went with the earlier set of AIPs. Given the nature of the AIP (that is, large-scale and government-dominated), member countries recognized the importance of wider private sector participation and co-operation among them in carrying out the development of ASEAN industry.

The AIC seemed to fit this co-operation modality. Just like the AIP, AIC projects are allocated among ASEAN countries. Unlike the AIP, however, AIC projects are private sector projects, presumably because private industry is more familiar with the market than governments are. Moreover, the configuration of the projects is complementary or industrially linked (forward or backward).

Basic agreement on the AIC came later than the AIP. Although the first AIC was approved in 1981, there were subsequent changes to it and it was only in 1983 when a package was finalized. This was an automotive complementation scheme wherein each ASEAN country produced complementary products (for example, diesel engines in Indonesia, transmissions in the Philippines, V-belts in Singapore, and body panels in Thailand). Since products in the AIC enjoy exclusive privileges for two years (for example, tariff preferences that are included in the PTA, mandatory sourcing, and local content), approval for AIC projects is necessary.

Like the AIP, the AIC defined procedures and criteria for identifying products and their allocation to ASEAN members. However, the participation of the private sector added more players to the negotiating table, thus requiring more time for deliberation and perhaps complicating the process further. A case in point is the second AIC package of new automotive products that was set aside in 1982 pending clearer guidelines to resolve the AIC's inherent problems. In the mean time, ASEAN officials considered an AIC variant, namely, Brand-to-Brand Complementation (BBC), the industrial co-operation mode that was considered in subsequent discussions on possible regional projects with Japanese manufacturers of cars, trucks, and motorcycles. The BBC scheme remains a co-operation modality for industry development among four countries, namely, Indonesia, Malaysia, the Philippines, and Thailand.

The AIJV, as the third industry co-operation modality, was essentially private sector–initiated and was also formalized in the early 1980s. The AIJV is closer to the AIP in the sense of being individual projects with more than one (country) market. Also, unlike the AIC, AIJV projects need not be complementary.

With the lessons of AIP and AIC, the AIJV modality reflected flexibility and practicality. Given an accredited AIJV product (as defined by ASEAN governments), investors can locate production facilities in any ASEAN country and need only two participating countries to form an AIJV company or entity. Only the approved AIJV company shall enjoy the AIJV privileges for the first four years of its operation. After that period, any other company in the participating countries producing the same product as the AIJV company shall also be entitled to the same AIJV privileges. Though the minimum ASEAN equity is set at 51 per cent and holds for the first four years, this is only for new AIJV products. This equity requirement is waived, however, if more than 50 per cent of output is exported.

Proposed AIJV products are submitted to the COIME by the ASEAN-CCI (see Chapter 4). Approved products are then publicized to generate investor participation. In 1984, examples of approved AIJV are automotive parts (for example, mechanical and power rack and pinion steerings, ball joints), motorcycle electrical parts (for example, speedometer assembly, headlight assembly, flasher relay assembly), and constant velocity joints. Recently, proposed AIJV products expanded to food processing. The MOP granted to AIJV products stands at 90 per cent.

The AIJV stimulates both ASEAN industrial transactions and investment. Part of the resolutions in the Third ASEAN Summit to enhance industry and investment was a relaxation of the minimum ASEAN equity requirement (51 to 40 per cent) while keeping the 5 per cent minimum equity for ASEAN partners.

As vehicles for private sector participation, the BBC and the AIJV are supposed to differ, the former as a variant of the AIC, and the latter, a variant of the AIP. Yet because of the differential in the MOP granted (50 per cent and 90 per cent, respectively), BBC applications were converted into AIJV applications.

Industrial co-operation in ASEAN, exemplified by these three modalities, went full circle in many ways. Government-dictated industrial allocation, through the AIP, eventually gave way to private sector–driven industrial joint ventures. The BBC, for example, encouraged vertical integration in ASEAN industrial arrangements. Taken together, intervention was gradually overtaken by reliance on market forces.

Critics may describe the results of these industrial co-operation modalities in ASEAN as inconsequential. After all, both the AIP and the AIC failed to gain a foothold in industrial interaction in ASEAN, and the BBC went through various amendments. Furthermore, it looks as if these may be superseded by the CEPT scheme, which now affects ASEAN's industrial development pace. The BBC and the AIJV were eventually phased out and replaced with the ASEAN Industrial Co-operation (AICO) scheme (see Box 2.2).

After more than fifteen years of directing the pace of industrial co-operation, there are clear lessons for ASEAN. First, resource allocation (especially at the regional level) can neither be pre-determined nor can industries be picked even with market support. The AIJV scheme, which is the most market-oriented among the modalities of industrial development co-operation, is a case in point. Second, the small number of approved AIJV products (only eighteen products were accredited between 1983 and 1990 and many are yet to go on-stream), is due more to the slow pace of the ASEAN accreditation process than lack of proposals from the private sector. After all, ASEAN governments' approval was necessary to avail of MOPs and other waivers. More importantly, though, the AIJV scheme proved that with free trade, intra-ASEAN investment would be stimulated.

Third, past modalities may have overlooked larger long-run impacts. Part of the reason why the gradual effects of co-operation efforts in ASEAN were hardly felt is the understandable apprehension of the competitiveness of individual countries. Since ASEAN states were more or less at the same pace and level of development, they produce the same menu of tradable goods. It was but natural to expect some hesitation in opening markets for the same products. Conversely, the rationale of resource pooling and market sharing entails an exchange of goods among ASEAN states based on their comparative advantages that would ideally bring about industry specialization and inter-industry

BOX 2.2: ASEAN INDUSTRIAL CO-OPERATION (AICO) SCHEME

The new scheme of industrial co-operation will retain some of the features of the BBC and AIJV schemes but offers more in terms of tariff and non-tariff incentives. The new ASEAN Industrial Co-operation (AICO) scheme shall be based on the CEPT scheme for AFTA; promote investment from technology-based industries; and enhance value-added activities.

The AICO is a scheme to encourage companies located and operating in different ASEAN countries to co-operate with one another in the manufacture of approved AICO products. A minimum of two companies in two different ASEAN countries (with a minimum of 30 per cent national equity) is required to form an "AICO arrangement", which is not a legal entity but merely an "umbrella association" under the scheme that entitles participating companies to enjoy AICO privileges. This would mean that existing companies meeting the AICO eligibility criteria may apply to form an AICO arrangement without having to create a new equity. An AICO arrangement would involve not only the physical movement of parts and components between participating companies and countries but also emphasize resource sharing between them.

The major privilege of the new scheme is that approved AICO products (which may be finished, intermediate, or raw materials, except those excluded from the CEPT scheme), output of an AICO arrangement, shall enjoy preferential tariff rates of 0 to 5 per cent immediately upon its approval. The 0 to 5 per cent tariff represents the final CEPT rate to be reached by ASEAN by the year 2003. Thus, with the immediate application of the 0 to 5 per cent preferential tariff rate, a headstart to AICO products (compared with non-AICO products) would have been provided. Other incentives include local content accreditation (where applicable) and other non-tariff incentives provided by participating member countries.

Although an equity condition is imposed as a criterion, it is not as stringent as that of the AIJV wherein a minimum of two ASEAN countries contribute at least 40 per cent of the total equity of the AIJV. Under the AICO scheme, national equity holdings of a member country in each of the participating companies is sufficient. Since two companies are required to form an AICO arrangement, each company must have its own national equity holding.

trade. This partly explains the inherent conflicts in the AIP and AIC and the apparent harmony of the AIJV.

The fact of the matter, however, is that the dynamic element of global, Pacific, and ASEAN trade is intra-industry trade with the exchange of goods belonging to the same industry group. As Table 2.6 shows, the degree of intra-industry trade in some of the ASEAN states expanded rapidly in the last twenty years. While the figures may be overall intra-industry trade, intra-ASEAN intra-industry trade undoubtedly increased in the process (see Box 2.3). In terms of producer or intermediate products, it may be trade in goods in their processed, semi- or unprocessed state. In terms of consumer goods, trade may be an exchange of different brands that expands choice.

The increasing magnitudes of intra-industry trade do not mean that comparative advantage, as a basis for ASEAN trade, is losing importance. Rather, it is an additional basis for trade. Indeed, advantages surface as new market niches in some specialized outputs are exploited through further processing, different brands, or differentiated products. With a more comprehensive basis for trade, even countries with similar resource endowments or levels of development, as is true in

Table 2.6
Indices of Intra-Industry Trade, 1970–90

	1970		1980		1990	
Country	All[a]	Mfts[b]	All[a]	Mfts[b]	All[a]	Mfts[b]
Indonesia	0.07	0.14	0.15	0.08	0.21	0.19
Malaysia	0.19	0.13	0.3	0.37	0.46	0.58
Philippines	0.08	0.07	0.3	0.17	0.39	0.42
Singapore	0.54	0.44	0.52	0.65	0.65	0.71
Thailand	0.1	0.05	0.22	0.24	0.36	0.39

[a] Indexes are calculated for intra-industry trade at the Standard International Trade Classification three-digit level.
[b] Mfts = Manufactures, including Standard International Trade Classifications 5 through 8.

Source: P. Drysdale and R. Garnaut, "The Pacific: An Application of a General Theory of Economic Integration", in *Pacific Dynamism and International Economic System*, edited by C.F. Bergsten and M. Noland (Washington, D.C.: Institute for International Economics, 1993).

BOX 2.3: INTRA-INDUSTRY TRADE IN ASEAN: A PHILIPPINE ILLUSTRATION

A significant part of global trade is increasingly intra-industry trade (that is, the exchange of goods that are similar but not identical). This phenomenon does not fit well with traditional frameworks (which are better in explaining inter-industry trade, for example, agriculture goods in exchange for industrial goods) but is explained more by imperfect competition. Intra-ASEAN trade is no exception and in fact illustrates this phenomenon. Table B2.1 shows intra-industry trade indices in manufactures (0 means that all trade is inter-industry; 1 means all trade is intra-industry) for the Philippines with four ASEAN members. The numbers indicate an expansion of intra-industry trade — between 21 per cent for Malaysia and 39 per cent for Singapore. This is quite an improvement over 1970 values.

When disaggregated by specific products, the magnitude of overlapping trade in some cases is large. Calculations of the indices for the Philippines in the fifteen products under the accelerated CEPT scheme show indices as high as 0.90 (chemicals and pharmaceutical trade with Indonesia; rubber products trade with Malaysia and Singapore; electronics trade with Singapore; and trade in leather products with Thailand).

The full potential of intra-industry trade is realized under free trade. This was the hallmark of trade in Europe. Although the theoretical prediction of what products a trading country specializes in are uncertain, there is much room for differentiated products, market niches, and scale economies.

The original modes of ASEAN co-operation in industry and trade such as the AIP and AIC were based on the notion of specialization and comparative advantage that would have required protection for industries to thrive. Intra-industry trade, on the other hand, evolves out of free trade. If this illustrative case of the Philippines is any indication, ASEAN will see an expansion of intra-industry trade in the future.

Table B 2.1
Intra-Industry Trade Indices: Philippines

	1970	1990
All commodities		
with world	0.08	0.39
Manufactures		
with world	0.07	0.42
with Indonesia	0.17	0.28
with Malaysia	—	0.21
with Singapore	0.15	0.39
with Thailand	0.17	0.22

Source of basic data: P. Drysdale and R. Garnaut, "The Pacific: An Application of the General Theory of Economic Integration", in *Pacific Dynamism and the International Economic System*, edited by C.F. Bergsten and M. Noland (Washington, D.C.: Institute for International Economics, 1993).

ASEAN, would profitably engage in trade, some in competitive products, others in terms of production complementarities.

In the light of global integration, ASEAN's industrial development and trade are taking on a new meaning beyond the narrow confines of competitiveness and industry specialization as envisioned in previous co-operation modalities. It is moving significantly into complementarities, vertically and horizontally, across industries and product groups. ASEAN's difficulties and problems with regional industrial development taught valuable lessons that will provide a firm foundation for the transition from competitiveness to complementarity.

C. Food, Agriculture, and Forestry: Security with Conservation

Agriculture remains an important part of ASEAN's development agenda. Whether as producer, processor, or trader, each of the ASEAN economies is involved in agriculture. Indeed, the ASEAN region continues to be important producers and traders of several agricultural crops (for example, rubber, rice, coconut). Despite its importance, however, the share of agriculture in GDP consistently and dramatically declined between 1970 and 1990, as shown in Table 2.7. This means more than just the absolute decline in agriculture value-added. Rather, the growth of other industries far outstripped that of agriculture. Table 2.8 makes a comparison of the agriculture value-added growth rate

Table 2.7
Share of Agriculture in GDP, 1970–95
(Percentages)

Country	1970	1980	1993	1995[a]
Brunei	n.a.	1	1	n.a.
Indonesia	35	24.1	18	16.3
Malaysia	n.a.	22.9	16	13.9
Philippines	28.2	23.5	23	21.9
Singapore	2.2	1.1	0	0.2
Thailand	30.2	20.2	12	10.5
Vietnam	n.a.	42.7	29	32.2

[a] Projected.
n.a. = Not available.

Source: Asian Development Bank.

Table 2.8
Growth Rates of Value-Added in Agriculture, 1971–94
(Percentages)

Country	1971–80	1981–90	1991	1992	1993	1994
Indonesia	3.6	3.1	1.6	6.6	1.4	1.6
Malaysia	4.9	3.9	0	4.3	3.9	0.5
Philippines	3.9	1	1.4	0.4	2.1	2.4
Singapore	1.1	–6.8	–9.4	1.1	0.1	0.2
Thailand	3.1	3.9	5.9	4.2	–1.7	2.9
Vietnam	n.a.	5.3	2.2	7.2	3.8	3.6
ASEAN[a]	3.3	1	0.4	0.9	0.2	0.4

[a] Excluding Brunei and Vietnam, 1991–94 weighted by population.

Source: Asian Development Bank.

between the decade of the 1970s and 1980s. The latter average for ASEAN is less than a third of the growth of the previous decade. When a comparison is made of Table 2.8 with Table 2.5, the reason for the decline of agriculture's share in GDP becomes apparent.

Of the seven ASEAN members, five have significant agricultural sectors (that is, Indonesia, Malaysia, the Philippines, Thailand, and Vietnam). Their respective agricultural sectors are broadly measured either in terms of cultivated land area, total forest and woodland area, or total freshwater resources. Within these agricultural sectors, there are differences across countries. Some have more diversified agricultural sectors than others. Also, for specific products (for example, rubber), ASEAN's share in total world production is large. There are also countries (at least three) that are petroleum exporters while the rest are net importers.

In terms of ASEAN agricultural value-added, two countries, Brunei and Singapore contribute less than half a per cent of the total. In overall agriculture, Indonesia accounts for more than 40 per cent; the Philippines and Thailand, about 18 per cent each; Malaysia, 16 per cent; and Vietnam, 6 per cent. In terms of particular agricultural products, ASEAN is important relative to total world production. For example, ASEAN contributes more than 19 per cent of rice production (from the five members), 77 per cent of rubber production (Malaysia, Indonesia, and Thailand), and more than 80 per cent of copra and coconut oil (the Philippines, Malaysia, and Indonesia). Similarly, palm oil, spices, sugar, and forest products are important ASEAN products in global agriculture.

Despite the rapid industrial development of ASEAN, agriculture remains important. The proportion of rural population to total population in 1993 ranges from 48 per cent for the Philippines to Vietnam's 80 per cent (excluding Brunei and Singapore). Agriculture's share of GDP (1993) for all of ASEAN is 29 per cent, ranging from 12 per cent in Thailand to 29 per cent in Vietnam.

Food production in ASEAN is a major concern in the region. Two members (Thailand and Vietnam) are consistent exporters of rice although Indonesia produces 47 per cent of ASEAN's rice output. Except for Thailand, these shares have remained stable since 1985. The same can be said for corn, the other major crop produced in ASEAN.

In recent years, some ASEAN countries (excluding Brunei, Singapore, and Thailand) have devoted larger areas to agriculture with a consequent rise in yields per hectare, as shown in Table 2.9. Thus, the source of output growth of food crops seems to be more through increases in area planted rather than yield. Thus, there may be potentials for yield increases from innovations since for most members, the closing of land frontiers suggest that increases in food output will have to come from increases in yield. In addition, the experience of substan-

Table 2.9
Planted Area: Output and Yield, 1983–92

	Area ('000 hectares)		Output ('000 metric tonnes)		Yield (metric tonnes)	
Country	1983	1992	1983	1992	1983	1992
Brunei	2	1	3	1	1.5	1
Indonesia	9,162	11,103	35,303	48,240	3.85	4.34
Malaysia	666	679	1,734	2,070	2.6	3.05
Philippines	3,141	3,198	7,295	9,129	2.32	2.85
Singapore	n.a.	n.a.	n.a.	n.a.	n.a.	n.a.
Thailand	9,608	9,558	19,549	20,180	2.03	2.11
Vietnam	5,611	6,475	14,743	21,590	2.63	3.33

n.a. = Not available.

Source: Economic and Social Commission for Asia and the Pacific, *Statistical Yearbook for Asia and the Pacific* (various issues).

tial post-harvest losses in the ASEAN grains sub-sector implies some potential for yield and output improvements.

The other element in ASEAN food production is the livestock sub-sector that links backward to crops, and forward to agro-processing and related activities. So far, among the ASEAN states, Thailand is a net exporter of meat. Yet, other states with significant agricultural sectors can just as easily go into exports of meat, especially the non-ruminant kind, depending on the level of their corn production (as an ingredient for poultry and hog feed).

The region also contains substantial freshwater and seawater fish resources. The ASEAN region is part of the larger Pacific area that has 65 per cent of the harvest value of major tropical tuna species in the world. Of particular concern in the region are management problems posed by transboundary fishery resources (even with the establishment of the Exclusive Economic Zone [EEZ]), which prevent exploitation of ASEAN marine resources.

In 1993, some 47.5 per cent of ASEAN's total area was forest and woodland, a rich source of timber resources. The proportion of forest area varies considerably among ASEAN states. For instance, the Philippines has 33 per cent; Thailand, about 26 per cent; Vietnam, 29 per cent; and Indonesia, 59 per cent.[14] Although almost all ASEAN countries have expressed a concern for ecological balance and conservation, the declining proportion of forest area in some states may indicate differences in the degree of importance attached to environmental issues.

In the agricultural and trade sectors, the similarities among ASEAN states (wherein there would be competition) and their differences (wherein there would be complementarities) did not deter the mutual pursuit of co-operation. At least in this sector, ASEAN agreed to the concept of a regional food security reserve early on.

The regional food security provision stipulates that each ASEAN member establish an emergency rice reserve, over and above its national reserve, for the purpose of meeting ASEAN emergency needs. This reserve started at 50,000 metric tonnes of rice, with Thailand contributing 15,000 metric tonnes; the Philippines and Indonesia, 12,000 metric tonnes each; Malaysia, 6,000 metric tonnes; and Singapore, 5,000 metric tonnes. The agreement further defines emergency as the condition in which an ASEAN member suffers external and unexpected natural or man-induced calamity and food needs cannot be met through its reserve or through normal trade.

The manner of calling on the food security reserve as well as the terms and conditions of assistance is bilateral rather than multilateral (that is, the country in need can directly request the reserve from another country or countries). Notice, however, is given to the ASEAN Food Security Reserve Board (AFSRB).

The AFSRB's mandate goes beyond just supervising and co-ordinating the implementation of food security reserve. It extends into the periodic evaluation of ASEAN's food situation in particular, and world-wide in general; the exchange of information on policies pertaining to production, consumption, and storage of basic food commodities such as rice; and a review of the size of the ASEAN emergency rice reserve. In line with this, in recent years the rice reserve was adjusted to 53,000 metric tonnes amidst developments in ASEAN and the accession of Brunei Darussalam to the Agreement in October 1986. With Vietnam's accession, the total earmarked reserve stock will be increased to 67,000 metric tonnes.

The AFSRB is one of the many mechanisms for promoting co-operation in food, agriculture, and forestry. Until recently, another ASEAN committee, the COFAF, covered the whole gamut of areas described earlier, including crops, fisheries, livestock, forestry, agricultural research, extension, training, and agricultural co-operatives. It also had the largest number of subsidiary bodies (sub-committees and working groups) and regularly met with other co-ordinating groups. The COFAF had over fifty combined short-term and long-term projects on food security reserve and food handling, among others. The role of the COFAF was taken over by the Senior Officials Meeting of the ASEAN Ministers of Agriculture and Forestry (SOM-AMAF), which is being supported by eleven subsidiary bodies, among them, the AFSRB.

Without exhausting all the programmes and projects in this sector, several activities clearly address regional interests. For one, ASEAN projects on grains post-harvest improvement recognized the importance of post-harvest losses to agricultural productivity. Various sectoral (completed) programmes, such as the Aquaculture Development and Co-ordinating Programme, Fisheries Post-Harvest Technology Development and Small-Scale Coastal Fisheries Development addressed the concerns on fisheries and aquatic resources. On the other hand, in forestry, the ASEAN Forest Seed Centre, ASEAN Institute of Forest Management, and Timber Technology Centre attend to co-operation in afforestation, forest, and watershed management, and timber technology. The first two projects are still ongoing and is expected to terminate by March 1997 and July 1997, respectively.

In the post–Fourth ASEAN Summit and with the dissolution of the ASEAN committees on economic co-operation, the programmes on food, agriculture, and forestry are more focused. The Ministerial Understanding on ASEAN Co-operation in Food, Agriculture, Fisheries, and Forestry include the following priority areas of co-operation: (a) strengthening food security, (b) facilitation and promotion of intra- and extra-ASEAN trade in agriculture, fishery, and forest products, (c) technology generation and transfer to increase productivity and develop agribusiness and silvobusiness, (d) agricultural, community, and human resource development, (e) private sector involvement and investment, (f) management and conservation of natural resources for sustainable development, and (g) strengthening ASEAN co-operation and joint approaches in addressing international and regional issues.

For each of the seven priority areas, member countries developed a sectoral action programme covering policy co-ordination, research, technology transfer, production, marketing, and investment promotion. The general objective is to enable member countries to manage their agricultural and forestry sectors efficiently, use the latest technology in production and processing, be made aware of market information, produce at competitive prices, and allow international market expansion, enter new markets, and exploit technological and organizational advantages. The sectoral action programmes are embodied in the 1995–99 Medium-Term Programme of Action for ASEAN Co-operation in Food, Agriculture, Fisheries, and Forestry, which was approved by the AMAF in 1994.

In the area of sustainable agricultural development, there is mention of aligning ASEAN's follow-up actions to Agenda 21 and the Statement of Principles on the Management, Conservation, and Sustainable Development of All Types of Forests as adopted by the United Nations Conference on Environment and Development (UNCED).

Other than this, the action plan urges the strengthening of institutional capabilities in integrated coastal zone management, conservation of marine resources and watersheds, and the monitoring, control, and surveillance of EEZs. It also advocates the development of regional policies on the conservation of biodiversity for the development of plants and animals for food and medicinal purposes.

Greater emphasis is given to the task of ASEAN co-ordinating its approaches on international and regional issues, particularly those that relate to farm subsidies and market access for agricultural and processed products, among others. Relatedly, ASEAN should strengthen its joint positions in (a) organizations such as the Food and Agriculture Organization (FAO) and the International Tropical Timber Organization (ITTO); (b) international fora such as the UNCED and the GATT; and (c) international agreements such as the International Natural Rubber Agreement (INRA). At the same time, ASEAN is encouraged to pursue enhanced co-operation with developed countries in training, research and development activities in food, agriculture, and forestry to find new uses for, and to upgrade the quality of, agriculture and forestry products.

Unprocessed agricultural products are to be included in the CEPT scheme for AFTA. All these products would either go into the Immediate Inclusion List or Temporary Exclusion List, with other arrangements worked out for sensitive unprocessed agricultural products not subject to CEPT scheme requirements. Although the details need to be fully laid out, including tariff reduction schedules and consistency with the CEPT scheme for 2003, there is no doubt that the inclusion of unprocessed agricultural products is a recognition of points of complementarity, benefits from scale economies, and free trade in agriculture.

Co-operation in forestry reinforces the larger context of the Jakarta Resolution on Sustainable Development, which highlights ASEAN common resources such as tropical rainforests, land resources, and the common seas. Thus, the forestry sector in ASEAN adopted "Towards Sustainable Forest Management in the 21st Century" as a central theme, addressing common strategies pertaining to the Convention on International Trade in Endangered Species (CITES), and adopting a common stand on the issue of timber product eco-labelling.

In addition, ASEAN is poised to take a common stand in agriculture and forestry promotion schemes to strengthen ASEAN's collective bargaining position in world markets, upgrade the quality of ASEAN agriculture, fisheries, and forestry products, and promote closer economic ties in ASEAN. Identified products include palm and coconut oil, carrageenan, frozen chicken, tapioca, frozen prawn, canned tuna, canned pineapple, cocoa, pepper, and forest products (timber and non-timber).

With the dissolution of the COFAF, the AMAF requested the ASEAN Secretariat to establish working groups on crops, livestock, fisheries, forestry, training and extension, and agricultural co-operation. The working groups' recommendation became the components of the 1995–99 Medium-Term Programme of Action for ASEAN Co-operation in Food, Agriculture, and Forestry, which identified sixteen projects to be implemented through networking arrangements among ASEAN member countries.

To facilitate the implementation of the action plan, an ASEAN sectoral co-ordinator in each sector will be held accountable to the SOM-AMAF and the ASEAN Secretariat. Each member country, on the other hand, shall appoint a national sectoral co-ordinator who will be accountable to the national SOM-AMAF leader. Individual projects at the national level shall have a focal point who is an expert or specialist in the area. An ASEAN Project Focal Point will be selected among the national focal points to facilitate implementation and exchange of information among national experts.

In summary, despite the changes in co-operation mechanisms, the wide array of subsidiary bodies on the sector, and the similarity of the agricultural structure among five of the seven ASEAN members, the substance of co-operation remains the same. Concern for food security, for instance, is strong with the AFSRB's close monitoring of ASEAN's food supply to determine an optimum size for an expanding ASEAN and its mandate to increase the size of the emergency rice reserve as conditions warrant. In addition, food security includes other essential food items, and as part of food safety in ASEAN, co-operation has concentrated on minimization of post-harvest food losses and trade expansion of food products.

The Jakarta Resolution on Sustainable Development of 1987

boosted conservation concerns. Through several projects, ASEAN maintains a common theme for the sector, a common strategy with respect to international issues, and operates forest-related centres in the region (for example, the ASEAN Forest Tree Seed Centre and ASEAN Institute of Forest Management).

ASEAN's co-operation in forestry fits well with its conservation focus. For example, ASEAN's environmental impact studies on the use of local drift nets and its evaluation of tuna catch on fisheries resources management highlight conservation concerns.

Given the array of efforts on food security and conservation, the dramatic decisions to include unprocessed agricultural products in the CEPT scheme for AFTA signals an integrated view of food, agriculture, and forestry in the region. Undoubtedly, as trade in agriculture expands and sectoral policies benefit from years of co-operation and information exchange, the concerns will become institutionalized.

There remains two apparent lacunae in co-operation activities so far. One, there has hardly been sustained efforts at addressing the importance of joint approaches to increase levels of productivity especially for crops. While attention to post-harvest losses as a factor that impinges on productivity has merit, equal attention should also be given to develop crop varieties suited to ASEAN, hence a corresponding reliance on indigenous ASEAN genetic experiments. As land frontiers are reached, incremental food sources will have to come from technological improvements in crop production. ASEAN is starting to explore options in this regard (see Box 2.4).

Second, while there is an acknowledged common theme for conservation, ASEAN needs to take further steps in co-operation towards a common agricultural policy in ASEAN. This will require a deeper understanding of ASEAN comparative advantages by member countries and a recognition of product specialization. Relatedly, common incentive schemes to promote a single agricultural structure for the region has to be adopted. With the incorporation of agriculture in intra-ASEAN free trade, one policy hurdle was overcome. It remains to be seen whether this will be followed by a comprehensive view of ASEAN agriculture that will address co-operation schemes to increase output and satisfy food security and conservation concerns.

BOX 2.4: FOOD IRRADIATION IN ASEAN

The ASEAN Secretariat and the International Consultative Group on Food Irradiation (ICGFI) recently organized a Seminar on Food Irradiation in Jakarta in 1995.

The Seminar assessed the need to adopt food irradiation as a method to reduce post-harvest losses, control food-borne diseases, and expand trade in food products of member countries. It also addressed the status of regulations, technological advances, and trade in, and consumer acceptance of, irradiated food globally and in ASEAN.

The holding of the Seminar was considered significant and timely in light of the rapid actualization of the ASEAN Free Trade Area (AFTA), the current efforts of member countries to establish greater transparency in their sanitary and phytosanitary (SPS) measures and to adopt harmonized quality standards to enhance trade, and the need for ASEAN to take a common position on the application of irradiation technology in overcoming non-tariff barriers to trade.

An important output of the Seminar was a recommendation that, among others, ASEAN (a) consider food irradiation as one option in addressing food-related issues; (b) prepare for trade opportunities that might arise as food irradiation gains wider acceptance; (c) consider food irradiation as a new area of co-operation in line with the directive of the Fourth ASEAN Summit to continually seek new initiatives to enhance regional economic co-operation; and (d) consider the Model Regulation on Irradiated Food for Asia and the Pacific for updating and refinement and as a basis of harmonized regulations on irradiated food within ASEAN.

D. Transport, Communications, and Tourism: Connecting ASEAN

ASEAN member states are not geographically contiguous. Only three of them (Malaysia, Singapore, and Thailand) are physically connected. The rest are separate from each other although parts of them may be connected (for example, East Malaysia and Brunei) and others are archipelagic. Yet, in part, what has driven the ASEAN organization is the identity of being one region. A critical area of ASEAN co-operation has therefore been in "connecting" the members together via transport, communications, and tourism.

A physical link among ASEAN states through road networks would be a tall order considering the enormous magnitude of required infrastructure. Even previous ideas of an ASEAN highway could not cover all ASEAN member states. However, advances in telecommunications and information technology, the development of inter-modal transport and market-initiated physical linkages appear to overshadow the need for a comprehensive regional infrastructure network. These sub-regional physical linkages (for example, the SIJORI, IMT-GT) becomes more cost-effective over time as market players take advantage of the ease with which trade transactions occur.

ASEAN's transport co-operation schemes were initially laid out by the ASEAN permanent committee that covered civil air transport, shipping, and land transport. These were consolidated into an Integrated Work Programme on Transport and Communications (IWPTC) and subsequently into a Programme of Action in Transport and Communications (POATC) for 1992–96. A Plan of Action is in place for implementation in 1996–98. In earlier periods, 1982–86 and 1987–91, programmes for the communications sector include the Business Reply Service, ASEAN submarine cable projects (linking the Philippines and Singapore, Indonesia and Singapore, and Malaysia, Singapore, and Thailand) and Inter-Country Remittance Services. In the transport sector, most of the projects were in the maritime sector, and the rest deal with civil aviation and land transportation.

In formulating these initiatives, ASEAN co-operation seemed to be guided by a major consideration — to facilitate ASEAN trade and investment flows. For example, the ASEAN Resolution on Shipping and Trade adopted by the AEM in 1980, and reaffirmed by the AEM a year later, recognized the importance of shipping and ports to the development and expansion of ASEAN trade and economy, among others. There were also calls for setting up an ASEAN Liner Service that was approved by the AEM in 1981. However, this required a realignment of national priorities in transport towards regional agreements (for example, reducing cabotage restrictions, broader cargo reservations, and so forth), thus the 1981 proposal was reviewed for several years without concrete agreement. Some priority programmes to implement the ASEAN Resolution through the New Initiatives in Shipping proceeded but the results were way below expectations due to internal and external factors. Even the 1987 Manila Declaration merely pointed to the principles of the ASEAN Liner Service proposal as the foundation of an overall ASEAN transportation network.

The subsequent 1992–96 Programme of Action in Transport and Communications identified co-operation areas in policy, economic, and technical studies, human resource development, institution building, and sharing of expertise and information. Later, the 1992 Singapore Declaration and the Framework Agreement on Enhancing ASEAN Economic Co-operation directs ASEAN to "further enhance regional co-operation to provide safe, efficient, and innovative transportation and communications infrastructure network and continue to improve and develop intra-country postal and telecommunications system to provide cost-effective, high-quality and customer-oriented services". To achieve these goals, the ASEAN Plan of Action in Transport and Communications, 1992–96, was officially adopted by the AEM in September 1995 and reaffirmed under the 1995 Bangkok Declaration. The time frame for implementation was, however, revised to 1996–98 during the First ASEAN Transport Ministers (ATM) Meeting in March 1996.

An important development of the meeting was the signing of a Ministerial Understanding to establish a formal co-ordination mechanism for the transportation sector. Transport ministers also directed the development of detailed action programmes for each of the seven theme issues under the 1996–98 Plan of Action, as follows: (a) Multimodal Transport and Trade Facilitation, (b) ASEAN Interconnectivity in Telecommunications, (c) Harmonization of Road Transport Laws, Rules, and Regulations, (d) Improvement of Air Space Management in ASEAN, (e) Safety of Maritime Transport and Prevention of Pollution from Ships, (f) Human Resources Development, and (g) Competitive Air Services Policy. The latter is an initial step towards an Open Sky Policy in ASEAN. This was considered in the Bangkok Summit in 1995.

Co-operation programmes in transportation and communications include the completion of the ASEAN Cargo Transport Study (ACTS), establishment of freight booking and consolidation centres, implementation of the ASEAN optical fibre submarine cable network, inter-country remittance services. There were also numerous training programmes in land transportation, shipping and ports, civil aviation and related services, and postal and telecommunications services.

Regional co-operation also included lowering of cable, telex, telephone, and postal charges among ASEAN states. The ASEAN Express Mail Service (EMS) is an illustration of this. In addition, co-operation activities include establishing an ASEAN Postal Track and Trace System for the ASEAN EMS, the continued promotion of philately, and enhancement of mail security. It is in telecommunications, however, that ASEAN co-operation appears to have lagged behind. The ASEAN Datacom Co-ordinating Group (with Malaysia as Secretariat) confines co-operation in data communications, public data networks and services, and packet switching. In recent years, however, ASEAN and the rest of Asia saw a revolution taking place in telecommunications. Driven by private sector initiative, distance among trading partners is now a minor concern as alternative and superior communication modes emerged. Rapid developments in the field "shrunk" ASEAN in terms of physical distance as fast and efficient communication links changed the pace of financial transactions and made possible interactive consultations among ASEAN businessmen, thus facilitating decision-making and consensus-building. As globalization of firms take place, and with ASEAN actively participating in the process, the notion of building physical linkages is more and more being applied to the movement of goods, rather than individuals, across state boundary lines.

Substantial growth in wireless communications — cellular, fixed radio, paging, and data services — in ASEAN is also impressive. Three ASEAN countries (Malaysia, the Philippines, and Thailand) are among the top ten markets in cellular services in Asia. Their quick installation at falling costs in what otherwise (that is, telephone) requires years of waiting in some countries is helped along by private sector co-operation and ASEAN governments' collective policies of deregulation, liberalization, and privatization. However, there is an urgent need to ensure interconnectivity and harmonization of telecommunications services between ASEAN countries and between ASEAN and the global network.

There are also dramatic changes taking place in other telecommunications media. Broadcast deregulation in the late 1980s reduced the number of public broadcasters while increasing the number of private broadcasters, introduced cable and satellite television, and created legal questions of individual dish ownership, intellectual property, and copyright protection. The collective ASEAN use of Indonesia's Palapa system contributed to a "borderless ASEAN". In fact, many major ASEAN programmes are simultaneously seen by all member states. In telecommunications, present co-operation is geared towards the creation of ASEAN programmes. On the other hand, developments in broadcasting and computing prompted telephone companies to transform themselves into full-pledged information service companies.

In civil aviation, the ASEAN broad agreement for enhanced co-operation is manifested in increased forms of private sector co-operation. Three of the seven ASEAN national airlines are among the most profitable world airlines. Over a third of their revenues depend on Asian passengers. Moves towards privatization opened alliance possibilities for many of them. ASEAN now utilizes a joint computer reservation system (ABACUS), and is a party to code-sharing arrangements.

On the part of ASEAN governments, there were joint consultations on alternatives to investments in tarmac via the Future Air Navigation System (FANS) (that is, the CNS/ATM system), in addition to independent airport capacity expansions in Malaysia, Singapore, and Thailand; joint training programmes on airport security, airport design and construction, disabled aircraft removal/recovery techniques; and navigational flight calibration aid systems.

In shipping and ports, further collaboration aims to increase capacities to implement multimodal transport systems, promote compatible and harmonized national legislation, regulation, and freight and cargo traffic. An ASEAN Framework Agreement on Multimodal Transport is also envisioned. In addition, there are joint training sessions on port planning and management to improve the ability of ASEAN members on port facilities' expansion, and the productivity and efficiency of port facilities.

Promoting ASEAN as a tourist destination among ASEAN and non-ASEAN nationals is the aim of co-operation in tourism. This involves joint marketing strategies and training programmes that highlight ASEAN's commonalities as well as distinct cultural and social heritage.

Among the more concrete measures implemented by ASEAN to

promote tourism are the holding of ASEAN trade fairs every two years (adopted at the AEM in 1978), reciprocal recognition of domestic driver's licences in ASEAN countries, establishment of an ASEAN Promotion Centre on Trade, Investment, and Tourism in Japan in 1981 to cater to the Japanese market, and the declaration of 1992 as the "Visit ASEAN Year". In addition, visas are no longer required for travel within ASEAN by ASEAN nationals. Indeed, there was a hefty increase in the number of total tourist arrivals in ASEAN from all countries in the last five years. Annual growth rates ranged from 32 per cent for Indonesia (1989–93) to 34 per cent for Thailand. Intra-ASEAN tourists also rose in recent years. Tourists (from the PATA area) for the period 1984–93 increased from 26.4 per cent in 1984 to 31.3 per cent in 1994 (about 72 million). Three countries, namely, Indonesia, Singapore, and Thailand are among the top ten destinations of the Pacific Area Travel Association (PATA). In 1995, foreign tourist arrivals to Indonesia was 4.32 million, bringing some US$5.9 billion in revenue (see Box 2.5).

ASEAN tourism efforts are complemented by promotional efforts from the industry itself. For example, there is an "ASEAN fare" package offered by ASEAN airlines and national tourism brochures feature other ASEAN destinations. The combination of inter-governmental measures and private sector initiative supported ASEAN tourism in the last twenty-five years. As indicated in the action plan, future co-operative efforts in tourism will be directed towards the provision of transport and tourism-related infrastructure and shall focus on promoting sustainable tourism development, preservation of cultural and environmental resources, simplification of immigration procedures and human resource development.

The main objective behind co-operation among ASEAN states in transportation, communications, and tourism is to connect ASEAN. Given the geographical diversity of its members, ASEAN has had to collectively come up with measures that enhance linkages among them, reduce distances for trade and interaction among themselves, and promote deeper appreciation of each other's social and cultural heritage.

The rapid transformation of the global economic environment, the convergence of many technological advances that facilitate trade, and the desire of progressive individuals to see more of their neighbours

BOX 2.5: TOURISM IN ASEAN

None of the ASEAN member countries rely on tourism as a major source of foreign exchange earnings. Tourism earnings in the region in 1993 amounted to US$18.9 billion, representing only 8.9 per cent of the region's total exports of US$211.8 billion for the same year. Although the growth of exports has been higher (at 10.3 per cent per year) than tourist arrivals (at 7.5 per cent per year) in the last decade, this does not mean that tourism is unimportant.

Tourism, especially intra-ASEAN tourism, is a vehicle for connecting people, assimilating culture, and promoting a common identity. Moreover, despite advances in telecommunications, the minimum physical infrastructure to "connect" ASEAN countries remains formidable, thus making tourism doubly important.

Some 41.6 per cent of tourist arrivals in ASEAN in 1993 were from ASEAN countries. This is the largest group followed by tourists from Japan (10.3 per cent of arrivals into ASEAN in 1993). However, this hides a wide variation within each of the ASEAN member countries. Over 90 per cent of tourist arrivals in Brunei were ASEAN in origin while in the Philippines, ASEAN tourists constituted just under 5 per cent of tourist arrivals.

Even if tourist arrivals from ASEAN had increased in recent years, the average length of stay in ASEAN (excluding Brunei and Vietnam) has not increased substantially during the period 1985–92: from 7.1 to 7.5 days. Thus, ASEAN tourism promotion should work at increasing not only the number of intra-ASEAN tourists or the number of ASEAN countries visited but also their length of stay.

have changed the scope and manner of ASEAN co-operation in transportation, communications, and tourism. Thus, despite continuing discussions in ASEAN of new co-operation modalities, the environment has had a dynamism of its own.

ASEAN co-operation was important in setting a pace for connecting ASEAN and linking its citizens together. The faster pace of other developments (in transport and telecommunications) has actually challenged ASEAN to increase its pace. That appears to be what matters in the next generation as ASEAN becomes more "connected" — electronically and physically.

E. Finance and Banking: Towards Financial Integration

An implied goal of ASEAN co-operation in finance and banking is not just developing ASEAN financial institutions but increasing the frequency and depth of transactions among member countries. A distinction has to be made, however, between what can be pursued by monetary authorities and the kind of relationships that take place among private financial and banking institutions.

One of the earliest and concrete expressions of ASEAN co-operation in this area was the Swap Arrangement agreed upon in 1977 (that has since been amended). The arrangements provide for a stand-by credit of US$200 million to member countries with short-run liquidity problems. Countries are allowed to purchase foreign exchange (on a spot transactions basis) with local currency and its forward sale (with the same local currency) is set at a future date for one, two, or three months, and a possible extension of another three months (maximum).

Beyond this form of co-operation, ASEAN also endeavours to foster greater financial interdependence among ASEAN countries. This requires a harmonized environment where no undue barriers to financial transactions exist. For its part, ASEAN's Committee on Finance and Banking (COFAB) convened three subsidiary bodies in support of this goal. These are the Working Group on Customs Matters, the ASEAN Meeting of Insurance Commissioners, and the Working Group on Tax Matters.

An ASEAN Customs Code of Conduct was signed in 1983 laying out the principles and standards regarding customs valuation, classification, and other supporting measures for intra-ASEAN trade. With the advent of the CEPT scheme, the link broadened to include the harmonization of tariff nomenclature.

The actions of the Asia-Pacific Economic Co-operation (APEC) appear to support ASEAN's co-operation on customs matters as it has convened customs officials in the region to arrive at region-wide standards on valuation methods, classification, and tariff nomenclature, among others.

The ASEAN Insurance Commissioners supported the private sector's ASEAN Insurance Council in creating an ASEAN Reinsurance Pool in 1982. For reinsurance transactions to thrive ASEAN-wide, the development of common standards, definitions, and other norms acceptable to ASEAN members is required. At the 19th AEM in 1987, an ASEAN Reinsurance Corporation was established with an authorized capital of S$20 million. At the succeeding AEM this was increased to S$30 million.

At the Third ASEAN Summit in Manila, an Agreement for the Promotion and Protection of Investments was drawn up, incorporating non-discriminatory provisions among ASEAN states on expropriation (where necessary), the guarantee of capital and earnings repatriations, subrogation, and arbitration procedures. The ratification of this Agreement reflected the importance of investment to the region.

In the end, co-operation in finance and banking should stimulate greater capital mobility within ASEAN. This can only be facilitated with greater trade within the region as financial integration follows greater trade transactions. In the late 1980s and early 1990s, ASEAN, along with the rest of Asia, saw the emergence of capital markets driven by the combination of government-led privatization and ASEAN firms seeking larger equity or joint venture partners. Indeed, ASEAN became a central part of the emerging capital market sought out by foreign investors.

A reconfiguration of capital markets in ASEAN took place. As member states gave greater importance to foreign investments, as Asia experienced rising wealth that created excess capital, as ASEAN conglomerates expanded, and as governments accommodated international equity, in short, by sheer market forces, the ASEAN region became integrated with global capital markets. The Philippines, for example, is host to investments of Thailand's Shinawatra Group while other ASEAN countries are partners to the increasing number of Singaporean corporate investors. Indeed, ASEAN, as a regional capital market, has come of age.

F. Minerals and Energy: Enhancing Co-operation

In the early 1970s, although there was a close association between growth, minerals development, and energy use, it had never been interwoven into the overall economic context of ASEAN, or for that matter, in the global economy. Though the two oil crises triggered independent actions in exploring alternative fuel sources, greater energy efficiency, and price adjustments, economic co-operation activities in this sector did not immediately follow suit.

Within ASEAN, this is partly explained by the organizational direction of sectors. Of the fifteen subsidiary bodies under COIME, only two focused on minerals and non-petroleum energy resources (each an Experts Group). Several other subsidiary bodies, however, impinge on minerals and energy.

The diverse nature of ASEAN countries with respect to these sectors has likewise constrained joint perspectives. Three members — Indonesia, Malaysia, and Brunei — are major producers of oil and gas while the Philippines, Thailand, and Vietnam depend, in large part, on imported oil. On the other hand, Singapore, as an oil-refining and trading country, imports crude oil and exports petroleum products.

ASEAN weathered the first oil crisis by a combination of appropriate macroeconomic policies, price adjustments, and conservation measures. The second oil crisis, however, affected ASEAN's economic performance more as some countries were, by then, burdened with debt, an adverse balance of payments, and inflation, among others. It was only during this period that concerted ASEAN efforts in energy co-operation went into high gear as countries shifted their energy demand away from oil sources and began to harness the natural gas deposits available in the region. As expected, the use of natural gas and coal increased and, since 1992, Malaysia began to supply piped gas to Singapore. More recently, a study initiated by the ASEAN-EC Energy Management Training and Research Centre (AEEMTRC) indicates that the Trans-ASEAN Gas Pipeline could be realized as early as 2010.

The Agreement on ASEAN Energy Co-operation of 1986 spelled out the six areas for co-operation — planning, energy development, conservation, training, energy supply, and information exchange. Details of the general agreement can be found in the 1986 ASEAN Petroleum Security Agreement. The definition of a shortage and oversupply situation is specified and conditions are identified under which ASEAN governments shall make available crude oil and/or petroleum products to a country in short supply or procure the same from a member in oversupply.

Under the recent reorganization, the three pillars of ASEAN's co-operation in energy are petroleum security, conservation, and the search for alternative fuels. Focus on these three areas reflects ASEAN's recognition that sustained economic growth requires considerable inputs of energy.

The ASEAN Medium-Term Action Programme on Energy Co-operation (1995–99) followed a review of the Programme of Action for Enhancement of ASEAN Co-operation in Energy, which in turn was endorsed by the ASEAN Economic Ministers on Energy Co-operation (AEMEC) in 1991. The Programme cites the need to develop specific measures for energy co-operation, strengthens previous modalities expressed in past agreements, and rationalizes related energy co-operation activities. Included in the latter is a forum on power utilities or authorities, a master plan on natural gas development and utilization, and energy management training and research.

Energy sub-sectors that require follow-up work include electricity, coal, oil and gas, geothermal resources, new and renewable sources of energy (NRSE), energy efficiency/conservation, diversification of energy sources, energy and the environment, and energy policy and planning.

In the electricity sector, the Programme calls for jointly developing and utilizing energy resources, strengthening interconnection development efforts leading to the realization of the ASEAN Power Grid and standardizing power equipment for its eventual manufacture within ASEAN. On the other hand, the ASEAN Council on Petroleum (ASCOPE) is focused on oil conservation and its activities include information exchange, exploratory studies on natural gas pipeline connection in ASEAN, and test correlation for fuels and engines.

There is a renewed emphasis on the commercialization of NRSE, mainly in the development of ASEAN manufacturing capabilities in the NRSE sector and the promotion of intra-ASEAN trade in NRSE products, namely, solar photo voltaic systems, solar thermal water heaters, and wind-energy equipment. Relatedly, as the key to sustainable energy development, energy policy and planning is pursued along the lines of energy conservation and environmental awareness. As in other sectoral Programme, energy planning is directed towards achieving national development and the promotion of economic co-operation and trade within ASEAN. This it hopes to achieve by an active exchange of country experiences in the formulation and implementation of energy policy, plans and measures, environmental impact assessment studies, and environmental standards. The latter provides material for an energy planning database from which a comprehensive regional energy co-operation plan could be formulated.

Implementation of in-country components of the Programme shall be the responsibility of a national focal point and various other focal points for each of the identified energy sub-sectors. Technical support shall be provided, as necessary, by the AEEMTRC, which will also participate in the planning and implementation of work plans for the ASEAN Energy Co-operation Programme.

Past co-operation activities in minerals were sporadic and limited in terms of organization, falling as they were under the COIME, which had other substantive responsibilities. In recent ASEAN history, however, the framework of co-operation in minerals is more focused as the sector is seen as particularly supportive of ASEAN's industrialization drive. Consequently, programmes are directed on the production and utilization of industrial minerals and its finished products, and their integration with the larger industrial sector.

In response to the restructuring of ASEAN institutions, ASEAN's co-operation programme in minerals for 1994–96 aims at the following: (a) rationalization of investment in mineral resources of ASEAN members, (b) production and utilization of industrial minerals and their finished products with due consideration for the environment, (c) integration of mineral resources development with industries within ASEAN members, (d) transfer of technology and exchange of expertise within ASEAN, and (e) participation of the private sector in trade and investment in industrial minerals.

Among the preparatory and initial activities was a November 1993 mineral legislation meeting in Indonesia to start a process of examining and amending mineral legislation in ASEAN to attract investments in the sector. This was followed by a consultative meeting on the deliberations of the ASEAN Experts Group on Minerals. Overall, it was recommended that co-operation be focused on industrial minerals, especially those needed by mineral-intensive sectors such as manufacturing and construction. More recently, there was a Forum on Trade and Investment in minerals that acknowledged the critical role of the private sector and called on governments of member countries to provide an environment that encourages private sector investments in mineral exploration, development, and utilization. While it is recognized that mineral resources are unevenly distributed in ASEAN, such regional collaborative efforts would benefit ASEAN in terms of supporting the region's industrialization programme and intra-ASEAN trade.

The dissolution of the economic committees after the Fourth ASEAN Summit paved the way for new institutional arrangements to handle ASEAN co-operation in minerals. Co-operation activities are to be carried out by the ASEAN Secretariat through the ASEAN Regional Development Centre for Mineral Resources with Indonesia as the lead country.

The scale of co-operation activities between minerals and energy is uneven, limited, and short of a regional potential. In the case of minerals, current co-operation is confined to upstream activities such as seminars, workshops, training, and research. There is still a dearth of programmes in mineral processing technology, product quality improvement, search of new industrial uses of minerals and harmonization of mineral grades and resource classification schemes. There is also limited co-operation efforts towards developing NRSE. As pointed out in the ASEAN Medium-Term Action Programme on Energy Co-operation (1995–99), there are limitations to focusing on ensuring petroleum security to the neglect of other energy sources, particularly as these relate to the bases of energy co-operation activities.

The integrative nature of energy and minerals co-operation to support the growth requirement of ASEAN augurs well for enhanced regional activities. These two sectors will reinforce each other in sustaining the growth momentum for all member countries whether energy-sufficient, energy-dependent, resource-abundant, or resource-deficient.

Many of the activities detailed in the 1996–98 ASEAN Programme of Action in Industrial Minerals Development, Utilization, and Marketing are implemented on a networking basis, and utilize national funds. Examples of activities include technology transfer, policy studies and information exchange, review of mineral legislation and management practices, and harmonization of industrial grades and standards. Succeeding three-year action programmes would be similarly formulated and developed collaboratively based on members' needs.

Organizational changes in ASEAN as it relates to co-operation in energy and minerals, and the ASEAN Secretariat's active involvement in the supervision of programme implementation (in collaboration with national mineral agencies) and in sectoral regrouping, indicate that a greater match between substance and form is expected. With master plans for each sector (though with varying timetables), clearer directions would be emanating from the ASEAN economic ministers (as in the case of energy) or focal institutions (as in the case of minerals).

III. Summary

The review and assessment of ASEAN economic co-operation covered several areas and sectors indicating past efforts and future plans. The magnitude and pace of economic co-operation were uneven across the areas examined since some had significant collective activities while others have yet to attain meaningful co-operation.

The three core areas for ASEAN economic co-operation cover (a) intra-ASEAN trade, (b) ASEAN industry, and (c) ASEAN agriculture. Across these three, economic co-operation activities were initially muddled by government bureaucracies and conflicting national mandates in terms of defining directions. Instances of "muddling through" include the roundabout procedures in determining products subject to PTA (and the degree of protection) and the manner in which industrial complementation schemes were arrived at amidst inherent conflicts between regional and national interests.

Yet, in these core areas, vigorous attempts at economic co-operation promoted greater familiarity among officials in ASEAN. In turn, this built mutual understanding of each other's economic systems and practices essential to developing joint concerns and efforts. The many meetings ASEAN officials went through to decide a course of action heightened familiarity and understanding. Indeed, one criticism of ASEAN co-operation is the enormous number of meetings officials had. Without doubt, there may have been excesses, but it appears mutual trust and confidence within ASEAN were outcomes of familiarity.

In formulating co-operation programmes in the three core areas, interventions (direct and indirect) in policy and programmes influenced the character of the sectors. Interventions ranged from pure protection (as in the case of the AIP) to incentives to improve efficiency (as in the case of ASEAN co-operation on post-harvest technology).

Realizing, in part, the weakness of heavy government intervention, co-operation in the core areas swung into reliance on private sector initiative. The rationale was that the private sector knows the market, is cognizant of its needs, and is quick to respond to potentials and opportunities. Thus, the private sector was at the helm in the development of joint industrial ventures and complementation in ASEAN. Many of the products for which MOPs were granted were supposedly generated from wide consultations with the private sectors of each ASEAN state. Despite this emphasis, government approval was still required to obtain tariff exemptions for joint ventures. In most cases, the government still determined the success of projects, even supporting those that have been determined to be non-viable.

Only in the last five years did a dramatic turnaround and transformation take place in co-operation in the three core areas. Rules were changed to eliminate discrimination and minimize intervention. In food, agriculture, and forestry, the emphasis towards infrastructure and conservation, for instance, improves the environment for the sector across the board. If AFTA becomes fully realized, natural market forces will direct resource allocation. Economic co-operation in the three core areas can then focus on improving the environment, increasing infrastructure, building human resource capacities, raising the levels of competence and technology and other support structures. When the three core areas become more integrated, the direction of co-operation will be towards a regional perspective.

The other sectors covered in the assessment of co-operation are, in a sense, supportive areas of the core, either as outcomes of the core's development or inputs to it. Though results are varied, they show a number of areas that are barely exploited and hold promise of further integration with core activities.

Some co-operation activities are quite limited in scope and do not relate to a larger context or to core areas. In part, this is attributable to the nature of the sector and the initial efforts put into it. Such is the case in the minerals sector, and in part, also energy. Subsequent changes in the action programmes, however, widened the scope of potential areas of co-operation and tied them to both the core areas and regional needs. Thus, both energy and minerals co-operation activities are viewed as supportive of the growth and industrialization drives of ASEAN.

Where initial co-operation activities were weak, external developments engendered closer interaction among ASEAN states, if not explicit co-operation modalities. The advent in the 1990s of electronic communications and satellite broadcasting linked member countries closer, well ahead of joint programmes and projects in the sector. Where infrastructure facilities and connections have yet to be set up, the integration they were supposed to make possible were partly met through technological advances. In fact, these advances encouraged the ASEAN private sector to enter into co-operative arrangements that would tap the region's technical compatibilities. Having been overtaken by private sector–led technologies, regional co-operation activities (at least in communications) may concentrate more on regulation than promotion.

In other supportive areas, the agenda includes improving the environment for ASEAN integration in the face of technological breakthroughs. For instance, greater financial interdependence in ASEAN requires more than just sophisticated telecommunications facilities but also a less restrictive environment that promotes substantive inter-ASEAN financial dealings, greater convertibility, harmonized taxes, and so forth. Many elements of these have yet to be worked out.

Co-operation in the supportive and core areas is also constrained by institutional weaknesses. These are either the ASEAN mechanisms (described in Chapter 1) that are regional in nature and inter-governmental, or national institutions that are unique to individual countries. In some cases (for example, minerals) the institutional umbrella is isolated from the larger regional set-up, or the organization was too dispersed as in the food, agriculture, and forestry sector.

In the final analysis, the review and assessment of economic co-operation bares out the need for a holistic view of the region and integration of programme objectives in various sectors. Although the core areas are the pillars of ASEAN's economy, they cannot be separated from the supportive areas, and vice versa. In addition, co-operation activities, to be successful, require a package of supportive programmes (legislation, organizational reforms, fiscal incentives, infrastructure, and so forth) other than modular elements.

This summary leads to a number of general observations. First,

ASEAN went through a long period of experimentation with alternative modalities of co-operation that had limited success. There was no hiatus in ASEAN co-operation although most of them were exercises to foster familiarity and understanding rather than achieving concrete results. ASEAN remained a sum of five and then six members instead of a unit composed of six components.

Second, despite the prolonged transition and the weak starts in co-operation, ASEAN, through its economic co-operation activities, managed to maintain mutual interest in the search for collective actions. Despite criticisms of its regional efforts, ASEAN officials were able to keep the co-operation momentum going. Indeed, increased familiarity and mutual trust kept ASEAN co-operation alive through all of twenty-five years and remain to date the longest-standing regional organization among developing countries.

Third, the challenge of the external environment, combined with regional confidence gradually, but cumulatively, transformed ASEAN dramatically into an organization with a regional perspective. ASEAN shed off its inhibition towards liberalization and collectively declared a free trade area, signifying a single market for the region but cautious in maintaining global openness.

Fourth, beyond its perspective transformation, ASEAN economic co-operation took on clear and bold initiatives not previously considered. These were in terms of direction, policy, and institutions. At the Fourth ASEAN Summit, the declaration of a free trade area in fifteen years was a major turnaround. Further, the acceleration of the effort from fifteen to ten years, as agreed upon at the Fifth Summit, along with the inclusion of unprocessed agricultural products, are even bolder steps. The associated measures taken in support of these bold initiatives are a signal that ASEAN's direction towards liberalized trade is unambiguous.

In terms of policies, ASEAN governments harmonized codes and other policies to minimize distortions and achieve homogeneity in rules and market systems. This is a sharp departure from previous ASEAN norms of exemption or the "6 – *x*" principle or some variant thereof.

Institutionally, the bold initiatives for economic co-operation were along three fronts. Dissolution of the five economic committees, though long in coming, paved the way for an integrated view of

ASEAN as an economic region. With the SEOM assuming leadership at the technical level, a holistic view is assured even as some *ad hoc* groups and committees evolved to take on specific tasks. The ASEAN Secretariat was reinforced, further professionalized, and given greater substantive responsibilities befitting a regional body. The Secretariat has a stronger mandate of co-ordinating some regional co-operation activities, formulating sectoral action programmes, and organizing meetings and groups of experts. The Secretary-General of the ASEAN Secretariat now holds the rank of minister and represents the region in external relations as ASEAN Secretary-General. All these institutional initiatives grant more responsibility and authority to the ASEAN Secretariat as a regional body.

NOTES

1. ASEAN also spawned a phenomenal growth in research — from books to journals — which cannot be exhaustively referred to here. In economic co-operation, the literature bunched up before the Third ASEAN Summit. A recent and useful starting point is in K.S. Sandhu et al. (1992).
2. See, for example, Chee Peng Lim and Jang-Won Suh (1988), and G. Naidu (1988), in K.S. Sandhu et al. (1992).
3. Gerald Tan, in Noordin Sopiee et al. (1987).
4. G. Naidu (1988), in K.S. Sandhu et al. (1992).
5. Chee Peng Lim (1984).
6. L.S. Cabanilla (1988), in K.S. Sandhu et al. (1992).
7. Hal Hill, in Noordin Sopiee et al. (1987).
8. Gerald Tan, in Noordin Sopiee et al. (1987).
9. Chng Meng Kng (1985).
10. The Group of Fourteen (1987).
11. F.A. Alburo (1990).
12. Chng Meng Kng (1985).
13. Chng Meng Kng (1985).
14. This is based on 1992 data.

3

Future Directions: New Areas of Economic Co-operation

I. Introduction

Many ASEAN activities related to economic co-operation during the first two decades of the organization's existence were implicitly dedicated to building confidence and increasing familiarity. Still, there were many instances of co-operation throughout the period.[1] Though no less important, these were mainly symbolic in character as they were part and parcel of the familiarization context. Over the years, ASEAN economic co-operation can be considered evolutionary and consistent with the region's culture. Absent were legal intricacies to ASEAN agreements, specific details to co-operation activities, and voluminous annexes.

Once confidence was built within ASEAN governments and mutual trust generated, the pace of economic co-operation accelerated, the substance deepened, and coverage widened. The bold initiatives that

ASEAN took in the last three years would have encountered scepticism if foundations were not concretized earlier. Although external factors played critical roles in the dramatic turning points in economic co-operation, the experience of working together for more than two decades facilitated ASEAN solidarity.[2]

The previous chapter reviewed and assessed in detail ASEAN economic co-operation since its founding. Even though initial attempts to forge closer relations among ASEAN countries fumbled around numerous arrangements, an underlying agenda was to accelerate economic growth through a more secure and stable environment in the region. Even in the midst of initial animosities between some countries, collective interests eventually prevailed towards ASEAN as it is today.

ASEAN economic co-operation originally covered traditional sectors. Short of being commodity-specific, core areas were later covered (that is, industry and trade). Eventually, other supportive areas were also included (for example, finance, minerals, energy, transport, communications, and tourism).

The solutions and approaches taken by ASEAN to forge economic co-operation were equally traditional. In agricultural or industrial production, for example, efforts were concentrated on increased output within ASEAN as early industrial schemes relied on production allocation. Technological exchanges also emphasized mutual benefits from sharing experiences as did other related schemes such as swap arrangements, food security, and so forth.

From the review, some weak spots in ASEAN economic co-operation emerged. In the core areas, products not produced in ASEAN received liberal concessions while there was reluctance to freer trade among those the members produce. There were also conflicts between national and regional interests as manifested by, among others, the growing list of exemptions to co-operation schemes. In addition, there was undue government intervention in the location of industries amidst the lack of attention to productivity problems in certain sectors (for example, agriculture).

A preoccupation of early ASEAN economic co-operation was fashioning (inter) governmental policies to direct regional growth. The range of policies, however, was more direct interventions (for example, industrial projects, MOP rates, and so forth) rather than indirect measures to make the environment conducive for market forces to function. Co-operation straddled between broad policies and infrastructure to "picking winners". The evolution of economic co-operation drew in the private sector, in active partnership, although for the most part, rules and discriminatory policies were still in effect.

The watershed of ASEAN economic co-operation occurred at the Fourth Summit as ASEAN abandoned its erstwhile cautious approach to liberalization and promulgated AFTA. Although not radically bold (in the sense of being set initially at a fifteen-year time frame), it nonetheless brought on a series of associated initiatives and complementary measures.

The new initiatives, within the framework of ASEAN's existing co-operation arrangements, rekindled and generated new interest on ASEAN especially from third countries and the international economic community. In almost all areas of potential co-operative endeavours, ASEAN forged some initial commitment to reinforce the region's capability to, for example, attract investments, upgrade the standards and quality of its products and services, harmonize pricing and customs procedures, protect intellectual property rights, sustain its infrastructure development programmes, and support small and medium enterprises (SMEs).

External interest on ASEAN reflects an appreciation of its importance in the Pacific Rim, the most dynamic part of the global economy. More important than this external interest, however, is the sustained interest among ASEAN members throughout the implementation of new initiatives in economic co-operation.

Sustaining interest within ASEAN brought about a second wave of co-operation modalities that go beyond traditional areas and the bold initiatives within them. The second wave defines new areas of economic co-operation that would sustain interest in the region and strengthen the underlying foundation of ASEAN's economic direction.

The new areas aim to enhance free and liberalized trade in the region. A focus on standards and quality (that is, the adoption of common standards for ASEAN products) would definitely support trade expansion. At the same time, common measures to protect intellectual property rights would preserve an important aspect in investment incentives.

The new areas address at least three things. One is the need to achieve compatibility and comparability among ASEAN members and with non-ASEAN trading partners in terms of traded goods (that is, to ensure that minimum and common product standards are met and the level of product quality is maintained). These require understanding and co-operation ranging from technical specifications, reciprocal recognition of tests, certification acceptability, and other schemes. This concern goes a step beyond trade liberalization and zero tariffs since tradable goods require a certain amount of standard of acceptability that is recognized not only within ASEAN and the Pacific but globally. Implicit is the argument that free trade alone is not sufficient for trade to take place.

Another is the need to provide a support system to the bold initiatives set out after the Fourth Summit. The system includes an infrastructure network to facilitate the movement of goods made possible by free trade. On the other hand, paying attention to trade in services partly attends to the appropriate complement to free trade in goods. Other supportive sectors were also part of early forms of ASEAN economic co-operation and their changes were noted in the previous chapter.

Thirdly, there is the need to address some of the weak spots in traditional co-operation areas. In particular, there is a lack of regional efforts to tap, and acknowledge, the potentials of SMEs in contributing to ASEAN trade and industrial development.

The next section describes ASEAN's directions along new areas of co-operation. These are in standards and quality, investment promotion, intellectual property, services, infrastructure development, and SMEs.

Being a rundown of future programmes, they are often at different stages of preparation. The directions, especially where relevant ASEAN committees or officials have yet to officially consider or finalize, are fluid although their basic rationale is clear. Thus, not all project proposals for specific areas outlined in this chapter are detailed. To highlight ASEAN co-operation schemes in the new areas, some projects are indicated for illustration. In many of these new areas, several activities are already taking place.

In the third section, a perspective to ASEAN economic co-operation is briefly elaborated on. For now, this serves to synthesize the review and assessment made in Chapter 2 and the directions of the region along new areas. A chronological summary of ASEAN economic co-operation caps this section.

II. New Areas of Economic Co-operation

A. Standards and Quality

ASEAN efforts to enhance economic co-operation among member countries go beyond merely facilitating trade in goods and services. Member countries are also looking into border and non-border areas of co-operation to supplement trade liberalization. These include technology and information exchanges, reciprocal recognition of tests and product certification, observance of rules for fair competition and the harmonization of standards.

The ASEAN Consultative Committee for Standards and Quality (ACCSQ) was formed upon the directive of the AEM in February 1993. Its role is to examine standards and technical barriers that deter the active promotion of intra-ASEAN trade. There are three technical working groups (TWGs) that assist the ACCSQ. TWG 1 focuses on standards and conformance, TWG 2 deals with conformity assessment and accreditation, and TWG 3 covers testing, calibration, and laboratory accreditation. These groups have since worked on regional co-operation programmes such as testing and accreditation of laboratories, technical information, harmonization of standards, and conformity assessment. Another group, called the Special Working Group on the Elimination of Non-Tariff Barriers, looks into the modalities of eliminating technical barriers to trade in AFTA. The task ahead for this special working group is determining measures to eliminate technical barriers in electrical appliances and machinery, base metals, plastics, and chemicals. These sectors were identified as priority sectors at the Eighth AFTA Council Meeting in December 1995 as the products in these sectors are widely traded in ASEAN.

The Committee implements co-operation activities to achieve common standards and uniform technical requirements in products to promote greater intra- and extra-ASEAN trade. Thus far, in September 1994, the International Standardization Organization (ISO) recognized the ACCSQ as the regional standards organization for Southeast Asia (see Box 3.1).

The ASEAN Standards and Quality Programme (ASQP) guides the ACCSQ's work. This programme has eighteen projects that disseminate information on technical standards. For example, two of its completed projects are "The Directory of ASEAN Contact Points for Standards and Technical Regulation" and "ASEAN Standards and Quality Bulletin".

Member countries of ASEAN are compiling a list of measures of technical barriers to trade on CEPT products. The purpose of the exercise is to take specific steps to eliminate these measures within a specific time frame of the implementation of AFTA.

In the area of food, agriculture, and forestry, the medium-term programme of action for ASEAN co-operation puts a priority in strengthening institutional capacities to standardize operation techniques for the control, surveillance, and monitoring of the EEZs, and in establishing and harmonizing ASEAN standards and quality assurance. At the same time, activities proposed for current funding to support the ASEAN programme of action for the minerals sector include, among others, a review of mineral legislation among various ASEAN countries and the harmonization of industrial grades and standards.

BOX 3.1: ASEAN AND THE INTERNATIONAL STANDARDIZATION ORGANIZATION

The ASEAN Consultative Committee for Standards and Quality (ACCSQ) links with the International Standardization Organization (ISO) on matters relating to standards. Collaborative programmes were also set up with dialogue partners such as the EC and Japan. In January 1994, for example, the ASEAN-Japan Standards and Quality Co-operative Programme was concluded. Its objective is to upgrade the level of understanding and implementation of the Total Quality Management concept, as applied to industry, through training and consultancy programmes, and using the ISO 9000 as a minimum platform. The project is currently at the technical formulation stage. On the other hand, the first phase of the ASEAN-EU Industrial Standards and Quality Assurance Programme (ISQAP) was completed in 1994. Funded by the EU, the ISQAP aims to help ASEAN manufacturers become more competitive by producing internationally accepted products.

On the other hand, the focus of the agenda for energy co-operation is to encourage the standardization of equipment for power development that will eventually lead to the manufacture of this same equipment within ASEAN. Furthermore, the goal to commercialize the NRSE includes exchange of experiences among ASEAN energy experts to strengthen national focal points on the NRSE, and the set-up of quality control standards for NRSE systems, equipment, and so forth. Both measures aim to encourage the participation of local manufacturers of NRSE components. In addition, utilizing the framework of sustainable development in the energy sector, there is an explicit directive to standardize the format and criteria of environmental assessment studies of various development projects in the region to facilitate comparison of environmental impacts. Related to this, there are also initiatives to harmonize methodologies for data reporting, demand forecasting, and development of future energy plans within ASEAN.

In infrastructure development, the action plan detailing ASEAN programmes on Investment, Transportation and Telecommunications, Environment, and Energy, reiterates the importance of establishing improved criteria to prioritize infrastructure investments, and uniform analytical frameworks to assess potential areas of co-operative industrial and infrastructure projects and the benefits to co-operating member countries. At the same time, the plan cites the need to have systematic guides on procedures and regulations relating to infrastructure investments to encourage private sector participation in its development. Relatedly, the working group on transport and communications emphasized harmonizing road transport laws, rules and regulations, motor vehicle construction and use, and traffic safety standards. There is also a similar emphasis on harmonizing standards and qualifications in the regulation of multimodal transport operators and maritime procedures and instruments on state control ports in ASEAN. Both are important theme issues referred to in the Singapore Declaration of 1992 and the Framework Agreement on Enhancing ASEAN Economic Co-operation.

There are also concrete co-operation activities with dialogue partners (as noted in Box 3.1). Initially forged with Japan and the EC, co-operation will extend to Australia and New Zealand under the broader ASEAN Free Trade Area–Closer Economic Relations (AFTA-CER) linkages. The focus on bilateral collaboration is useful in identifying specific areas of co-operation that can later be multilateralized.

In January 1995, Vietnam started out as an observer in the ACCSQ. As a formal ASEAN member and as it phases into the CEPT scheme, issues of standards and quality will eventually be integral to its schedule.

B. Investment

ASEAN's much admired economic growth and industrial development is due, in large part, to its ability to attract foreign direct investment (FDI). However, the relative share of ASEAN countries of total FDI started to decline by 1990. This is due to a number of factors, namely: (a) the emergence of massive trade blocs such as NAFTA and the EC, (b) the unprecedented increase in the number of countries competing for FDI, and (c) the comparative cost advantage of many non- ASEAN developing countries. In light of the latter, there is agreement that ASEAN should not be promoted as a group of individual countries but as a regional market that, through AFTA, can offer opportunities for production efficiencies. This can be achieved through the region's various complementary and comparative location-specific advantages, not to mention its total market of 410 million, a great number of whom have experienced increases in gross disposable incomes due to their countries' rapid economic growth.

Under the Framework Agreement on Enhancing ASEAN Economic Co-operation, member countries agreed to increase investments, industrial linkages and flexibility for new forms of industrial co-operation schemes. Although ASEAN co-operation in industry and investments proceeded at a modest pace since the 1992 Summit, significant progress in identifying new areas for ASEAN co-operation was made.

In the field of investments, the First Consultative Meeting on the Promotion of Foreign Direct Investment in ASEAN was held in February 1993. At that meeting, a Memorandum of Understanding among the Authorities of ASEAN Countries Responsible for Investment Promotion was signed to promote investment co-operation within the region. A Working Group on Investment Matters was established that drew up the terms of reference for an ASEAN Agreement on Investment Co-operation and Promotion. In addition, a draft ASEAN Plan of Action on Co-operation in the Promotion of FDI for 1996–98 was proposed for consideration by the Working Group on Industrial Co-operation Programme (WGICP) and subsequent endorsement by the SEOM.

The action plan identified possible co-operative endeavours to increase investment flows to the region and among member states. It stipulated the implementation of joint programmes on publicity, image building, and marketing of ASEAN's investment regimes; continuous consultation; information and experience exchanges among investment agencies within the region; training programmes for investment officials; the creation of an ASEAN Investment Monitoring, Policy Review and Analysis Unit and the promulgation of an ASEAN Investment Code, embodying investment procedures and policies that are simplified, uniform, and transparent. This proposal was reiterated in the Fifth ASEAN Summit where the revised plan of action on the Promotion of Foreign Direct Investment and Intra-ASEAN Investment was endorsed. The revised plan aims to project ASEAN as a single investment region. In this regard, an ASEAN Investment Area (AIA) was proposed to encourage greater investments in the region through, among others, adoption of simpler and more transparent rules, standardization of procedures relating to the collection and recording of investment data, and the removal of barriers to capital flow. Other than external investment flows, the action plan also called for joint efforts to promote intra-ASEAN investments and regional production based on the principle of resource pooling and intra-regional division of labour.

Whilst efforts to promote ASEAN as an ideal investment location entails encouraging existing investors already familiar with ASEAN to expand their operations or locate new projects in other areas (the so-called favourable experience effects), promoting FDI in infrastructure-related and higher technology-based industries, in SMEs, and in services are likewise indicated as priority areas in the action plan to support the AFTA process. At the same time, these activities would also enhance ASEAN's investment environment by providing efficient conditions for operations and cost-effectiveness for intra-regional procurement activities.

In the December 1995 Summit, a new industrial co-operation scheme called ASEAN Industrial Co-operation (AICO) was endorsed, replacing both the BBC and AIJV schemes. The CEPT-based AICO scheme was developed with private sector participation and is aimed at encouraging mainly private sector–led investment in technology-based and higher value-added industries (see Box 2.2, Chapter 2).

Other suggested modes to promote FDI would be through joint-venture schemes and greater networking and linkages with various chambers of commerce, industry clubs, and professional and trade associations. The latter can be utilized to promote greater intra-ASEAN investment where regional investment and business information and opportunities in the region, including information on potential joint-venture partners, can be disseminated. Relatedly, regional research projects may be undertaken by the proposed ASEAN Investment Monitoring, Policy Review, and Analysis Unit within the ASEAN Secretariat. Some of the suggested regional themes include looking at ASEAN's complementary location advantages and approaches to promote greater business linkage between ASEAN and non-ASEAN investors. A UNDP-funded comprehensive review of FDIs in ASEAN currently under way and supervised by the ASEAN Secretariat may provide a useful starting point (see Box 3.2).

C. Intellectual Property

With the recently concluded agreement on trade-related aspects of intellectual property (TRIPS) under the GATT Uruguay Round, senior economic officials, under the umbrella of the SEOM, created a Working Group on Intellectual Property Co-operation. Recognizing the importance of protecting intellectual property rights (IPRs) and enhancing collaboration in this area, the working group at its September 1994 meeting concluded an ASEAN Framework Agreement on Intellectual Property Co-operation. This is a recent development in intra-ASEAN relations, although links with similar international organizations were already in place. Examples of institutional co-operative programmes include the ASEAN-World Intellectual Property Organization (ASEAN-WIPO), which focuses on improving the legislative framework of intellectual property, the ASEAN-European Union (ASEAN-EU), which emphasizes patents modernization and trademarks administration, and ASEAN-Japan, which covers the human resource development aspect of IPR. These programmes aim to modernize and strengthen administration and the enforcement of IPRs.

BOX 3.2: POLICY STUDY ON FDI IN ASEAN

The aim of the comprehensive FDI review is to determine, among others: (a) how ASEAN and international investors regard ASEAN's investment environment in the present international setting; (b) what are the investment strategies of multinational enterprises (MNEs) with regard to their operations in the region; (c) whether ASEAN is being regarded as an investment region in its own right; (d) the motivations and locational decisions of investors intending to operate or are already operating in ASEAN; (e) the implication of regional schemes, such as the CEPT-AFTA and the AIJV, on FDI decisions; and (f) future investment plans of existing investors operating in the region. In addition, the survey also addresses certain issues on MNE operation towards technology transfer and management practices in ASEAN host countries.

The methodology employed in the collection of primary data for the comprehensive review is two-pronged: a case-study approach conducted through interviews with chief executive officers based in ASEAN, and a comprehensive postal survey carried out via questionnaires to over 7,500 foreign-owned and ASEAN MNEs.

In order to conduct the FDI survey effectively, the ASEAN Secretariat has to establish a comprehensive database of ASEAN and non-ASEAN investors operating in the region. From this database, the Secretariat is planning to publish a compehensive list of investors in a set of business directories categorized, among others, by industry groupings. It is hoped that such publications will help facilitate and foster greater trade, business, and investment linkages, as well as activities in the region.

The ASEAN Secretariat in 1996 convened a "High-Level Experts Seminar on FDI in ASEAN in the context of AFTA". ASEAN investment officials and FDI experts within and outside ASEAN deliberated on various issues pertaining to FDI flow to and within ASEAN/AFTA.

Taking a cue from the ASEAN-EU programme, the Framework Agreement urges ASEAN to consider the possibility of setting up an ASEAN Patent System and an ASEAN Trademark System, and if feasible, common offices.

Since 1993, WIPO has assisted ASEAN co-operation in intellectual property. The activities jointly implemented by the two organizations include a comparative study on ASEAN IPR legislation, a seminar on the enforcement of intellectual property, and a forum on the role of intellectual property in ASEAN economic development.

In January 1995, an informal ASEAN Working Group on Intellectual Property discussed the request by the ASEAN Music Industry

Association (AMIA) for a Memorandum of Understanding among ASEAN countries. Though member countries agreed that protection of IPRs should be extended to the sound recording industry, there was also recognition of the different rights in various member countries. In this regard, member countries agreed to survey existing legislation to serve as input to a formal agreement.

An *Ad Hoc* Working Group on Intellectual Property Co-operation completed the ASEAN Framework Agreement on Intellectual Property Co-operation as an initial output of ASEAN co-operation in the protection of intellectual property. Such an agreement was signed by the appropriate ASEAN ministers at the Fifth ASEAN Summit. The framework calls for specific activities to enhance intellectual property enforcement and protection, strengthen intellectual property administration and legislation, promote human resource development, and public awareness of IPR. To carry these out, the Framework also included the possibility of ASEAN setting up its own Patent and Trademark System through an ASEAN Patent Office and an ASEAN Trademark Office. Once these activities are institutionalized, ASEAN countries can expect to make higher royalty payments for intellectual property as rules and penalties relating to it are strengthened and enforced. The harmonization of intellectual property standards will have significant immediate costs to dealers and consumers in ASEAN.

From the above, ASEAN co-operation in intellectual property will not only adhere to the World Trade Organization (WTO) agreement to which ASEAN countries have acceded to but also add an ASEAN dimension in terms of enforcement, legislation, and larger public awareness.

As a member of ASEAN, Vietnam is expected to be a signatory to the Framework Agreement even if it has not yet been admitted into the WTO and thus a party to the TRIPS agreement.

D. Services

In the third meeting of the *Ad Hoc* Working Group on Services held in Manila in 1995, specific sectors were identified as possible areas of co-operation in services, among them, financial and business services, construction, tourism, and transport. Member countries were asked to review the inventory of ASEAN efforts in services and to pass this on to the ASEAN Secretariat for further discussion.

This is not the first time ASEAN paid attention to the services sector. There was a previous call at the Third ASEAN Summit in Manila in 1987 and initial co-operation in financial services was well under way. At the 25th AEM (June 1994), an *Ad Hoc* Working Group on ASEAN Co-operation in Services was created to enlarge the scope of co-operation in services. The 1995 ASEAN Plan of Action on Co-operation and Promotion of Foreign Direct Investment and Intra-ASEAN Investment, which was endorsed at the Fifth Summit, stipulates that efforts to promote FDI should not only focus on the manufacturing sector but also include the services sector. As defined, this includes banking and financial services, insurance, health, hospitality and management consultancy.[3] In recognition of the importance of co-operation in services to enhance the overall investment climate in ASEAN, a Working Group on Co-operation in Services was established to look at possible co-operative endeavours.

The identification of the above sectors is part of a Framework Agreement for ASEAN Co-operation in Services. Such a framework is in accordance with the WTO General Agreement on Trade in Services. Since all ASEAN members of WTO participated in negotiations affecting ASEAN trade in services as covered by this agreement, there were already initial commitments in place.

The formulation of an ASEAN Framework of Co-operation in Services that is consistent with the General Agreement on Trade in Services (GATS), when incorporated into AFTA, would expand the current agreement on the CEPT scheme for AFTA. As it is, the CEPT covers only trade in goods, and proposes such measures as liberalization of tariffs and elimination of non-tariff barriers and quantitative restrictions as the main mechanisms for liberalization.

ASEAN co-operation in services aims to promote intra-ASEAN trade in services as integral to AFTA. At the 26th AEM, the basic elements and principles of the draft Framework Agreement on Services were discussed. The final draft was prepared by the *Ad Hoc* Working Group during its Eighth Meeting and subsequently adopted by the SEOM in November 1995. The Framework Agreement comprises provisions on objectives, areas of co-operation, liberalization, negotiations of specific commitments, mutual recognition, denial of benefits, settlement of disputes, supplementary agreements or arrangements, modification of the schedule of specific commitments, institutional arrangements, amendments, accession of new members, and other related provisions (see Box 3.3). Recognizing the fact that many of the existing ASEAN co-operation efforts in services are activities of the private sector, the Agreement carries a preamble encouraging participation and co-operation among the private sector.

ASEAN member states made a clear distinction as to who can and cannot benefit from the implementation of the Framework Agreement. The service suppliers eligible for benefits are:

1. natural persons of member states with or without substantive business operations in the territory of member states;
2. juridical persons owned or controlled by persons of member states with or without substantive business operations in the territory of member states;

BOX 3.3: THE ASEAN AGREEMENT ON SERVICES

The ASEAN Agreement on Services is made up of two parts: The first part covers "Co-operation", which identifies current regional efforts as potential areas to expand co-operation. A general mandate to strengthen ASEAN co-operation in this regard includes the improvement of infrastructure, research and development, exchange of information and technologies, and joint marketing and purchasing arrangements. "Liberalization Measures" is contained in the second part, which enjoins members to abide by the principles of the General Agreement on Trade in Services (GATS). This means eliminating all market access limitations and existing discriminatory measures among member countries to a substantial degree and prohibiting the emergence of new forms of market discrimination and/or access limitations. In this respect, member states need to set specific scheduled commitments with respect to the terms, limitations, and conditions on market access, and where appropriate, also a timeframe for implementating such commitments. General mandates should also be laid down to cover the progressive liberalization of capital movement (for both investment and payments) and persons supplying services. Moreover, mandates for national treatment and provisions on government procurement and subsidies, among others, would have to be made. Certain service subsectors (such as professional services) may be singled out for preferential provisions. Subject to future negotiations, member countries may also provide specific arrangements for each sector and consider integration possibilities, for example, of its financial services sector.

3. juridical persons owned or controlled by persons of non-member states and constituted under the laws of member states who have substantive business operations in the territory of member states; and
4. natural persons of non-member states who have substantive business operations in the territory of member states;

while the following category of service suppliers are not eligible for benefits:

1. natural persons of non-member states who do not have substantive business operations in the territory of member states; and
2. juridical persons owned or controlled by persons of non-member states and constituted under the laws of member states but who do not have substantive business operations in the territory of member states.

In the Fifth ASEAN Summit on December 1995, member countries signed a Framework Agreement on Services to enhance co-operation in the services sector and begin a process of preferential liberalization of trade in services. It is expected that ASEAN countries shall also enter into negotiations of specific commitments on market access, national treatment, and additional commitments covering all services sectors and all modes of supply that go beyond those made by ASEAN member states, as inscribed in their Schedules of Specific Commitments under the GATS. The first round of negotiations began on 1 January 1996 and is expected to conclude no later than 31 December 1998. The negotiation gave emphasis to seven services sectors, namely, financial services, maritime transport and telecommunications (where all ASEAN member states made commitments), air transport, tourism, construction, and business services. Of these sectors, there was agreement at the Summit that the process of negotiations in telecommunications, financial services, and tourism will be completed within eighteen months.

The AEM sets directions for future negotiations, including identification of sub-sectors for negotiation, as ASEAN member states undertake subsequent rounds of negotiations until a higher level of liberalization is achieved. All negotiations are conducted bilaterally or plurilaterally among member states on the basis of request-and-offer lists. In this connection, member states are given the flexibility to determine the extent to which sectors are to be negotiated and the duration of the negotiation but are not to take measures to improve their negotiating position and leverage.

To facilitate the implementation of the ASEAN Framework Agreement on Services, member states agreed to enhance transparency of their multilateral and bilateral agreements and existing regimes in the services sector. This is already ongoing through an exchange system co-ordinated by the ASEAN Secretariat. Member states submit their list of multilateral and bilateral agreements in the services sector to the ASEAN Secretariat, who in turn collates and formats these according to the U.N. Central Product Classifications (CPC) and then distributes the formatted lists to all members. Member states would continue to submit notifications on changes in their services sectors to the ASEAN Secretariat for collation, format, and distribution to all members.

Through the Working Group on Co-operation in Services, ASEAN received an offer from the United Nations Conference on Trade and Development (UNCTAD) to assist in the establishment of a statistical database at the ASEAN Secretariat on member countries' policies, regulations, and measures affecting trade in services. The Working Group recommended the offer to SEOM, indicating that the exercise would entail the preparation of a project document by UNCTAD for consideration by the SEOM.

E. Infrastructure Development

Infrastructure is recognized as essential to the growth and efficiency of trade and investment in AFTA. It was therefore not a coincidence that during the September 1994 AEM Meeting held at Chang Mai, the directive for an Infrastructure Plan of Action came in the light of AFTA. It was recognized that the mandate should take into account ASEAN action plans on infrastructure development, transport and communications, and on energy, among others, to support the growth and efficiency of trade and investment under AFTA.

Initial ASEAN infrastructure co-operation was limited to providing infrastructure, and mainly funded by the government, to specific sectors and special development zones for trans-border industries. The

Infrastructure Plan of Action, on the other hand, explicitly promotes and facilitates private sector investment in infrastructure services within and/or by ASEAN member countries.

The strategies to promote infrastructure development and mobilize greater private sector participation therein include: (a) the conduct of a regional policy dialogue on public-private sector partnership in infrastructure, with focus on the needs and capabilities of the private sector as users and providers of infrastructure; (b) infrastructure provision that takes advantage of regional complementarities; (c) the creation of a more conducive environment for private sector participation in the provision of infrastructure to, among others, special development zones; (d) enhancement of personnel and plant mobility to increase efficiency in infrastructure provision; and (e) establishment of centres of excellence and human resource development co-operation in infrastructure and private sector investment.

The ASEAN plan aims at capitalizing on existing capacities within each of the member countries. The next step is to create the mechanisms, the forum, and the region-wide dialogue for such national capacities to bear on a regional infrastructure programme.

In support of the policy dialogues to be undertaken, an ASEAN infrastructure information network needs to be institutionalized to provide ASEAN members with databases on infrastructure planning, opportunities, and capacities. The lack of information and the uncertainty that goes with it caused inefficiencies in infrastructure planning, provision and utilization and directly affected the region's overall investment and economic efficiency. The task envisions a dialogue process among national infrastructure agencies to develop jointly analytical techniques to improve supply and demand projections in the databases, improve co-ordination, and provide useful exchanges of information, expertise, and experience.

At the policy level, several actions are envisioned. To increase capacity mobility, for example, a progressive removal of national barriers and procedures that constrain or inhibit the mobility of corporate participants, managers, selected professional and technical and other skilled manpower is a necessary step. Relatedly, exploring means to harmonize investment incentives among ASEAN member countries and identifying common grounds in formulating national policies in infrastructure development and private sector participation also requires regional follow-through. Finally, the development of an ASEAN network of centres of expertise in infrastructure policy and planning analysis, funds and investment mobilization, and related technologies will provide baseline information to develop practical mechanisms for co-operation and mutual support in infrastructure investments.

An ASEAN Plan of Action for Infrastructure Development was endorsed at the Fifth Summit for implementation over the next few years. The action plan covers development of port facilities, utilities, and road networks. The endorsement of the Plan is a reflection of the importance given by ASEAN leaders to the enabling role of infrastructure in supporting domestic and regional economic goals.

F. Small and Medium Enterprises Development

Small and medium enterprises (SMEs), defined as enterprises employing less than one hundred workers, account for a majority (nearly 90 per cent) of manufacturing establishments in ASEAN. They are a source of employment and savings, serve as "training ground" for developing industrial skills and entrepreneurial creativity, support the underground economy, and provide linkages among industries. Despite their significance in ASEAN, SMEs as a viable sector are bypassed in most ASEAN economic meetings and their potentials are not fully realized due to various constraints that have unfortunately not been addressed in early regional consultations.

In ASEAN, many formal institutions downplay the importance and viability of SMEs. In most cases, SMEs run into the same problems as newly established business enterprises do — inability to access commercial bank credit, and training, management, and marketing expertise, and so forth. Other than lack of access to institutional credit, SMEs are often dependent on obsolete or traditional technology, a condition that is spawned by their inability to acquire large and modern, often expensive, types of machinery and/or production methods. In addition, inadequate management skills and poor customer service orientation, largely unskilled workers, poor quality standards, and marketing arrangements have all contributed to low productivity and production standards.

Efforts to attend to the needs of SMEs are notable only at the level of individual ASEAN governments. Indonesia and Malaysia, for example, incorporated SMEs in their respective development plans. Furthermore, SME policies are either implemented by formal government agencies, quasi-government entities or by non-governmental organizations (NGOs). This is true in both Singapore and Thailand, where key agencies are involved in policy implementation. However, there is no explicit regional ASEAN programme for SMEs, much less a formal ASEAN unit, despite acknowledgment that collaborative efforts to modernize SMEs in ASEAN entail common goals and strategies.

The directions for ASEAN development of SMEs include networking related SME agencies among ASEAN members through resource pooling and exchange of information and experience, and public and private sector co-operation in such areas as policy analysis, financing arrangements, training, technology selection, marketing, linkages between multinational corporations (MNCs) and SMEs, and between ASEAN and non-ASEAN SMEs. An initial objective would be to thresh out "best practice" policies and programmes from experiences of individual member countries that will support SME development. This can be followed by efforts to mobilize financial resources, either through ASEAN channels, such as the ASEAN Finance Corporation (AFC) or through a regional credit guarantee fund that would tap the resources of ASEAN's dialogue partners. Later on, joint training programmes for entrepreneurs, managers, and technical workers can be implemented in selected fields where regional efficiency can best be achieved.

ASEAN may consider establishing an ASEAN Regional Clearing House for Technology Information for SMEs. Upgrading of technology will need action on a number of fronts, for example, dissemination of information about the technology shelf and potential gains from the use of such technology, skills training, extension services, and so on. Since a number of ASEAN countries already made strides in some of these areas, disseminating such information to other member countries would be an important core of regional co-operation activities. Results of research studies and technological advances in industries where SMEs are dominant, (for example, handicrafts, textiles, metal products, and so forth), that are carried out on a joint basis could also be channelled through the Clearing House for use by member countries.

In a private sector–sponsored AFTA Convention in December 1995, the ASEAN Secretary-General called on the ASEAN-CCI to work with ASEAN in helping SMEs meet the challenges of AFTA. He also urged private associations to facilitate intra-regional trade by providing regular inputs to the ASEAN Trade and Investment Database, an undertaking that could provide additional opportunities for private sector–led investments in SMEs.

Co-operation could also take the form of joint marketing of products produced by SMEs for export. Although some conflict of interests exists as ASEAN countries are competing with each other in the international market, some joint effort on export promotion can still be worked out. Among the possible areas are the provision of information on market opportunities for SME products in different ASEAN countries, sharing of information on changing demand patterns in major foreign markets, and joint trade exhibits of SME products (for example, handicrafts).

ASEAN industrial co-operation schemes are largely based on the development of large-scale enterprises. Despite huge investments in both capital and manpower, such schemes were generally unsuccessful, as in the case of the AIP. More significantly, because of long gestation periods, the benefits of such projects on the majority of people in ASEAN are in doubt. On the other hand, SME development and its attendant co-operative action, requires a smaller amount of resources, yet is expected to bring immediate benefits to the vast majority of entrepreneurs and industrial workers in ASEAN. Given that a majority of industrial enterprises in the ASEAN region are SMEs, their development should have priority in new schemes for ASEAN industrial co-operation. The new thrust will assist SMEs realize their full potential as significant players in ASEAN economic development.

III. A Perspective

Future direction in terms of new areas of ASEAN economic co-operation is invariably fraught with risk. The enormity of the task and the scope of programmes and projects may be too ambitious for each ASEAN member to pursue individually or even collectively. There may be problems of synchronization and timing among components and preparatory actions may not be forthcoming.

This brief exposition into ASEAN's new areas of economic co-operation, however, suggest several implications. The first is that they support the other initiatives of ASEAN economic co-operation described in Chapter 2, indicating a tight fit with core areas. For instance, attention to standards and quality ensures more efficient trade transactions within ASEAN and with the rest of the world. A well-planned infrastructure programme enhances greater mobility of both resources and goods in ASEAN while liberalization of services supplements the liberalization of goods trade. An affirmative action on SMEs, on the other hand, reverses a bias in industrial co-operation in the region. The new areas clearly dovetail with the bold initiatives of ASEAN in the traditional areas.

Second, the new areas reflect aggressive "ASEAN-plus" co-operation activities. ASEAN members are signatories to global agreements on services and intellectual property, among others, and made liberalization commitments to these. Their additional commitments to ASEAN in the same areas reflect a firm regional identity without being inward-looking. Indeed, even as ASEAN pursues new agreements beyond WTO, it maintains a free trade philosophy.

Finally, the drive for comprehensiveness in these new areas led to the adoption of a broader framework for action and co-operation. In this sense, co-operation areas are deliberately considered in terms of interaction with other sectors (for example, infrastructure with energy) and the synergistic effects of joint implementation.

These new areas of economic co-operation appear to be essential complements to ASEAN's bold economic initiatives, as set out in Chapter 2. When viewed in an integrated manner, they do not appear to be too ambitious or difficult to achieve. On hindsight, these directions serve to highlight the chronology of economic co-operation in ASEAN.

The First ASEAN Summit was held in Bali in 1976. It called for intensifying co-operation in economic and social development and taking co-operative action in national and regional development programmes. Resources available in ASEAN are to be used to broaden the complementarity of member countries' economies.

The Declaration of ASEAN Concord, the principal co-operation instrument of the First ASEAN Summit, clearly delineated the economic areas (for example, establishment of large-scale industrial projects, food security, and establishment of the PTA). These roughly reflected the desired complementarity of the ASEAN economies. Food and energy, industry, and trade were traditional areas and progress made in these areas since the First Summit was traced in the previous chapter. More recent initiatives, however, tell of significant transformation in the substance of co-operation.

The Second ASEAN Summit held in Kuala Lumpur in 1977 declared, among others, that efforts should be intensified and the pace of economic co-operation accelerated with greater vigour. There was a call for the private sector to: (a) intensify efforts towards the implementation of industrial complementation schemes and projects and general industrial development in the region; and (b) take measures to stimulate the flow of technology, know-how, and private investments among member countries.

Although private sector importance was highlighted in this period, agreements arrived at finalized the earlier thrusts of the First Summit. Examples are the ASEAN Food Security Reserve in 1979, the Agreement on ASEAN industrial projects in 1980, and the 1981 Agreement on ASEAN industrial complementation.

The Third ASEAN Summit held in Manila in 1987 noted that ASEAN regionalism, founded upon political, economic, and cultural cohesion, is more vital than ever for the future of Southeast Asia. Member states were called to strengthen intra-ASEAN economic co-operation to maximize the realization of the region's potential in trade and development, increase ASEAN's efficacy in combating protectionism and countering its effects, and promote an environment wherein the private sector can play an increasing role in economic development and in intra-ASEAN co-operation.

In the Fourth ASEAN Summit held in Singapore in 1992, member countries were urged to accelerate efforts in enhancing intra-ASEAN economic co-operation and adopt appropriate new economic measures (as contained in the Framework Agreement on Enhancing ASEAN Economic Co-operation) towards sustained ASEAN economic growth and development, as these are considered essential to the stability and prosperity of the region.

As pointed out in Chapter 2, the Fourth Summit was the watershed in economic co-operation as ASEAN took bold moves in its declaration of AFTA. In addition, new areas of co-operation were fashioned out to take policy initiatives a step further.

Apart from intra-ASEAN economic co-operation, ASEAN has extensive economic linkages with its dialogue partners, third countries and international organizations through various economic co-operation programmes and activities on trade, investment, development assistance, and other economic issues. However, ASEAN's ability to consolidate its position on a number of regional and international economic issues is in part due to the active advocacy role of the ASEAN-CCI to make the ASEAN machinery more efficient and focused. The Committee on ASEAN Development, for example, was created by the ASEAN-CCI in response to the 1992 ASEAN Summit directive for the organization to encourage co-operation among ASEAN private sector and between ASEAN and non-ASEAN private sectors.

NOTES

1. For an illustration of these, see Hans Indorf (1975), Chia Siow Yue (1980), and Narongchai Akrasanee et al. (1981).
2. Early proposals for free trade in ASEAN can be discerned from academic writings, for example, Seiji Naya and Michael Plummer (1991), Mari Pangestu, Hadi Soesastro, and Mubariq Ahmad (1992), and Pearl Imada, Manuel Montes, and Seiji Naya (1991).
3. For an overview of ASEAN co-operation in services, see Robert Teh (1995).

4

The ASEAN Private Sector and Regional Co-operation

I. Introduction

The official ASEAN machinery is supplemented by a network of regional non-governmental organizations (NGOs) that help promote the objectives of ASEAN co-operation. These networks are the mechanisms for national private sector organizations to link with their ASEAN counterparts to assist their governments in pursuing ASEAN goals and objectives. The network of regional NGOs forms a cluster of transnational linkages that increase the centrality of ASEAN and provides the infrastructure for better communications and enhanced co-operation in various fields.

In a broad sense, NGOs are organizations formed by the business sector and by professional and other non-profit associations. In the ASEAN context, NGOs include (a) the ASEAN-CCI, serving as the official link between ASEAN governments and the private sector engaged in commerce and industry; and (b) other private organizations that help promote ASEAN objectives in the social, cultural, economic, and scientific fields. ASEAN provides for a system of official affiliation of NGOs in the region to bring their activities closer to the workings of ASEAN structures and to promote ASEAN objectives (see Box 4.1).

II. ASEAN Chambers of Commerce and Industry (ASEAN-CCI)

The ASEAN-CCI, formed in April 1972, is the largest and most significant private sector organization in the region. Being the official channel between the private sector and ASEAN governments, its founding represents member countries' recognition that regional economic co-operation can only succeed through the active participation of the private sector. On the other hand, it also reflects the positive response of the business community to the political initiatives of ASEAN leaders in promoting regional co-operation.

The initial ASEAN-CCI organization was composed of five national chambers, namely, that of the original five member countries (that is, the Kamar Dagang Dan Industri Indonesia [KADIN], the National Chamber of Commerce and Industry of Malaysia [NCCIM], the Philippine Chamber of Commerce and Industry [PCCI], the Singapore Federation of Chambers of Commerce and Industry [SFCCI], and the Joint Standing Committee on Commerce, Industry and Banking [JSCCIB] of Thailand). The National Chamber of Commerce and Industry of Negara Brunei Darussalam (NCCI-NBD) and the Chamber of Commerce and Industry of Vietnam (CCIV) became the sixth and seventh national chambers when Brunei Darussalam and Vietnam joined ASEAN.

Over the years, the ASEAN-CCI evolved to facilitate inter-country private sector interaction other than being a channel for dialogue with official ASEAN bodies. It also institutionalized official links with the private sectors of ASEAN's dialogue partners to promote trade and investments in ASEAN. Moreover, the ASEAN-CCI established and maintained close relations with a number of regional and international organizations.

BOX 4.1: PROCEDURES AND GUIDELINES

ASEAN has been promoting NGOs that can perform a regional function consistent with the objectives of ASEAN co-operation. In particular, special efforts are being made to bring ASEAN NGOs under the wing of the official ASEAN machinery through the process of affiliation. Affiliation is encouraged to draw the NGOs into the mainstream of ASEAN activities so that they are kept informed of the major policies, directives, and decisions of ASEAN and are given the opportunity and privilege of participating in ASEAN activities. Affiliation also ensures fruitful interaction between existing ASEAN bodies and NGOs. An NGO would establish a working link with an ASEAN committee or with any other construed body of ASEAN (referred to as "link body") through the ASEAN Secretariat.

A set of guidelines, implemented by the ASEAN Secretariat, governs the process and privileges of affiliation. Under the present set of guidelines, an ASEAN NGO is defined as "a non-profit-making association of ASEAN persons, natural or juridical, organized to promote, strengthen, and help realize the aims and objectives of ASEAN co-operation specifically in the social, cultural, economic, and scientific fields". An ASEAN NGO has to have membership from a majority of the ASEAN countries to qualify as an ASEAN NGO.

The process of affiliation involves the following principal steps:

1. The NGO files a formal application for affiliation with the ASEAN Secretariat accompanied by all information on the NGO, including its aims and nature of operations, its constitution and by-laws, and its functions and activities.
2. The Secretariat reviews the application and recommends its approval if the guidelines are met.
3. The Secretariat's recommendation is forwarded to the ASEAN Standing Committee for approval.

The ASEAN Standing Committee considers applications using the following criteria:

1. As a rule, only NGOs whose membership is confined to ASEAN nationals may be considered for affiliation with ASEAN.
2. Approval of application for affiliation of an NGO with ASEAN shall be based primarily upon the assessment of the positive contribution that such NGO could make to the enhancement, strengthening, and realization of the aims and objectives of ASEAN.

FOR NGO AFFILIATION WITH ASEAN

3. Affiliation status with ASEAN may not be granted to an NGO if its objectives, activities, or projects are contrary to or inconsistent with the aims and objectives of ASEAN as embodied in the Bangkok Declaration and the Declaration of ASEAN Concord.
4. An NGO whose membership comes from a relatively even spread of the ASEAN member countries may be allowed affiliation, provided that ASEAN is satisfied that the NGO merits affiliation and the non-participating member countries have given their consent to the NGO, and provided further that membership shall remain open for other member countries.

Affiliated NGOs enjoy in addition the following privileges:

1. It may use the name "ASEAN" and display the official ASEAN emblem in correspondence, communications, and its official meetings, so long as the intention of displaying the emblem is non-commercial in nature.
2. It may submit written statements or recommendations and views on policy matters or on significant events or regional or international concerns, to the ASEAN Standing Committee through the ASEAN Secretariat.
3. It may submit its own project proposal for third party funding to be channelled through the ASEAN Secretariat to the ASEAN Standing Committee for approval.
4. It may initiate programmes of activities for presentation to its link body for appropriate action.
5. At the discretion of the chairman of the link body, it may, through its representative, attend meetings of the link body for consultation on matters and issues of direct concern to the NGO.
6. For purposes of doing research for its projects, it may be allowed access to ASEAN documents on a selective basis in consultation with the ASEAN Secretariat and/or its link body.
7. Subject to rules and regulations, it may be allowed the use of the facilities of the ASEAN Secretariat for its official meetings and other official activities in Jakarta.
8. It shall be encouraged to be self-reliant in terms of its material requirements.

A. Objectives

The objectives of the ASEAN-CCI as stated in its constitution are:

1. to effect organized private business sector co-operation and co-ordination in keeping with the objectives of ASEAN;
2. to accelerate economic growth and progress in the region through joint approaches, endeavours, and actions in order to strengthen the foundation and co-ordination for the enhancement of the communities of ASEAN;
3. to foster closer relations and co-operation between and among the constituent members and mutual assistance in matters of common interest in the solution of economic problems in the area; and
4. to maintain closer relations and co-operation with regional and international organizations having similar aims and objectives.

B. Organizational Structure

The ASEAN-CCI structure is four-tiered. At the highest level is the Council that governs and administers the organization while the next level consists of various working groups. The next tier is the regional industry clubs (RICs) and the regional commodity clubs (RCCs). The fourth tier is composed of national industry clubs (NICs) and national commodity clubs (NCCs). The presidency of the ASEAN-CCI follows the ASEAN principle of rotation among member countries in alphabetical order. It has an interim Secretariat that rotates with the presidency until a permanent Secretariat was established in April 1996.

The Council is composed of the ASEAN-CCI president, the six vice-presidents (each representing a constituent member organization), six other individuals from each of the constituent members, and the Secretary-General who is appointed by the president subject to the confirmation of the Council. Council members hold office for two years, meet at least once a year, and hold special meetings as deemed necessary.

The second level consists of various working groups, principally, the working groups on industrial co-operation, trade, agribusiness and agro-industry, transportation, communication and tourism, finance, banking and insurance, and more recently, sustainable development. The organization of the working groups parallels those of the ASEAN economic committees (that existed prior to their restructuring in 1992) to facilitate interaction with ASEAN bodies. The working groups are governed by their respective mother organizations and working procedures.

The third tier consists of the RICs and RCCs. The RICs are under the jurisdiction of the Working Group on Industrial Co-operation while RCCs are under the jurisdiction of the Working Group on Trade (see Box 4.2). These clubs are involved in formulating proposals for co-operation in their respective areas. To achieve its objectives, the RICs conduct studies to identify opportunities, products, and projects that may be suitable for joint ventures. It plays a lead role in encouraging studies for harmonizing expansion plans within the region. The clubs also deal with questions on incentives, tariffs, and other forms of promotional measures for particular projects and products. Among the industries covered by the RICs are agricultural machinery, aluminium, automotive, cement, ceramics, chemicals, electrical and electronic, food processing, furniture, glass, industrial machinery, iron and steel, leather-based products, panel products, pharmaceuticals, plastics, printing and publishing products, pulp and paper, rubber, and textiles. In addition, the RICs search for new markets outside ASEAN and take joint approaches on issues of common interest affecting a particular industry.

The fourth tier is made up of the NICs and NCCs, components of the RICs and RCCs. Regional clubs are considered an integral part of the ASEAN-CCI and hence work closely with their national constituent members. The NICs initiate the identification of possible projects for economic co-operation and recommend them to the RICs. The recommendation is processed by the relevant working group for endorsement by the ASEAN-CCI Council.

C. Joint Business/Economic Councils with ASEAN's Dialogue Partners

Apart from the multi-level structure of the ASEAN-CCI, it sponsors private sector representation in business/economic councils with dialogue partners of ASEAN. The ASEAN-CCI is currently active in the ASEAN-Australia Business Council (AABC), ASEAN-Canada Business Council (ACBC), ASEAN-EC Business Council (AEBC),

BOX 4.2: GUIDELINES ON PRIVATE SECTOR

The third meeting of ASEAN Heads of Government held on 14–15 December 1987 in Manila decided to encourage and improve private sector involvement both in extra-ASEAN co-operation and in ASEAN dialogue relations in view of the importance of the role of the private sector in both areas. Pursuant to this decision, private sector participation in ASEAN meetings and activities was given due consideration, while taking cognizance of the fact that in the normal proceedings of ASEAN meetings, items relating to policy matters shall be discussed solely by ASEAN officials concerned. There are, however, other items in which the private sector could participate. In this regard, the extent of involvement of the private sector in the dialogue process could be based on the response of each dialogue partner. In light of the above, the following recommendations have been adopted as guidelines for private sector participation in the ASEAN machinery.

A. ASEAN Economic Ministers Meetings

1. The president and the six vice-presidents of the ASEAN Chamber of Commerce and Industry (ASEAN-CCI) should be invited to attend all open sessions of the AEM.
2. To encourage free-wheeling exchange of views between the AEM and the private sector, the president of the ASEAN-CCI could be invited for consultations during AEM meetings. The outcome of the consultation in the form of a record of discussion should also be prepared. The host country would be responsible for the preparation of such session and of the topic of such consultations.

B. ASEAN Functional Committees

1. National secretariats of ASEAN committees could closely consult with the private sector concerned in the preparation for meetings of the committee, including sub-committees and working groups, and in following up the decisions or actions taken at such meetings.
2. Representatives of national chambers of commerce and/or affiliated NGOs could attend meetings of ASEAN committees, sub-committees, and working groups, as and when necessary on the understanding that such participation is in accordance with paragraph 3 below.
3. Where there are agenda items deemed to be of direct interest to the private sector, the private sector could be invited to consult with the committee in such meetings.
4. Where deemed appropriate, the private sector should be encouraged to contribute in the process of the formulation of relevant ASEAN project proposals by ASEAN committees.

PARTICIPATION IN ASEAN MEETINGS AND ACTIVITIES

C. Dialogue Process

1. There should be close co-ordination between ASEAN national secretariats as well as other agencies concerned and their respective private sector in the preparation and implementation of the result of dialogue meetings.
2. Identification of specific agenda items for the private sector to participate in dialogue meetings should be made during the preparatory stage of such meetings.
3. The private sector should be given the opportunity to propose agenda items and submit position papers as deemed necessary well in advance for the consideration of officials of both ASEAN and dialogue partners, particularly in highlighting problem areas on policy matters that require public sector attention.
4. The country co-ordinators should give sufficient time to dialogue partners and the private sector from dialogue countries to consider and have initial exchange of views on the agenda items proposed by the private sector of ASEAN member countries.
5. Business associations of ASEAN and their counterparts in respective dialogue countries should be informed of such dialogue meetings and encouraged to meet before the scheduled dialogue meetings.
6. The country co-ordinators should invite the president of the ASEAN-CCI and the relevant co-chairmen of the business councils to attend the dialogue meetings after having ascertained that the dialogue partners concerned have no objection.
7. The issues that the private sector could be involved in are as follows:
   a. International and regional economic issues of interest to ASEAN and the dialogue partners which are of direct interest to the private sector.
   b. Commercial co-operation and industrial and investment co-operation. However, discussion of policy matters will be confined to the officials concerned only. The private sector will be invited to participate only in the discussion on practical aspects of these issues, including implementing procedures.
8. In view of the benefits of private sector participation in the dialogue process, funding from dialogue partners could be sought for projects that are of interest to the private sector.

ASEAN-India Business Council (AIBC), ASEAN-Japan Business Council (AJBC), ASEAN-Korea Business Council (AKBC), ASEAN–New Zealand Business Council (ANZBC), and the ASEAN-U.S. Business Council (AUSBC). These councils complement the work of other ASEAN-CCI bodies and their activities support ASEAN objectives.

The structure of the business/economic councils parallels those of ASEAN and non-ASEAN sections, with each having a co-chairman. Regular meetings are convened jointly between the two sections. In general, the councils help to ensure an awareness of bilateral relations through business leadership and enhancement of business relations and contacts between the two business communities. They also provide a forum to advance solutions to economic, financial, and commercial problems and promote trade and investment.

D. ASEAN-CCI's Role in ASEAN Co-operation

The ASEAN-CCI plays an active role in enhancing ASEAN's efficiency and effectiveness as an organization. It prepared four major papers/reports on ASEAN co-operation and put forward a number of important recommendations for consideration by ASEAN leaders. More importantly, it played a major role in influencing the shape of ASEAN economic co-operation programmes especially in trade and industry.

The first comprehensive report was prepared in 1982 by a Special Review Committee created by the 13th ASEAN-CCI Council in 1980. Noting the slow pace of ASEAN co-operation at that time, the ASEAN-CCI tasked the Special Review Committee to identify and address the bottlenecks impeding the progress of ASEAN co-operation. Among others, the report dealt with the role of the ASEAN-CCI, the relationship between the ASEAN-CCI and ASEAN governments, ASEAN relations with non-ASEAN countries, and improvements in industrial and trade co-operation.

The second major contribution of the ASEAN-CCI was its inputs to the 1982 Task Force on ASEAN Co-operation. Created at the ASEAN Ministerial Meeting in July 1982, the Task Force, comprised of three senior individuals from each member country (and chaired by Anand Panrayachun of Thailand), made a comprehensive review and appraisal of ASEAN co-operation. The Task Force also made a number of significant recommendations to improve the ASEAN organization.

At the wake of preparations for the Third ASEAN Summit in Manila, the 28th Meeting of ASEAN-CCI Council held in July 1986 established the G-14 to study and recommend measures to advance ASEAN economic co-operation. The Group made recommendations in four areas, namely, in key economic sectors (trade, industry, primary commodities, transport, tourism, energy, and finance); the management of ASEAN's external economic relations; the institutions that govern ASEAN processes; and how to foster ASEAN consciousness.

More recently, following the Fourth ASEAN Summit, ASEAN-CCI, in its 47th Council Meeting, created a Committee on ASEAN Development. The Committee was created in response to the directives of the Fourth Summit encouraging co-operation and exchanges among ASEAN private sectors and between ASEAN and non-ASEAN private sectors. The Committee report proposed a proactive orientation for the ASEAN-CCI and wide-ranging institutional reforms, including the restructuring of its organization.

Related to the ASEAN-CCI advocacy for a more efficient ASEAN, various ASEAN-CCI working groups that parallel the ASEAN committee structure provided the mechanism for the private sector to participate actively in the design and implementation of ASEAN co-operation schemes in various sectors. In particular, the Working Group on Trade and the Working Group on Industrial Co-operation made important contributions to the ASEAN PTA, AFTA, and various ASEAN industrial co-operation schemes.

ASEAN industrial co-operation is the fulcrum of the private sector's participation in ASEAN. On the whole, the modest achievements of various ASEAN industrial co-operation schemes depended largely on the extent to which the private sector was willing to participate in these programmes. For instance, the failure of the AIPs was primarily attributed to the absence of private sector consultations in investment decisions pertaining to the establishment of large-scale industrial plants.

Owing to the failure of the AIPs, ASEAN's industrial co-operation scheme shifted to industrial complementation, drawing heavily from private sector contributions and initiatives. Launched in 1980, the ASEAN Industrial Complementation (AIC) programme, in allocating different stages of vertically integrated industries to realize economies of scale, required the active participation of the private sector. In this respect, the ASEAN-CCI became the official channel for identifying and proposing products in the AIC package before they are approved by ASEAN governments.

Difficulties encountered in the implementation of the initial AIC packages prompted the private sector to introduce a new scheme of industrial co-operation in the form of the AIJV. The AIJV concept was introduced at the 14th ASEAN-CCI Council Meeting in 1980, and in 1983, ASEAN member countries signed the Basic Agreement on ASEAN Industrial Ventures. The AIJV scheme was intended to cover projects (outside of the AIC) whose implementation was agreed upon by at least two member countries. This system avoided the lengthy negotiations (characteristic of the AIC) since only potential joint venture partners have to agree on business details (for example, equity sharing, financing, and so forth). After consultations with their respective governments, joint venture partners submit their application to the SEOM (previously to the COIME) through the ASEAN-CCI or the host ASEAN government. The impetus provided by the private sector to the AIJV scheme was cited as important to the programme's relative success.

More recently, the ASEAN-CCI Working Group on Industrial Co-operation proposed modifications in the basic agreements on the AIJV and the BBC schemes to make them compatible with AFTA. Since then, they have worked closely with ASEAN officials in devising new schemes of industrial co-operation as AFTA will eventually render the present programmes redundant. This is the ASEAN Industrial Co-operation (AICO) scheme (see Box 2.2, Chapter 2).

In the implementation of the ASEAN PTA, and its successor, the CEPT scheme, the ASEAN-CCI Working Group on Trade served as an effective sounding board on the coverage, depth, and pace of tariff programmes. Although national chambers have sought to promote their own interests with their respective governments, the ASEAN-CCI generally supported the policy of liberalizing trade within the region. In addition to the removal of tariff barriers, it also recognized the need to address non-tariff measures. In this regard, however, the private sector, in trying to avoid undue disclosure of their business operations, was not forthcoming in providing information on specific non-tariff measures that they have encountered.

E. ASEAN-CCI and ASEAN Governments

In the early years of the ASEAN-CCI, there was limited communication with governments and the channels of dialogue were not properly instituted. As the AIC and the AIP schemes began to take shape, the private sector felt that closer and more systematic interaction with the government was essential to improve its effectivity in responding to these programmes and help ensure the viability of ASEAN co-operation schemes. In 1978 the ASEAN-CCI requested attendance in all appropriate ASEAN meetings discussing matters involving the private sector. It also asked the AEM to allow direct consultations between the ASEAN-CCI working groups and the economic committees and the setting of a specific period for consultations whenever appropriate government committees met.

Several specific proposals to improve co-operation between the ASEAN private sector and ASEAN governments were made by the ASEAN-CCI in the past. In the G-14 report, the following recommendations were made: (a) an annual meeting between the ASEAN-CCI and the Standing Committee; (b) the participation of ASEAN-CCI representatives in preparatory meetings before each dialogue session; and (c) the participation of the ASEAN-CCI President (as a member of the ASEAN delegation) in the ASEAN dialogue process.

During the Third ASEAN Summit held in Manila in 1987, due consideration was given to private sector participation in ASEAN meetings. The Meeting adopted a set of guidelines that currently govern private sector attendance and representation in various ASEAN meetings (see Box 4.2). In general, while the private sector will be invited to attend ASEAN meetings, policy items will be discussed solely by government representatives. As regards ASEAN meetings with third countries, the extent of private sector involvement in dialogue meetings will depend on the response of the dialogue partner.

The private sector believes that the participation of the ASEAN-CCI in the AEM and SEOM can be made more meaningful if ASEAN-CCI representatives are taken in as full-pledged, non-voting members of the government delegation, except in forums where sensitive issues are discussed. The July 1995 report of the ASEAN-CCI's ASEAN Development Committee reflected this view and recommended the private sector's involvement in policy formulation so that, having participated in the process, the private sector can accept and abide by these policies, thus ensuring their effective implementation.

The ASEAN-CCI's ASEAN Development Committee also proposed a Memorandum of Understanding (MOU) to define the working relationship between ASEAN governments and the private sector so they can effectively complement each other in promoting the objectives of ASEAN co-operation. The proposed MOU covers: (a) attendance in ASEAN meetings at various levels; (b) access to reports, studies and communications; (c) relationship with the ASEAN Secretariat, and (d) policy advocacy. To forge a closer relationship with the ASEAN Secretariat, a permanent secretariat for the ASEAN-CCI is now housed at the former's headquarters in Jakarta. This is part of the Committee's proposal to enable effective day-to-day co-ordination (between ASEAN and the ASEAN-CCI) and the efficient use of available resources at the ASEAN Secretariat.

Notwithstanding improvements in ASEAN-CCI participation in the ASEAN organization, its formal participation in ASEAN decision-making is an outstanding organizational issue. Although ASEAN governments accepted the need to incorporate the views of the private sector in their decision-making, ASEAN governments remain cautious in allowing them to participate in the process. Thus, on the whole, the co-operation process among ASEAN private sectors moved on to a different track from the official process, with its own speed and direction.

There are a number of reasons why ASEAN governments are cautious in allowing full private sector participation in decision-making. First, unlike ASEAN governments, the private sector is not accountable to the peoples of ASEAN. Moreover, the motivations and the ambit of competence of the ASEAN-CCI differ from that of ASEAN governments. Second, and perhaps more fundamentally, the interests represented by the ASEAN-CCI are not necessarily synonymous with the interests of private enterprises. Some private enterprises could be driven by competition, while others could be motivated by rent-seeking activities. Third, ASEAN member countries have different economic philosophies, political cultures, and (government–private sector) interaction dynamics. Because of this, it is difficult for the ASEAN-CCI to arrive at a regional consensus. The intrinsic difficulties of involving the ASEAN private sector in official decision-making underscores the need to improve consultation mechanisms and channels of communication between the ASEAN-CCI and ASEAN. Finally, the absence of a mechanism in the ASEAN-CCI internal structure to gather inputs from its members and other private sector bodies undermines its responsiveness and weakens its representation to governments on issues of interest to the private sector as a whole.

The ASEAN-CCI recognized the need to attain a higher degree of internal consensus if it is to influence national and regional policy-making. This could be achieved through closer co-ordination with national government counterparts, rather than merely relying on ASEAN-CCI representation to official ASEAN bodies, to adequately reflect private sector views in national positions. At the same time, however, this has to be balanced by a wider regional perspective that goes beyond national concerns.

F. Linkages with Regional and International Organizations

The ASEAN-CCI recognizes the need to extend co-operation both within and outside the region. At its Fourth Council Meeting in 1975, the ASEAN-CCI agreed to affiliate with other regional and international organizations to enhance its ability to work on issues of mutual interest, and to contribute to mutually beneficial programmes. In implementing this decision, the ASEAN-CCI followed an approach parallel to that of ASEAN — pursuing relations with regional and international organizations that have similar objectives. To date, the ASEAN-CCI is affiliated with the International Chamber of Commerce (ICC) and its Commission on Asia-Pacific Affairs (CAPA), the ISO, and the Pacific Basin Economic Co-operation Council (PBEC).

III. Other Private Sector Organizations

Apart from the ASEAN-CCI, there are other private organizations that implement important initiatives to promote ASEAN co-operation, by their significant contributions in the areas of banking and finance, shipping, and tourism, among others. In many cases, these organizations forged closer links among national players in specialized areas and provided the structural means for greater bargaining ability with external actors.

In 1991, the private sector initiated the establishment of the ASEAN Institute, a non-profit organization composed of about 250 ASEAN-based companies whose corporate earnings are largely dependent on ASEAN capital, management, and labour. Unlike the ASEAN-CCI whose membership comprises the national chambers of commerce and industry of member countries, the membership of the ASEAN Institute is at the firm level. The ASEAN Institute aims to generate closer business ties among ASEAN companies and promote joint ventures through an Advisory Unit within the organization. The Unit identifies opportunities, provides advice on tenders and disseminates economic information and intelligence, among others. In 1994, the Institute was renamed the ASEAN Business Forum. It organizes an annual event where government ministers, senior officials, and leading executives are invited to exchange views on regional developments. The Forum also organizes an annual roundtable meeting among ASEAN chief executive officers.

In the field of banking and finance, the ASEAN Bankers Association (ABA) provides the vehicle for co-operation among ASEAN bankers. Leadership of the ABA is vested in the ASEAN Banking Council (ABC), which was formed in 1976 to promote friendship and co-operation among ASEAN bankers, address common threats to ASEAN banking, and identify opportunities and common ventures in the interest of ASEAN banks. Although the ABC does not fall under the organizational ambit of the ASEAN-CCI, it stands out among ASEAN private sector organizations for its concrete accomplishments (see Box 4.3).

Perhaps the most tangible proof of co-operation among ASEAN bankers was the establishment of the ASEAN Finance Corporation (AFC). The formal proposal for an "ASEAN merchant bank" was made as early as 1976 at the First ASEAN Banking Conference but it was only at the fifth ABC meeting that the proposal was accepted. The proposal was subsequently endorsed by the ASEAN COFAB and the AEM. The AFC was finally incorporated in Singapore in 1981 and began operations in June of that year.

BOX 4.3: ASEAN BANKING CONFERENCE

The ASEAN Banking Conference is held biennially to draw out ideas to attain the objectives of the ASEAN Bankers Association and to present desirable ones to the ASEAN Banking Council for more detailed deliberation and subsequent implementation.

The ASEAN Banking Council, being the executive arm of the Association, meets annually to formulate policies and co-ordinate activities of the Association.

The 11th ASEAN Banking Conference and the 26th ASEAN Banking Council Meeting were held in July 1996. The Conference attracted more than 200 participants from ASEAN countries, namely, Brunei, Indonesia, Malaysia, the Philippines, Singapore, Thailand, and Vietnam. The Vietnam Bankers Association, the seventh member of ASEAN Bankers Association, attended the Conference and Meeting for the first time.

A Memorandum of Understanding was signed to launch the Second ASEAN Fund, following the highly successful First ASEAN Fund. The Second Fund, to be named ASEAN Supreme Fund Limited, will have a minimum size of US$100 million and will initially be listed on the stock exchanges of Singapore and Osaka and when appropriate on other stock exchanges in ASEAN as well. The Fund will invest in listed and unlisted securities of corporations in ASEAN for long-term capital appreciation. The Fund is fully underwritten by members of the ASEAN Bankers Association and Nomura Singapore and will be managed by Jardine Fleming Singapore.

The Association also launched the inaugural issue of its official newsletter, *The ASEAN Banker*, which will be published on a quarterly basis, highlighting issues of interest on ASEAN banking. To facilitate the dissemination of information amongst ASEAN banks, the Council has endorsed the proposal to use the Internet as a communication channel.

The 27th ASEAN Banking Council Meeting will be hosted by the Association of Banks in Malaysia in 1997 and the 12th ASEAN Banking Conference will be hosted by the Thai Bankers' Association in 1998.

Source: ASEAN Bankers Association.

The AFC was set up to finance ASEAN industrial co-operation projects and to provide venture capital to ASEAN entrepreneurs. It is owned by commercial banks in ASEAN member countries and provides loan and equity capital to ASEAN-based enterprises. Although the AFC's performance was hampered by structural and operational difficulties, it remains an important source of loanable funds for ASEAN enterprises.

In the field of insurance, the ASEAN Insurance Council, whose affiliation with ASEAN started in 1983, helps to promote the development of the insurance industry in the region through collaborative projects in training and information networking. Council members are recognized associations and organizations of insurers in ASEAN member countries. They hold seminars and workshops to propagate the insurance concept and its technical aspects among members and their counterparts from ASEAN dialogue partners.

National shippers' councils in ASEAN recognized early on that to become more effective in representing their interest in shipping, it would be advantageous to form an ASEAN federation. Thus, the Federation of ASEAN Shippers' Councils (FASC) was established in 1972 to represent its members in shipping conferences and negotiations with shipping lines, governments, and international organizations. The Federation also promotes co-operation in the improvement of shipping services to achieve efficient and economic carriage of goods among member countries.

The FASC represents ASEAN shippers' organizations in conference-negotiations on general rate increases with major liners serving the region. Other than being involved in the determination of competitive freight rates for exports, the FASC also ensures that freight competitiveness is not achieved at the expense of efficient fleet operation. Together with the ASEAN Committee on Transport and Communications, the FASC is involved in formulating ASEAN approaches to co-operation in shipping.

The FASC works closely with the Federation of ASEAN Shipowners' Association (FASA), an organization that is concerned with the development of shipping lines and the efficient and effective carriage of goods by sea. FASA members collaborate to represent their collective interest with shippers' councils, port authorities, governments, and international organizations. FASA programmes cover the provision of joint shipping services, ship financing, and joint bulk shipment.

An ASEAN Ports Authorities Association (APAA), which was formed by port authorities of ASEAN countries in 1975 based on the recognition that ports and harbours serve as vital links in the flow of cargoes, vessels, and passengers within the region. The APAA provides a vehicle for regional co-operation in port and harbour development, operations, and management. More specifically, the APAA is party to collaborative activities in the areas of cargo handling, port procedures and documentation, port statistics and port information systems, and administration of port personnel. It also maps out co-operative schemes with private agencies involved in the business of ports. Among the concrete projects implemented by the APAA are (a) simplification of port documents, (b) handling of dangerous goods, (c) assistance in container terminal operations, (d) comprehensive studies on containerization, and (e) feasibility studies on multimodal transport systems.

The ASEAN International Airports Association (AAA) is APAA's counterpart in the civil aviation sector. Formed in 1973, the AAA aims to promote efficient airport operations and management and engineering practices among its members through collaborative activities. The AAA also seeks to achieve, as far as practicable, uniform rules and procedures on common and identical matters, and to facilitate the formulation of joint positions on questions of common interest. Exchanges of information through technical tours, mutual provision of information on available airport facilities, and procedures for collaborative action on the removal of disabled aircraft are some of the concrete projects implemented by the AAA.

The ASEAN Tours and Travel Association (ASEANTA) was formed in 1971 to promote co-operation in travel, marketing and joint research, and publicity. In particular, ASEANTA undertakes activities to facilitate tourism in the region, further develop the tourist industry, and encourage collaboration with international transport, hotel, and travel agency associations. The Association also promotes closer relationships among tour operators and travel agencies, and helps establish the industry's ethical and disciplinary standards.

The ASEAN Fisheries Federation (AFF) is the private sector group encompassing the fishing industry in ASEAN. It has regularly met (as the AFF Council) in the last several years and its meetings are attended by delegations of business executives in the region. The Federation is important to ASEAN as indicated by the fact that most of its annual meetings are graced by either the Head of State or agriculture ministers as keynote speakers. It is the first NGO to have a secretariat based at the ASEAN Secretariat, an indication of its seriousness in drawing up ASEAN co-operation projects.

The AFF has four active working groups. These are (a) Working Group on ASEAN Shrimp Club, (b) Working Group on ASEAN Tuna Club, (c) Working Group on ASEAN Seafood Restaurant/Promotion, and (d) Working Group on Other Fisheries Interests. The AFF's recent recommendations include calls for greater liberalization of imports of raw and canned tuna in the region, formulation of unified marketing strategies, and development of ASEAN common dishes.

IV. ASEAN Centres

Over the years, a number of ASEAN regional centres were established to promote specific programmes and co-operation projects among member countries. Most of these regional centres were originally established to implement collaborative activities funded by dialogue partners. They provide the modality for realizing economies of operation through networking or specialization that could be accessed by member countries. In some cases, the hosting of a regional centre by a member country provided it with the opportunity to acquire facilities that would otherwise be too expensive to obtain unless used on a regional scale. Institutions that serve as regional centres can be either public or private institutions. Invariably, these centres could be institutionalized into self-sustaining organizations or transformed into inter-governmental institutions once dialogue partner assistance is terminated.

At present, there are fourteen regional centres in ASEAN involved in agriculture, energy, social and institutional development, culture, tourism, and science and technology. Most of these centres are highly dependent on external funding support and are not expected to continue operations after the completion of dialogue partner assistance. In general, plans for sustaining the activities and financing of these centres were not considered in the design stages of the project. In most cases, there seems to be a presumption on the part of both project participants and sponsors that the centres would be converted into national institutions after the termination of dialogue partner support. ASEAN member countries who expressed concern about the sustainability of these centres have, however, formulated policy measures to address their continued viability.

The ASEAN Centres contribute significantly to the enhancement of ASEAN co-operation in various areas. Many centres established in the field of agriculture and forestry, for instance, provide member countries with support in research, training, information exchange, networking, and project implementation. Centres operating in the energy and tourism sectors also serve as important resources to member countries.

The ASEAN Timber Technology Centre (ATTC), funded by the EU and established in 1986, provides services to the timber processing industry in such areas as applied research, training, and technical information services. Currently, the Centre implements a co-ordinated regional programme of applied research in specific areas of timber technology. Its recent training programmes covered, among others, finishing techniques for wooden furniture, maintenance of woodworking machines, and jigs production for wood machining. The Centre also conducts international symposia on topics of interest to timber producers and processors, for example, on investment opportunities in the wood industry, waste disposal from wood milling, rubberwood processing and finishing, and so forth. To keep the industry current on regional and global developments affecting the sector, it established databases and developed a media network within and outside ASEAN.

The ASEAN Institute of Forest Management (AIFM) is now in its second phase of operations with joint funding from Canada and ASEAN member countries. Established in 1986, the AIFM aims to develop expertise among ASEAN member countries in sustainable forest management and to disseminate such expertise to national forest administrations through pilot projects. The Institute, apart from providing training to key personnel, develops the capacity of member countries to adapt methods of securing forest resource information for application to sustainable forest management. It also serves as an information and networking centre to facilitate the transfer of appropriate technologies for resource inventory, monitoring, and management.

Primarily funded by the Australian Government, the ASEAN Food Handling Bureau (AFHB) is one of the most successful regional centres that managed to sustain operations since its establishment in 1981. Through the years, it established itself as an excellent technical and administrative centre for food handling projects through the provision of consultancy and advisory services to project implementors in different ASEAN countries. With the new mechanism for economic co-operation under the SEOM, the AFHB Management Board and the ASEAN Secretariat jointly exercises oversight functions for the Bureau until it becomes self-sustaining.

The ASEAN Centre for the Development of Agricultural Co-operatives (ACEDAC) in Jakarta was established in 1991 and is funded solely by the Indonesian Government. The Centre promotes the development and growth of agricultural co-operatives as a means of improving the living standards of small farmers and fishermen. To attain this objective, the Centre engages in exchanges of information and experience among member countries, and promotes research and development programmes. Among the activities it undertakes, with much success, are study visits to agricultural co-operatives in ASEAN, the preparation of case-studies on (successful) agribusiness, and the preparation of an agricultural co-operatives directory.

The ASEAN Rural Youth Development Centre was established in 1991 in Bangkok to act as the Secretariat of the project "Preparing Rural Youth for a Better Future in Agriculture". The project, which is funded by Japan under the Japan-ASEAN Exchange Programme (JAEP), seeks to enhance agricultural and rural youth development in ASEAN by increasing the income and productivity of rural youth. This it does through the conduct of research studies on the current status and future prospects of rural youth in agriculture, implements exchange visits of youth leaders and youth development officials, and organizes training programmes in various aspects of agricultural enterprises. The project, now on its second phase, aims to institutionalize the implementation, co-ordination, monitoring, and evaluation of future programmes and projects, and to serve as a repository of information on ASEAN rural youth.

The ASEAN Poultry Disease Research and Training Centre (APDRTC) was established in 1986 to carry out collaborative research on poultry diseases in ASEAN and serve as a regional reference centre for poultry pathogens and diseases. The Centre produces and supplies biological materials for diagnosis and vaccine production, and conducts training for poultry technicians and researchers in the region. As funding assistance is nearly completed, all operating costs of the Centre are currently funded by the Malaysian Government.

The ASEAN Forest Tree Seed Centre (AFTSC) was established in

1981 in Thailand with funding assistance from the Canadian Government. Its objectives are to increase the supply of quality forest tree seeds and materials for vegetative propagation of trees required for ASEAN reforestation programmes, and to protect the genetic diversity of ASEAN forests. In working towards these objectives, the Centre conducts research and development activities, provides operational support to ASEAN reforestation programmes, conducts training, and promotes information exchange through networking. Its notable achievements include the development and adoption of seed testing and certification standards for the region and the preparation of a manual on rapid viability testing for tropical tree seeds. The Centre also maintains a seed bank, a seed exchange programme, and a registry of genetic resources.

In the field of energy, the ASEAN-EC Energy Management Training and Research Centre (AEEMTRC) was established in 1980 in Jakarta. In 1994, the first phase of operations was completed and planning for the second phase is now under way with joint funding support from the EU and the ASEAN Fund. The AEEMTRC's activities involve the development of innovative methodologies in resources evaluation, production optimization, and energy utilization, with due consideration to environmental concerns. The Centre also assists member countries in developing the capabilities of energy professionals, improving energy information systems, and developing energy databases.

To support collaborative activities in tourism, national tourism organizations established the ASEAN Tourism Information Centre (ATIC) in Kuala Lumpur in 1988 to serve as a reference centre on tourism information in ASEAN. More specifically, the ATIC disseminates information on member countries' tourist attractions, evaluates and monitors the marketing programmes of the six ASEAN Promotional Chapters for Tourism (APCT), and supervises and monitors technical assistance programmes in manpower training and marketing. In addition, the Centre undertakes promotional activities within and outside ASEAN and maintains rapport with the travel trade and mass media.

V. Implications

This chapter's review of ASEAN private sector and regional co-operation bares out several important implications.

The first is the existence of a wide array of private sector groups in ASEAN that either evolved on their own or work closely with ASEAN governments. As Appendix D shows, the list of NGOs affiliated with ASEAN (that is, those that follow the procedures for NGO affiliation with ASEAN as detailed in Box 4.1) is varied — from finance, trade and industry groups to youth, sports and co-operative groups. These groups, which encompass national organizations within each ASEAN member state, indicate the strength of the private sector in the region. The list does not include other ASEAN groups that have not sought official affiliation with ASEAN to be within its network yet undertake regional co-operation activities and pursue ASEAN objectives. This shows the vast potential of harnessing the private sector for expanding the scope of ASEAN economic co-operation towards one region and a single economy, emphasizing the free flow of goods, services, and resources among members. Private sector groups cover a wide range of sectors, hence, they can also be tapped to promote economic co-operation in the traditional areas promoted by ASEAN.

Second, these ASEAN NGOs can become potential vehicles for the regional processes that officials go through in considering co-operation activities. For one, they can be independent feedback mechanisms about co-operation modalities that ASEAN governments initiate. The NGOs can provide an evaluation of existing programmes and suggest measures to make them more "implementable" and effective. For another, they can be active participants in deliberating on suggested ASEAN co-operation schemes reflecting the views of private citizens in member states without being officially involved. The NGOs may know of alternatives and options to push co-operation efforts in the region. Finally, the NGOs can be organized in ways that parallel official ASEAN organizations, as what the ASEAN-CCI did, enabling it to quickly respond to, and actively participate in, ASEAN matters. To the extent that NGOs have extensive networks within each country, regional perspectives may be heard. If the various ASEAN committees and working groups systematically interact with appropriate NGOs, the regional identity may be further advanced. For instance, in the CEPT scheme for AFTA, the entire ASEAN NGO community may be mobilized to stimulate and sustain interest in the scheme, disseminate the programme to a wider constituency, and increase the use of the scheme.

BOX. 4.4: ASEAN CALLS FOR GREATER PRIVATE SECTOR PARTICIPATION

ASEAN governments continue efforts to open additional avenues for more active dialogue between officials and private businessmen. At the 27th AEM Meeting held in September 1995 in Brunei Darussalam, a half-day session was allocated for free-flowing discussion between private sector representatives and economic ministers on topics that were of mutual interest. At that meeting, the ministers called on the ASEAN-CCI to reach out to all captains of industry in ASEAN so that their participation in ASEAN programmes can be effective and meaningful.

For his part, the Secretary-General of ASEAN, Dato' Ajit Singh, in his keynote address at the private sector–sponsored AFTA Convention in Bangkok in 1995, called on the ASEAN-CCI to assist ASEAN in publicizing details regarding the CEPT scheme for AFTA, to work with ASEAN in helping small and medium enterprises meet the challenges of AFTA, and to facilitate intra-regional trade by providing regular inputs to the ASEAN Trade and Investment Database. The Secretary-General also underscored that through various initiatives and co-operation activities, ASEAN governments have opened opportunities for the private sector, opportunities that the ASEAN-CCI and its members are encouraged to take advantage of and, whenever applicable, to take the lead in implementation.

The call for greater private sector participation was further echoed by His Majesty, the Sultan of Negara Brunei Darussalam in his Opening Address at the 27th AEM. In that address, His Majesty said: "Communication and interaction between the officials and private sector players need to be strengthened. Let both sides explore and propose how best to have more private sector inputs into ASEAN's economic co-operation programme. Such inputs from the private sector will help ASEAN remain ahead of its competition in the global market place."

These are the primary reasons why ASEAN officials opened the avenues for greater NGO participation in ASEAN (see Box 4.4).

Finally, the proliferation of ASEAN Centres that cater to a wide spectrum of interests highlights some concerns. The fourteen ASEAN Centres located in different ASEAN capitals fared well in terms of achieving their objectives. There is no doubt they perform functions that contribute to ASEAN's regional co-operation efforts. However, it appears that the creation of a number of these centres was donor-driven (from bilateral or multilateral sources) and not derived from a systematic assessment of regional concerns that lead to specific co-operative actions (for example, the creation of a centre). In addition, the most apparent pitfall in the creation of these centres is the lack of attention given to the centres' viability (hence sustainability) beyond the donor's initial funding. Moreover, once created, ASEAN or the host country, allocates resources for the Centre's eventual maintenance without fully deliberating on alternative opportunities for regional co-operation and their relative costs. Thus, ASEAN may need to take stock of these centres, review their functions, and decide the appropriate centres to establish and maintain before seeking donor resources.

5

Co-operation within a Narrower Framework: Growth Triangles in ASEAN

I. The Emergence of Growth Triangles

The emergence of growth areas in Southeast Asia is best seen against the broader context of increasing economic integration in the region. As the rise of the newly industrializing economies (NIEs) shifted the location of industries from high-cost to low-cost countries, investments and technology became more interdependent, resulting in production linkages and increased intra-industry trade flows. As a result, East and Southeast Asian economies came closer together regardless of formal institutional ties.

ASEAN economies are among the beneficiaries of the investment-trade nexus driving economic integration in Southeast Asia. The fast-paced growth of ASEAN economies required that development processes go beyond national limits to free the constraints posed by domestic

BOX 5.1 GROWTH TRIANGLES:

Growth Triangles involve economic co-operation based on encouraging specific and limited linkages of complementary economic activities across borders. It is a pragmatic response to the practical problems of formal economic integration among nations that require fundamental changes in national institutional and administrative arrangements, as with NAFTA, the EC, or AFTA. Growth Triangles, as sub-regional economic co-operation modes, need not involve entire countries, but simply adjacent areas within countries that have complementary capabilities and resources.

The concept is essentially a simple one: link adjacent areas with different factor endowments and different comparative advantages — such as differences in the levels of technology, labour (quantity and quality), natural resources, financial capital — to form a sub-region of economic growth that is driven by market dynamics. The intention is to have specific linkages across borders, rather than just complementarities in respective national economic structures. Sub-regional economic co-operation essentially involves initiatives in limited or localized economic integration that create transborder "economic neighbourhoods". In its various forms, it has a number of characteristics:

1. Sub-regional economic co-operation tends to be consistent with the evolution of "natural economic linkages" among neighbouring countries, building on increasing formal and informal local trade and investment linkages. It "goes with the flow" in the very real sense, both responding to and facilitating emerging transborder economic activities.
2. Since Growth Triangles are limited in both substantive and geographic scope, the political and economic complexities (and related risks) are generally more manageable than those associated with more formal and extensive regional arrangements or "blocs".
3. The more modest scope of regional co-operation allows tangible benefits of co-operation to emerge more quickly and with less uncertainty, compared with larger, more formal arrangements. Furthermore, it allows one country to participate in several Growth Triangles at the same time, both testing different approaches to economic co-operation and tailoring them to specific conditions.
4. Sub-regions tend to be outward-looking investment zones, shifting from national comparative advantage to sub-regional comparative advantage, with a focus on trade creation. Countries and enterprises outside the sub-region can benefit from both the expanded market and investment zone nature of the Growth Triangles.

THE RATIONALE

5. Within participating countries, sub-regional co-operation can expand to other adjacent areas, becoming a key element of domestic development and of more extensive transborder economic co-operation. In this way, for countries and firms — both inside and outside the sub-region — Growth Triangles can become the building blocks of a broader regional strategy.
6. Sub-regional economic co-operation can become the building block of (or linked to) more general forms of regional co-operation such as AFTA (for example, all ASEAN countries are now involved in pursuing one or more such sub-regional initiatives with other member countries).

Sub-regional economic co-operation in eastern Asia is intended to be primarily market-driven, generally taking the form of investment-led integration, with the private sector providing capital, technology, training, and marketing channels. In this, intra-industry flows are to play a key role, linking firm-level activities such as investment, sourcing, production, and distribution across borders and taking advantage of sub-regional economic complementarities. The key supporting role of the government should not be overlooked, and in some cases the government emerges as the catalyst. An important characteristic of sub-regional economic co-operation is the symbiotic relationship between the public and the private sectors. This goes beyond traditional roles, and increasingly involves forging new types of partnerships and collaboration between them.

Infrastructure is seen as the critical success factor, "the necessary condition" for transforming geographic proximity to economic linkages. In this, the government plays a key role including that of creating a framework for investment, though the participation of the private sector is increasingly central. In addition to "hardware", governments must also provide "software" in the form of institutional frameworks required to anchor and sustain sub-regional co-operation. This includes (often in localized and limited form) the legal, regulatory, and policy frameworks and (perhaps limited) transborder agreements relating to areas such as customs, immigration, repatriation of capital, foreign exchange transactions, fiscal incentives, investment guarantees, and so forth. More generally, the government plays an important role as facilitator in sub-regional economic co-operation as political commitment at the highest levels is likely to be necessary.

(Note: Excerpts from a paper presented by George Abonyi, National University of Singapore, at the Fourth Southeast Asia Roundtable on Economic Development: "Growth Triangles in Southeast Asia: Strategy for Development", 27–28 June 1994, Kuala Lumpur. *For reproduction in any form whatsoever please seek the permission of the author.*)

economies and to take advantage of opportunities offered by other economies in the region. AFTA is the formal vehicle for strengthening economic co-operation and integration. However, other forms of economic co-operation have emerged, operating with less institutional formality that characterizes conventional economic arrangements, and largely motivated by market forces.

As economies adopted outward-looking policies to promote or accelerate economic growth, economic exchanges between geographically contiguous but politically separate border areas increased. The propensity among proximate localities to do business with their neighbours is driven by lower transport, communication, and other transactions costs. Furthermore, geographically proximate areas often (but not always) share a common ethnicity, language, culture, and kinship ties. This makes it easier for investors to operate in different political, legal, and bureaucratic settings.

Within the context of increasing economic integration in the region, sub-regionalism emerged as a new phenomenon in Southeast Asia. Sub-regionalism took a number of forms, among them sub-regional economic zones, transnational economic zones, and extended metropolitan regions. A dominant example of transborder economic sub-regionalism is that of Hong Kong, China, and Taiwan.

Within ASEAN, similar developments took place. An example is the Singapore-Johor-Riau (or SIJORI) Growth Triangle, also known as the Southern Growth Triangle. It was recently joined by two other Growth Triangles, the Indonesia-Malaysia-Thailand Growth Triangle (IMT-GT), also known as the Northern Growth Triangle, and the East ASEAN Growth Area (EAGA), also known as the Eastern Growth Triangle (or Quadrangle since four countries comprise it, namely, Brunei, Indonesia, Malaysia, and the Philippines).

The term Growth Triangle is now part of the ASEAN terminology to refer to growth areas. The term evolved from the phrase used by then Singapore Deputy Prime Minister Goh Chok Tong in 1989 when he proposed that Singapore, Batam (in Riau), and Johor form a "triangle of growth within ASEAN in the decade ahead". Since then, the term Growth Triangle became firmly established in the jargon of regional politics. The use of the labels "southern", "northern", and "eastern" to refer to the growth areas already established clearly denote a geographical reference to ASEAN — thus reinforcing the fact that the Growth Triangles are considered ASEAN sub-regional institutions.

The idea underlying a Growth Triangle or growth area is to take advantage of differences in factor endowments in adjacent locations. The concept is workable because benefits accruing to growth areas spill over state boundaries into areas that are relatively less developed than "original" growth areas. Apart from economic considerations, however, a large degree of political influence is also crucial in the development of growth areas. Where benefits accruing to a participating country fall short of expectations, there should be larger political motivations to support the growth area concept. In addition, social influences, such as ethnic and cultural ties, could also impact on the pace and character of development of a growth area.

Figure 5.1 shows the various regional and sub-regional arrangements existing in the Pacific area. Nine Growth Triangles are identified, of which three are in ASEAN, and fall within AFTA. The figure also indicates two free-trade agreement areas.

II. The ASEAN Experience with Growth Areas

A. Singapore-Johor-Riau Growth Triangle (SIJORI)[1]

ASEAN's initial experience with Growth Triangles developed through sub-regional co-operative arrangements among Singapore, Johor, and the Riau Islands, otherwise known as the SIJORI Growth Triangle. Singapore, Johor, and the Riau Islands lie on the strategic sea route passing from the South China Sea to the Indian Ocean through the Straits of Malacca (see Figure 5.2). Johor, the second largest state in peninsular Malaysia, has good infrastructure facilities and devotes huge areas to plantation agriculture. Riau Islands is part of Indonesia's Riau province and is one of the country's largest producers of oil and natural gas. The Riau Islands comprise Batam, which is nearest to Singapore, Bintan to the east, Bulan to the southwest, and other smaller islands. SIJORI covers a total land area of 20,000 square kilometres and a population of 6 million.

The formation of the SIJORI Growth Triangle evolved through a combination of politically motivated and market-driven factors. Between 1979 and 1988, the Indonesian Government undertook various

Figure 5.1
Map of Growth Triangles in the Pacific Area

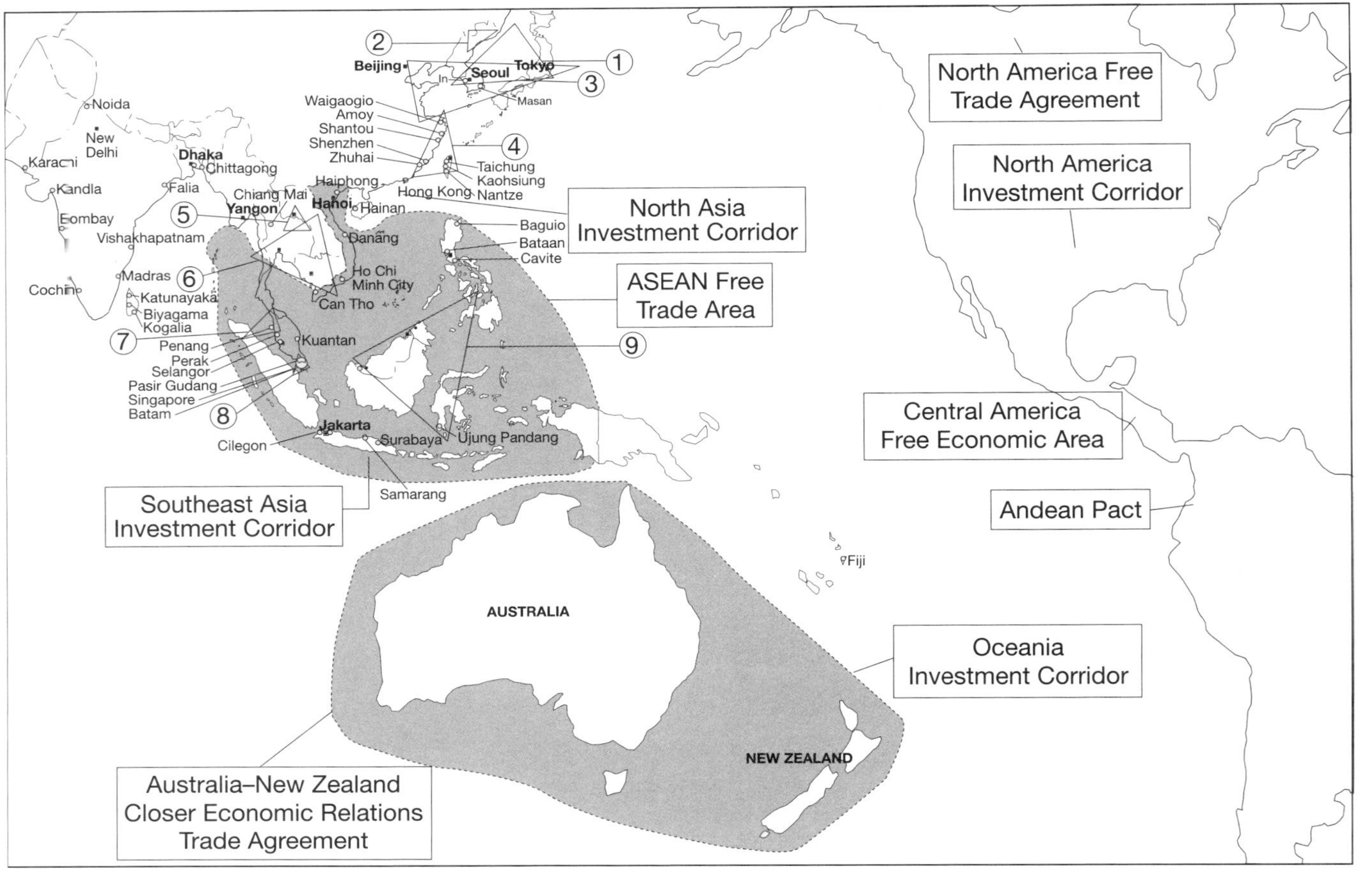

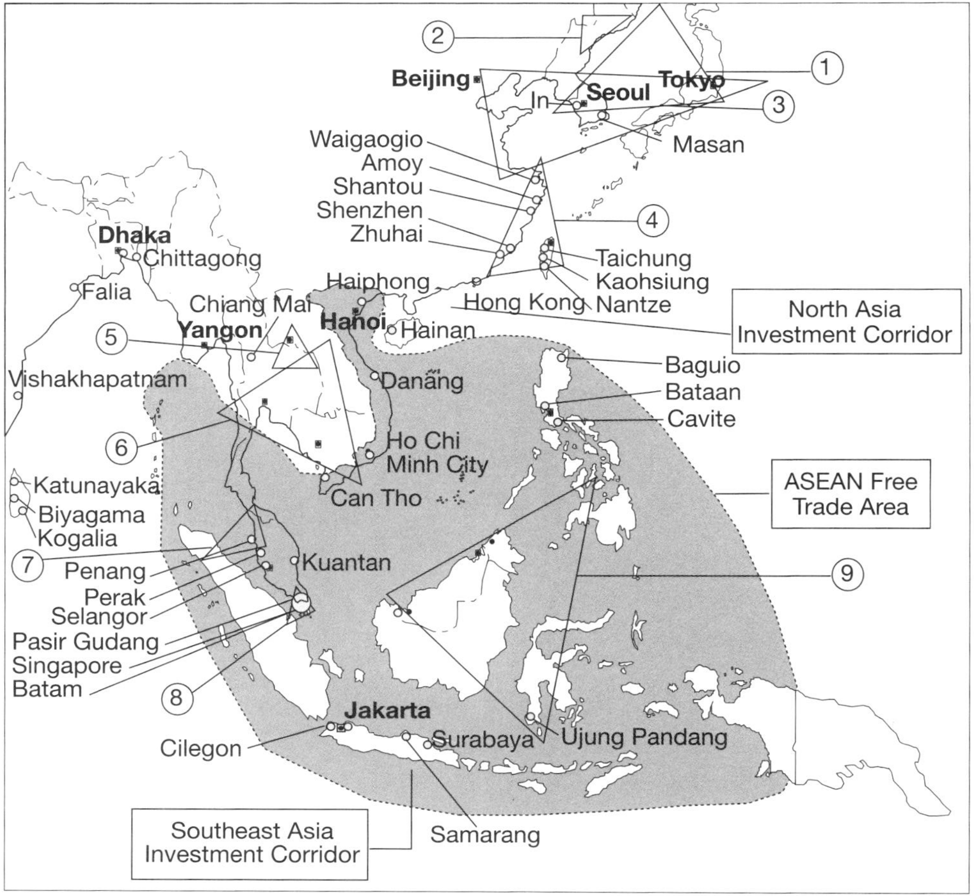

Source: Compiled by the Sakura Institute of Research.

Figure 5.2
Map of SIJORI

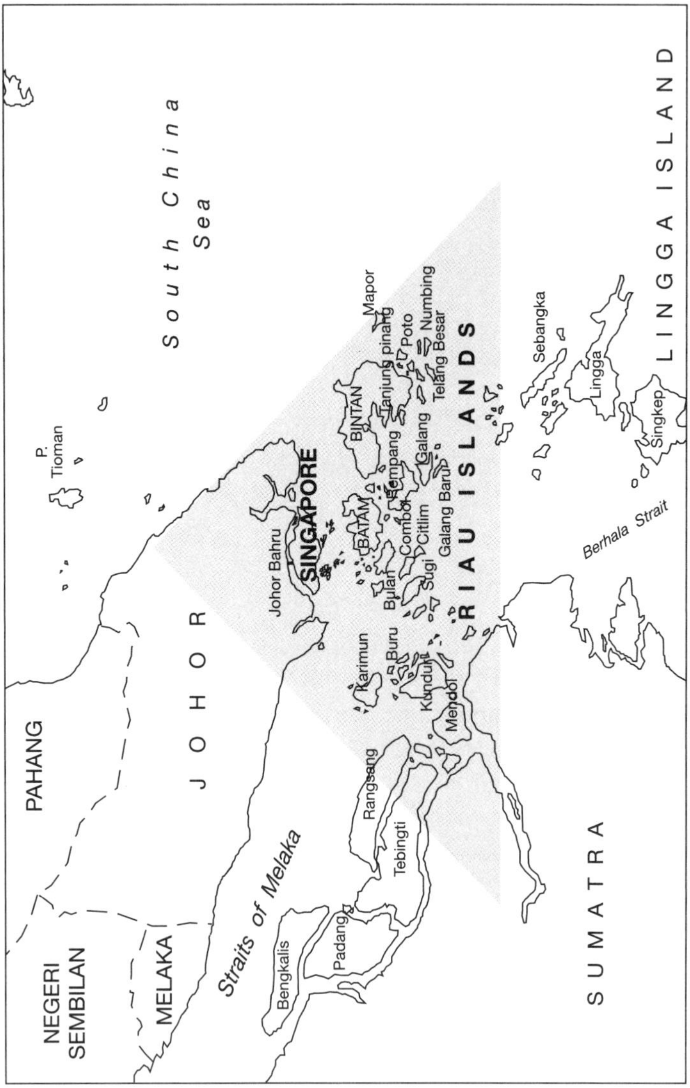

initiatives to develop Batam (in Riau) and to establish co-operative arrangements with Singapore. However, it was not until after 1988, when Indonesia began to improve its foreign investment regulation that economic activity between the two states accelerated. Changes in the investment policy regime allowed the private sector to set up industrial estates in Batam, which led to the establishment of the Batam Industrial Park, a joint venture between Indonesia's private sector and Singapore's state-owned enterprises. Subsequently, Japanese and other MNCs based in Singapore began to locate their investments in Batam and Bintan.

Singapore and Indonesia entered into three bilateral agreements in 1990 and 1991 providing for the joint development of Riau. A Joint Ministerial Committee co-ordinates the development efforts in Riau, including improvements in the policy and regulatory framework, and co-operation in immigration procedures. Government and private sector investment in Indonesia, such as infrastructure and inter-island transport links, supported the rapid growth of business in Riau.

Economic activity between Singapore and Johor antedates the formal institutional arrangements for the Growth Triangle, owing to historical ties between the two. The causeway that physically links Johor is two kilometres across the straits to Singapore and is an important means for the carriage of goods and people. Thus, even without the benefit of a formal institutional arrangement among governments, companies in Singapore moved into Johor as early as the 1980s. Johor benefited from its close proximity to Singapore and from Malaysia's relaxation of foreign investment rules and regulations.

The Johor-Riau link is the weakest in the "triangle". Investment from Johor to Riau and vice versa did not materialize to a significant degree. Moreover, investment and trade links did not develop at the same pace as other nodes of the triangle because of lack of complementarity and the physical distance between Johor and Riau. To strengthen this link in the triangle, there is a need to identify and implement more co-operative projects in various sectors in the two areas.

The "triangle" concept eventually emerged from the Singapore-Johor and the Singapore-Riau bilateral relations. The possibility of a three-way relationship was first suggested in 1989 by then Deputy Prime Minister Goh Chok Tong of Singapore. The concept attracted serious discussion by government leaders in Malaysia and Indonesia as there were perceived advantages in plugging their economies to the global market via Singapore's economic base, thus expanding the international reach of the two areas. On the other hand, Singapore would become more commercially attractive by combining its resources with those of its neighbours.

The Singapore-Johor-Riau Growth Triangle represents a unique blend of government initiative and private entrepreneurship. Apart from the political initiatives taken by the Governments of Indonesia, Malaysia, and Singapore, market forces were also at work in shaping the Growth Triangle. The overall cost of doing business in Singapore rose sharply in recent years due to limited labour and land supply, causing firms to either upgrade their activities, redistribute labour-intensive operations, or both. The proximity of Johor and the Riau Islands provided the opportunity for such redistribution to take place. Johor has extensive land and semi-skilled labour while the Riau Islands has low-cost labour. Further, the relative costs of factor endowments are attractive for industries relocating to Johor or to Riau. With such complementarities in factor endowments, it was possible for manufacturing firms to achieve vertical integration in their operations.

Apart from vertical integration, scale economies can also be captured within the Growth Triangle. Singapore's well-developed and internationally linked financial markets and business services provide the required support services to enterprises locating in the growth area. To the extent that enterprises avail of these services, greater transactional efficiencies are achieved due to scale economies brought about by a larger network. Johor and Riau can tap into Singapore's facilities without duplicating infrastructure expenditures.

With Singapore's highly skilled labour force, it was possible for MNCs to maintain knowledge-intensive operations in Singapore, and labour-intensive and spatially driven operations in Johor or Batam. Singapore's well-developed infrastructure also made it possible for MNCs to efficiently handle trans-shipment of goods, and monitor and control their operations. All told, the creation of a wider manufacturing base with different factor endowments in each area provided an investment incentive for MNCs to consider the ASEAN region a whole. This trend led to a self-augmenting process that led to the expansion of the initial Growth Triangle to other contiguous areas.

The amount of investments generated in SIJORI is significant. The magnitude of cumulative investments in Batam island alone reached US$4.2 billion as of 1994. These investments were poured into machinery, basic metals, chemical and electronics industries, trade and services, and agribusiness. On the other hand, about US$6 billion was invested in Johor as of 1994.

B. Indonesia-Malaysia-Thailand Growth Triangle (IMT-GT)[2]

The IMT-GT, which is sometimes referred to as the Northern Triangle, represents the second major effort at linking three complementary locations comprising northern Sumatra and Aceh in Indonesia, the states of Perak, Kedah, and Perlis in northern Malaysia, and Songkla, Satun, Yala, Narathiwat, and Pattani in Thailand (see Figure 5.3). The Indonesian part of the triangle is the largest component, constituting 70.5 per cent of the total area of the triangle and 64 per cent of the population. Northern Malaysia and northern Thailand contribute 17.9 per cent and 11.6 per cent of the total area, and 22.1 per cent and 13.4 per cent of the population, respectively. The total land area of the IMT-GT is 180,000 square kilometres, with a population of 22 million.

The natural resource endowments of the IMT-GT present a considerable economic potential that could be realized through sub-regional co-operation. The surrounding seas consist of the Gulf of Thailand on the eastern coast of Thailand, the Strait of Malacca, which form the coastline of the four Malaysian states, the Andaman Sea on the eastern coast of Aceh, and the Indian Ocean on the western coast of northern Sumatra. These seas provide important shipping routes among the coastal areas of the region, resources for offshore exploration in oil and gas, and scenic routes for tourism. The Triangle shares common mountain ranges, soil systems, and a hot and humid climate ideal for tropical agriculture. The IMT-GT area is also well endowed with mineral resources, such as tin, oil, and natural gas. However, although agriculture is seen as important to the economies of the three regions in terms of its contribution to GDP, there is little by way of complementarity in this sector that can catalyze economic activity.

Economic activity in the Northern Triangle is sparked by the comparative advantage of the areas that comprise it and by seasonal

Figure 5.3
Map of IMT-GT

scarcities that result in significant price differentials across borders. Trade within the IMT-GT area occurs both formally and informally. Among some of the facets of formal trade in the area are north Sumatra's exports of fresh vegetables, coal and coke to north Malaysia; south Thailand's imports of rubber and tin ingots, which are shipped through Penang; and south Thailand's fish exports to Malaysia. Informal trade also occurs in the area, largely among residents whose long-established family and business ties transcend national borders. Due to price differences, a substantial amount of informal trade occurs in rice and other agricultural products that are smuggled from Thailand to Malaysia and essential oils from Malaysia to Thailand.

Investments within the IMT-GT are motivated by a number of factors. For one, many MNCs based in Penang, experiencing rising costs of land and labour, opted to relocate to lower-cost sites to remain competitive. Similarly, north Thailand and northern Sumatra, as a source of cheap raw materials, attracted many resource-based investors. Agriculture-related investments are also taking place between Indonesian and Malaysian joint-venture companies in the establishment of palm oil estates and milling factories.

Although there are existing transport routes that facilitate the carriage of goods and people within the IMT-GT, there is consensus, particularly among the private sector, on the need to expand and improve infrastructure facilities to support economic activity. For instance, because of unsatisfactory facilities at Songkhla Port, exports from south Thailand (for example, rubber, marine produce, and canned food) are routed to the Penang port (where trucking services are inadequate) and then hauled on to the rail system that connects south Thailand and north Malaysia. In addition, although direct telecommunication links are possible among the north Malaysian states, south Thailand, and north Sumatra, there is scope for expansion in the submarine cable and microwave systems links.

In the utilities sector, there are forthright efforts worth mentioning. For instance, there is an interchange of electricity supply between south Thailand and Malaysia that enables reduction in on-line reserve carrying capacity, improved distribution, and better systems security. Plans are also under way for Malaysia to supply piped gas to Thailand.

However, there is no current interconnection with Indonesia, although there is a long-term plan to link the power grid of Sumatra with that of peninsular Malaysia.

About US$3.25 billion worth of projects were signed in the IMT-GT area in infrastructure-related areas like power stations, industrial estates, roads, oil and gas pipelines, and construction of railway facilities. Malaysian investments into Thailand is recorded at US$2.5 million in industries such as rubber gloves manufacturing, and palm oil and seafood processing.

C. East ASEAN Growth Area (EAGA)[3]

The East ASEAN Growth Area (EAGA) was formally established in March 1994 among the Governments of Brunei Darussalam, Indonesia, Malaysia, and the Philippines, to jointly harness and develop the potentials of the following areas: Brunei Darussalam; the provinces of North Sulawesi, East Kalimantan, and West Kalimantan of Indonesia; Sabah, Sarawak, and Labuan of Malaysia; and Mindanao and Palawan of the Philippines (see Figure 5.4). The growth area is referred to as the BIMP-EAGA or EAGA for short. There was a conscious effort, especially on the part of the Philippines, to realize the concept of the EAGA as President Fidel V. Ramos took the initiative to enlist the participation of the Philippines' ASEAN neighbours. BIMP-EAGA covers 1 million square kilometres of land and has a population of 31 million.

There are factors working in favour of developing the EAGA into a growth area. These include the area's rich natural resources such as the forest and timber resources of Brunei, Kalimantan, Sabah, and Sarawak; oil and gas in Brunei, East Kalimantan, Sabah, and Sarawak; and marine resources and agricultural products in Mindanao, Palawan, and North Sulawesi. These sites are also potential tourist attractions. In addition, participating areas in the EAGA have a long tradition of intra-regional trade and family ties. For example, barter trade between Mindanao and Sandakan, Brunei and Labuan, Labuan and Mindanao, and Davao and Manado traces its roots from historical times.

In the short term, the EAGA's role in the larger southeast ASEAN region and its development thrust, as perceived by participating coun-

Figure 5.4
Map of EAGA

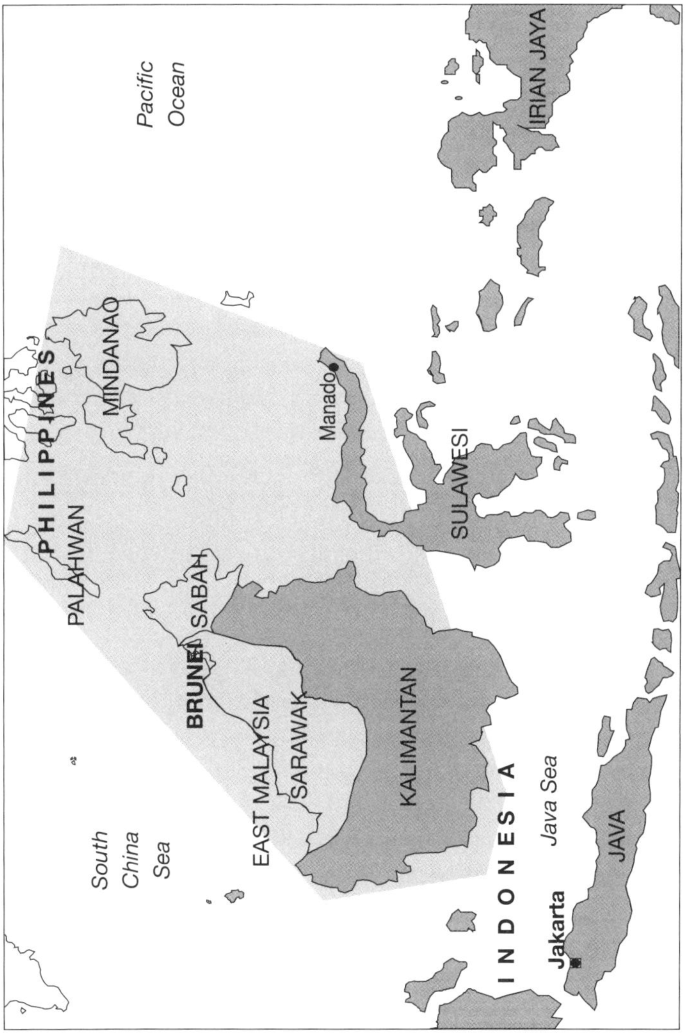

tries, is geared towards access to markets of prosperous nations by trading on goods in which it has a comparative advantage (that is, in light manufacturing, resource- and labour-based goods, skilled manpower and eco-tourism). Moreover, with a market-friendly policy environment, investments and financing from capital-exporting countries in East and Southeast Asia could be attracted to the EAGA.

The geographical proximity of commercial and trading centres in the EAGA region serves as a positive factor to increase trade in the subregion. Present trade within the EAGA region is principally in fish imports, consumer durables, and packaging materials. As is true in the IMT-GT area, a critical gap that must be addressed is the establishment of shipping routes to link key trading areas covered by the EAGA. Given existing trade links, a regional shipping operation could be established within the areas of Sandakan, Labuan, North Sulawesi, Maluku, Zamboanga, Cotabato, Davao, and General Santos. The synchronized upgrading of port facilities could complement joint shipping operations.

Prior to the formal government agreement establishing the EAGA, several government and private sector missions explored trade and investment opportunities. Initial agreements include the development of Samal Island by the Philippine Department of Tourism and a Malaysian private firm, Ekran Berhad, and the introduction of commercial flights linking Labuan and southern Philippines. Several activities were also lined up in the following areas: (a) expansion of air and sea linkages and transport and shipping services; (b) expansion of fisheries co-operation; (c) joint tourism development; (d) environmental protection and management; (e) energy development; (f) construction and construction materials development; (g) telecommunications development; (h) forestry and agro-industry; (i) capital formation and financial services; and (j) human resource development and labour mobility.

The EAGA was established in recognition of the importance of a market orientation and the principle of comparative advantage. Such is the basis of trade and investment flows in the area. The East ASEAN Business Council was formed to support this principle and spearhead private sector involvement in the growth area. On the other hand, the government organization overseeing the EAGA is highly decentralized, with a high-level council under the chairmanship of a minister for each participating country.

III. Problems of Integrated Development

Despite their relative success in fostering economic co-operation at the sub-regional level, growth areas continue to be confronted with a number of political, economic, and social challenges. For instance, there is lack of proper understanding of (a) the concept of growth areas at the sub-national level, (b) the complexity in decision-making structures, (c) border formalities as they affect labour mobility, and (d) the effects of inadequate infrastructure.

A. Perception of Unequal Benefits

To be sure, support of growth areas stems out of the conviction that complementary benefits accrue to states or provinces that are part of the growth area. This perception, however, may not be shared at the sub-regional level, especially by local government officials. One underlying reason may be the lack of understanding of the growth area concept, which may lead to a short-sighted perspective of the benefits of co-operation and thus hinder the progress of long-term co-operation. Differential economic gains could accrue to member countries depending on their roles in the vertical or horizontal integration of specific projects. Countries experiencing lower economic benefits need to be politically motivated to continue their participation and commitment to the growth area although in the long run comparative advantage can shift to alter the distribution of benefits. In the mean time, it is important to promote a clear understanding of the concept of growth areas and to clarify the focus and direction of collaboration in the short, medium, and long term.

B. Inadequate Infrastructure

Despite the advantages of proximity, inadequate infrastructure poses a serious setback to the development of growth areas. If the degree of infrastructure development is uneven among participating areas, the flows and patterns of investment are hindered and distorted. To be sure, participating countries are committed to develop infrastructure facilities in the growth areas but these projects may have to compete with other priorities at the national level. Within the growth area, the planning and timing of the construction of infrastructure projects is crucial and requires close co-ordination among participating governments. Besides physical infrastructure, regional air and sea links are equally important to facilitate the movement of people, goods, and capital.

C. Complex Decision-Making Structures

Decision-making structures in growth areas cut across national and provincial boundaries and can lead to a complicated and cumbersome process. In addition, the translation of national policies at the provincial or state level may be difficult or, in some cases, not feasible. This difficulty could also apply in the reverse case where provinces or states are constrained from instituting required policy changes that would require decision at the national or federal level. A related problem could be inadequate dissemination of information from the national to the provincial or state level and vice versa. Apart from the problems associated with government structures, it is also important to address mechanisms for private sector participation at various stages to ensure that programmes are responsive to market-driven initiatives.

D. Labour Mobility and Welfare

Differences in immigration policies and procedures hinder the movement of labour within the growth area. Without transparent policies and procedures, especially in acquiring and developing adequate skilled workers for the growth area, economic activities, even if they are well conceived, will not be successfully implemented. Relatedly, social security policies affecting migrant labour must be adequately addressed to avoid discord among participating countries.

IV. A Concluding Note

The emergence of Growth Triangles is a fairly recent development in ASEAN and the rest of the developing world. Yet they have a particular appeal, especially among contiguous areas that belong to different political states. In ASEAN the sub-regional arrangements are natural evolutions that were facilitated by the stability of the regional group and its flexibility in accommodating co-operation among component parts.

BOX 5.2: ASEAN REGIONAL INTEGRATION AND GROWTH POLYGONS

"The sub-regional growth areas can be regarded as building blocks for the ASEAN-wide co-operation and integration process. They will not only complement ASEAN economic co-operation at the regional level, but will also complement each other since each has its own unique characteristic. It would also be wrong to assume that the sub-regional growth areas are competing with one another. On the contrary, the success of any one sub-regional growth area will generate benefits which will spill over to the rest of ASEAN.

"It is too early to assess the performance of these growth areas, although SIJORI seems to have had a headstart over the others, primarily because it started earlier. The interest shown by the private sector in the various growth areas and the fact that billions of dollars have been invested in them, attest to their relevance and their importance in bringing development to the more remote areas in the respective ASEAN countries. Ultimately, it would lead to a more balanced growth in the countries concerned and to greater social and economic stability. That is why I believe that the growth areas are here to stay and we can expect, in the future, some of them to locate in the CLV countries (that is, Cambodia, Laos, and Vietnam), once the first two have joined ASEAN. The Fifth Summit has already endorsed Malaysia's proposal for ASEAN to participate in the Mekong Basin Polygon, involving the two ASEAN countries, Thailand and Vietnam, and the three non-ASEAN countries, China, Cambodia, and Laos. Even amongst the growth areas, the borders could be expanded to include new states or provinces, as has happened in the case of SIJORI, with the recent decision by the Ministers of the three countries concerned, to include West Sumatra in Indonesia and Malaca, Negeri Sembilan, and the state of Pahang in Malaysia.

"There is no institutional link between the three growth areas and the ASEAN Economic Ministers Meeting or the ASEAN Secretariat. There is also no formal co-ordinating link among the three growth areas. Co-ordination is done mainly at the country level between officials and the Ministers of the participating countries. Separate meetings are convened for each of the three areas. This arrangement has its advantages in that it is flexible and enables quick decisions to be made. The last thing that one would attempt in such an arrangement is to introduce red-tape, which would result in unnecessary delays and impediments. So far, the system has worked well but I do believe that there is a need for a link, no matter how unofficial, between the growth areas and the ASEAN Economic Ministers Meeting, to enable the Ministers to keep track of the activities and the progress of the areas concerned."

March 1996 — Dato' Ajit Singh
Manila — *Secretary-General of ASEAN*

It is too early to give any systematic judgement of the impact of Growth Triangles. SIJORI began only in 1979 while the EAGA is not yet fully operational. However, the prevailing view in ASEAN is that the growth areas or polygons are here to stay. As ASEAN economic co-operation deepens and the regional grouping expands, more sub-regional arrangements are expected to emerge (see Box 5.2).

Still, some critical concerns need to be addressed. Among them is the institutional machinery that promotes co-operation in narrower areas, carries out programmes and projects that support Growth Triangles and polygons, and provides an iterative feedback to the larger policy framework of ASEAN. In 1994, Indonesia, Malaysia, and Singapore formalized the establishment of a consultative mechanism to oversee SIJORI. In the other two growth areas, regular consultations among sectoral ministries concerned dictate the manner of interaction but the eventual shape of their institutional umbrellas is yet to evolve. Neither is there a formal link between the growth areas and the larger official ASEAN bodies. What is clear, however, is that these are contributing to meaningful economic co-operation in ASEAN. With the expansion in the area and coverage of these triangles (which reflects efforts and activities from the "bottom up" and the broad set of economic co-operation activities ASEAN is implementing "top down"), regional integration will undoubtedly be more balanced and take place faster and more efficiently.

NOTES

1. The SIJORI experience and its potential as a model for other areas is explored in Lee Tsao Yuan (1991).
2. Tan Min Tang and Myo Thant (1994) reviews the experience of Growth Triangles in the context of the IMT-GT.
3. The ADB recently completed a large study on the potentials of the EAGA along with individual country reports focusing on the EAGA components and the regional programmes and projects that can be derived from co-operation.

6

Co-operation within a Wider Framework: ASEAN External Relations

I. Introduction

Although ASEAN was established primarily for the purpose of intra-regional co-operation, the need to develop external relations with developed countries emerged in the early 1970s in the field of trade and commodities. It was during this time that ASEAN was prompted to take collective action *vis-à-vis* its major trading partners on pressing international economic issues — one related to the effects of synthetic rubber on ASEAN exports of natural rubber to Japan, the other on tariff preferences on ASEAN-sourced products from the European Union. Consequently, at UNCTAD IV in 1976, ASEAN participated actively in the establishment of the Integrated Programme of Commodities and took effective collective approaches to promote member countries' interests in the Association of Natural Rubber-Producing Countries as well as in the International Tin Agreement.

At the First ASEAN Summit Meeting in Bali in 1976, the ASEAN Heads of Government affirmed the importance of establishing relations with third countries and reflected this in the Declaration of ASEAN Concord. In a specific provision, the Declaration states that the principle of ASEAN co-operation on trade shall also be reflected on a priority basis in joint approaches to international commodity issues and other world economic problems such as the reform of the international monetary system, and the transfer of real resources, with a view to contributing to the New International Economic Order. The Declaration calls upon member states to give priority to the stabilization and increase of export earnings of those commodities produced and exported by ASEAN through commodity agreements, including buffer-stock schemes and other means.

The principles of ASEAN external relations contained in the Declaration of ASEAN Concord were confirmed at the Second ASEAN Summit held in Kuala Lumpur in 1977. The following years saw the establishment of dialogue relations with the EU, Australia, and New Zealand. Relations with Japan, Canada, and the United States followed subsequently. Dialogues with the EU and Canada were formalized through the signing of Co-operation Agreements in 1980 and 1981, respectively. In addition to its major trading partners, ASEAN also accorded dialogue partner status to the UNDP, the only multilateral agency that provides regular and substantial technical assistance to ASEAN.

ASEAN took further steps to expand external relations with the emergence of a new economic order towards the late 1980s, which saw the rise of Asia's NIEs and a shift in the dynamics of world trade towards the Asia-Pacific region. At the Third ASEAN Summit held in Manila in 1987, the Heads of Government agreed that an overall approach should be considered for ASEAN relations with additional countries or groups of countries and international organizations. Such relations need not reach full dialogue status and cover co-operation only in specific sectors. In particular, the Heads of Government recognized the need to promote co-operation with industrialized developing countries in the Pacific region, and the possible expansion of co-operative efforts in the context of South-South co-operation.

In 1989, a sectoral dialogue was established with the Republic of

Korea, which was subsequently raised to the status of a "full" dialogue at the AMM in July 1991. Following the Third Summit, ASEAN also considered the establishment of relations with other regional groupings such as the European Free Trade Association (EFTA). In recent years, a number of regional groups indicated their desire for a dialogue with ASEAN, among others, the South Pacific Bureau for Economic Co-operation (SPEC), the Nordic Counties, and the Economic Community of West African States (ECOWAS). Other groups such as the South Pacific Forum, the Gulf Co-operation Council (GCC), the Economic Co-operation Organization (ECO), the South Asian Association for Regional Co-operation (SAARC), and the Rio Group, also approached ASEAN to explore the possibility of establishing formal relations.

At the Fourth ASEAN Summit held in Singapore in 1992, the ASEAN Heads of Government recognized that new forms of dialogue are necessary in an increasingly interdependent world. In addition to intensifying co-operative relations with dialogue partners, ASEAN leaders agreed to engage in consultative relationships with interested non-dialogue countries and international organizations. In the following years, China and Russia became consultative partners of ASEAN. Sectoral dialogue relations were also established with India and Pakistan, thus broadening the ambit of ASEAN dialogue to other parts of Asia.

As it has evolved through the years, ASEAN relations with third countries are presently at three levels: full dialogue, sectoral dialogue, and consultative partner. There are existing guidelines covering the establishment of full dialogue with third countries and regional organizations, with the qualification that all future dialogues should be developed on a stage-by-stage basis beginning with sectoral co-operation (see Box 6.1). A separate set of guidelines is applicable in cases of developing countries and groupings of developing countries (see Box 6.2). The considerations for establishing consultative relations, however, are not explicit and formalized.

ASEAN relations with regional or sub-regional organizations are established on a organization-to-organization basis through the ASEAN Secretariat. Initially, all such relations are co-ordinated by the Secretariat under the supervision of the ASEAN Standing Committee. After a specific period, this interim arrangement is reviewed and, subject

BOX 6.1. GUIDELINES FOR THE ESTABLISHMENT OF FUTURE DIALOGUES WITH THIRD COUNTRIES OR REGIONAL GROUPINGS

The establishment of a dialogue between ASEAN and third countries or regional groupings, in future, should be dependent on the assessment of whether the dialogue would achieve all or some of the following objectives for ASEAN.

1. the securing of technical assistance and/or development assistance, particularly for ASEAN co-operation projects;
2. the promotion and development of mutually beneficial trade and economic relations between ASEAN and the particular third country or regional grouping;
3. the enhancement of any aspect of existing ASEAN co-operation;
4. the strengthening of ASEAN political relations with the particular third country or regional grouping; and
5. the enhancement of the international standing of ASEAN as a viable regional organization.

In addition to making sure that the establishment of relations with a third country or regional grouping will achieve the above objectives, ASEAN should ensure that

1. such relations shall not adversely affect ASEAN's existing programmes and projects; and
2. it shall not involve ASEAN in controversial issues relevant to the particular country or grouping that would be detrimental to the interest of ASEAN.

While such dialogue relations should preferably be established with a grouping of countries rather than individual countries, ASEAN should not preclude the prospect of dialogues with particular third countries where such dialogue would be of mutual benefit. However, in regard to dialogue relations with third countries that are deemed to be developing countries, it shall be guided by the decision previously taken by the ASEAN Standing Committee at its meeting in Jakarta on 14 September 1978.

All future dialogues should be developed on a stage-by-stage basis. To begin, relations should be confined by mutual agreement to specific areas of co-operation or sectoral co-operation of mutual interest. Provision should also be made for such relationship to be extended to other areas of co-operation at a later stage, by mutual agreement.

Where a dialogue relationship confined to specific areas of co-operation or sectoral co-operation with a third country or regional grouping is assessed, after a reasonable period, to have been sufficiently beneficial to ASEAN, it may by mutual agreement be elevated to the status of a full dialogue relationship, with regular meetings held.

ASEAN's relations with third countries or regional groupings should in general be initiated by the third country or grouping concern. However, in special circumstances, where there is consensus that ASEAN could obtain positive benefits by establishing dialogue relations, particularly with a regional grouping, the initiative may be taken by ASEAN through the Chairman of the Standing Committee.

BOX 6.2: GUIDELINES FOR THE ESTABLISHMENT OF DIALOGUES WITH DEVELOPING COUNTRIES OR GROUPS OF DEVELOPING COUNTRIES

The First Meeting of the ASEAN Standing Committee in September 1978 held the view that dialogues with developing countries or groups of developing countries should promote the objective of developing mutual economic and technical co-operation. To implement this principle, the following guidelines were adopted:

1. ASEAN's relations with developing countries shall in general be initiated by the developing countries and groupings of developing countries.
2. Approaches from them to establish relations with ASEAN shall be addressed to the chairman of the ASEAN Standing Committee through the Secretary-General of the ASEAN Secretariat with specific proposals.
3. For developing countries that belong to regional or sub-regional organizations, where possible it is preferable for ASEAN to establish dialogue with that organization or on an organization-to-organization basis.
4. In considering such approaches, the following points need to be observed:
   a. ASEAN's relations with developing countries or groupings of developing countries shall not adversely affect ASEAN programmes and projects.
   b. ASEAN's relations with developing countries or groupings of developing countries shall not involve ASEAN in controversial issues detrimental to the interest of ASEAN.
   c. The dialogue should be confined to certain specific areas of co-operation and should be limited to matters of mutual interests only.
   d. Either party should obtain prior consent of the other if it wishes to raise any item outside the agreed area of co-operation.
   e. The dialogue should be at the official level.
   f. Consideration should also be given to establishing in the other country an ASEAN committee that could serve as a link and represent ASEAN at meetings with the host country and thereby minimize the need for ASEAN countries to send representatives for meetings that are technical in nature.

to complaints with specific considerations as provided in the guidelines, the dialogue relations may be elevated to full status.

As regards limited or sector dialogues with third countries, the ASEAN Committee in the particular third country serves as the link and represents ASEAN at meetings with the host country, under the guidance of the ASEAN Standing Committee (ASC). Where co-operation involves a specific project, its co-ordination is assigned to the relevant technical committee.

At the Fourth Meeting of the 28th ASC in March 1995, ASEAN member countries agreed to review existing guidelines for establishing relations with third countries or regional groupings due to an increasing number of initiatives (from third countries and/or regional organizations) to establish relations with ASEAN. Member countries, however, felt that ASEAN's responses to these initiatives must be weighed against the resources needed to manage these relations.

Although ASEAN dialogue relations were initiated with the original objective of improving market access for ASEAN commodities, the dialogues gradually expanded as a forum to obtain other trade and economic concessions and to articulate ASEAN's position on issues of common interest in international organizations. The dialogues also served as a framework for consultations on a broad range of international political issues, strengthening political relations with dialogue partners, and boosting ASEAN's standing as a regional organization. The dialogues were also utilized to secure development assistance in various areas such as agriculture, trade and investment, science and technology, environment, transport and communications, human resource development, and drug abuse prevention and control.

Developed countries are important trading partners of ASEAN countries primarily because of the complementarity of their economies. The United States, Japan, and the EU are important destinations of ASEAN exports and major sources of ASEAN imports, followed by Australia, Canada, and New Zealand.

ASEAN's external trade underwent significant changes especially in the past two decades. In particular, the share of manufactures in ASEAN exports increased significantly. The share of intermediate and capital goods in ASEAN's import basket also grew in importance. Although the EU is still a major trading partner of ASEAN, there is clear evidence in recent years that the direction of ASEAN trade is gravitating from the Atlantic towards the Pacific. The Asia-Pacific share of ASEAN's total exports reached about 77 per cent in 1993. Among the Pacific countries, the United States represents the most important market for ASEAN exports while Japan remains the leading supplier of ASEAN's imports. In recent years, however, the share of East Asian NIEs (for example, Hong Kong, Korea, and Taiwan) to ASEAN exports steadily increased from 5.5 per cent in 1970 to 9.8 per cent in 1989, while that of ASEAN imports, from 3.8 to 10.3 per cent during the same period.

Amidst these changes concomitant with the gradual opening of ASEAN economies, protectionism continues to pose a threat. As tariffs were reduced, protection became less transparent through non-tariff barriers, both formal and informal. Over the years, ASEAN was seriously affected by the imposition of non-tariff barriers on food and textile imports by its major trading partners. Quantitative restrictions and food and drug regulations, for instance, adversely affected the exports of certain products such as canned tuna, fish, shrimp, crabmeat, and pineapple.

Notwithstanding the continuing importance of trade issues, the content of ASEAN dialogue meetings changed substantially in recent years. In earlier years, the agenda of dialogue meetings was largely confined to economic, commercial and technical assistance issues. More recent dialogue meetings, however, covered international economic issues, especially in the aftermath of the Uruguay Round. Among the regional security issues discussed were the Kampuchean problem, the Korean peninsula, Myanmar, and the South China Sea.

Over the past twenty-eight years, ASEAN dialogue partner relations reflected ASEAN's growing maturity and confidence in managing its external relations. The principle of mutual benefit was accepted by ASEAN as the central guidepost governing its relations with dialogue partners. ASEAN showed preparedness to shift inter-governmental dialogues towards issues of mutual market access. While taking a stronger hand in articulating its views on international economic issues, ASEAN acquired the flexibility to work with values and objectives shared by dialogue partners in addressing global challenges.

II. The Dialogue Process

The annual Post-Ministerial Conferences (PMCs) held after the AMM is the centrepiece of ASEAN's meetings with its dialogue partners. As ASEAN Foreign Ministers meet with their counterparts from dialogue countries, a holistic approach at the political level is taken with the multi-faceted agenda of the dialogues.

Dialogue meetings at the sub-ministerial level take place every eighteen months. To prepare for this, an ASEAN preparatory meeting is held under the auspices of the ASC during which the agenda for the dialogue, and ASEAN positions on various agenda items, are discussed. In the case of some of the dialogue countries (that is, Canada, Republic of Korea, and New Zealand), there are existing structures such as joint management committees to oversee the more detailed operational aspects of programme and project implementation.

Under present arrangements, an ASEAN member country is assigned the responsibility for co-ordinating ASEAN's dialogue relations with a particular dialogue partner on a rotational basis. The ASEAN Secretariat co-ordinates relationships with the UNDP on a permanent basis. The ASEAN member country, or country co-ordinator, makes the official representation on behalf of ASEAN to the dialogue partner, and serves as the official channel of communication for ASEAN dialogue partner activities. As chairperson of regular meetings with the dialogue partner, the country co-ordinator provides direction in the conduct of dialogue relations, both in its broad dimensions and in specific projects.

Rotating the country co-ordinatorship every three years provides the advantage of shared responsibility and exchange of experiences among member countries on dialogue relations. It has also prevented familiarity and the risks of complicity between a permanent co-ordinator and a dialogue partner. On the other hand, rotation does not provide an incentive to the country co-ordinator to engage in long-term strategic planning on ASEAN relations with a particular dialogue partner. This task, however, could now be performed by the ASEAN Secretariat under its expanded mandate.

In addition to the designation of country co-ordinators, ASEAN committees in third countries were formed and made directly responsible to the ASC. These committees are composed of ASEAN ambassadors posted in the capitals of the third country. The ambassador of the ASEAN member country holding the country co-ordinatorship for the dialogue partner acts as chairman of the committee and is responsible for co-ordinating with various officials and making representations on behalf of ASEAN to the host country, subject to the directives of the ASC.

A. ASEAN-Australia

Australia was the first developed country to establish relations with ASEAN. The first ASEAN-Australia Forum took place in Canberra in April 1974. Over the years, both established a number of working groups to give focus and depth to various fields of co-operation. At present, there are six working groups covering trade and investment, telecommunications, education and training, environment, industry and technology, and culture and information. The 16th Forum, held in Canberra in 1994, took stock of the progress made under the dialogue relations and discussed a number of outstanding issues in economic co-operation.

The growth of ASEAN imports from Australia outpaced the growth in ASEAN exports. ASEAN imports from Australia grew by 12.4 per cent on average from 1989 to 1993, compared with the average growth in exports of 9.2 per cent (see Figures 6.1 and 6.2). Two-way trade between ASEAN and Australia grew at an average rate of 10.36 per cent from 1989 to 1993 (see Figure 6.3). For the past five years, the balance of trade was in Australia's favour.

ASEAN's trade imbalance with Australia is largely accounted for by non-tariff barriers encountered by ASEAN products in the form of anti-dumping and countervailing duties. The passage of the Australian anti-dumping legislation in 1993 provided further incentives to Australian domestic industries to lodge dumping/subsidy complaints for protection against imports. In addition to anti-dumping and countervailing duties, quarantine measures also restricted the access of ASEAN agricultural products to Australia. These products include frozen chicken, fresh fruits, and vegetables, and condensed milk.

Australian investments in ASEAN comprise only 7 per cent of Australia's foreign investments in 1993. Areas identified by ASEAN for possible Australian investments include food production and

Figure 6.1
ASEAN Exports to Dialogue Partners, 1989–93
(US$ million)

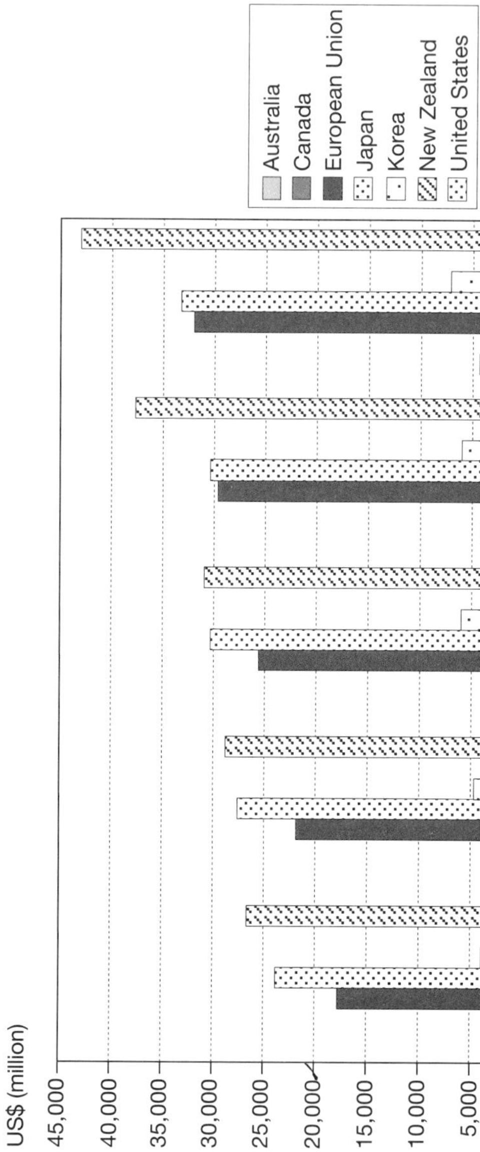

Source of basic data: International Monetary Fund, *Direction of Trade Statistics* (1994).

Figure 6.2
ASEAN Imports from Dialogue Partners, 1989–93
(US$ million)

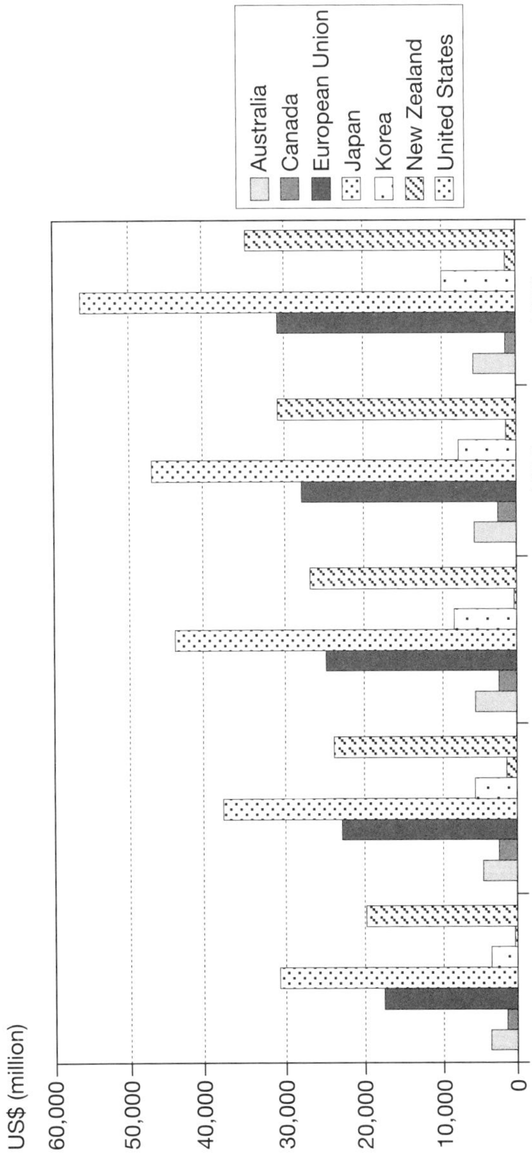

Source of basic data: International Monetary Fund, *Direction of Trade Statistics* (1994).

Figure 6.3
Growth Rates of Total ASEAN Trade with Dialogue Partners, 1990–93
(Percentages)

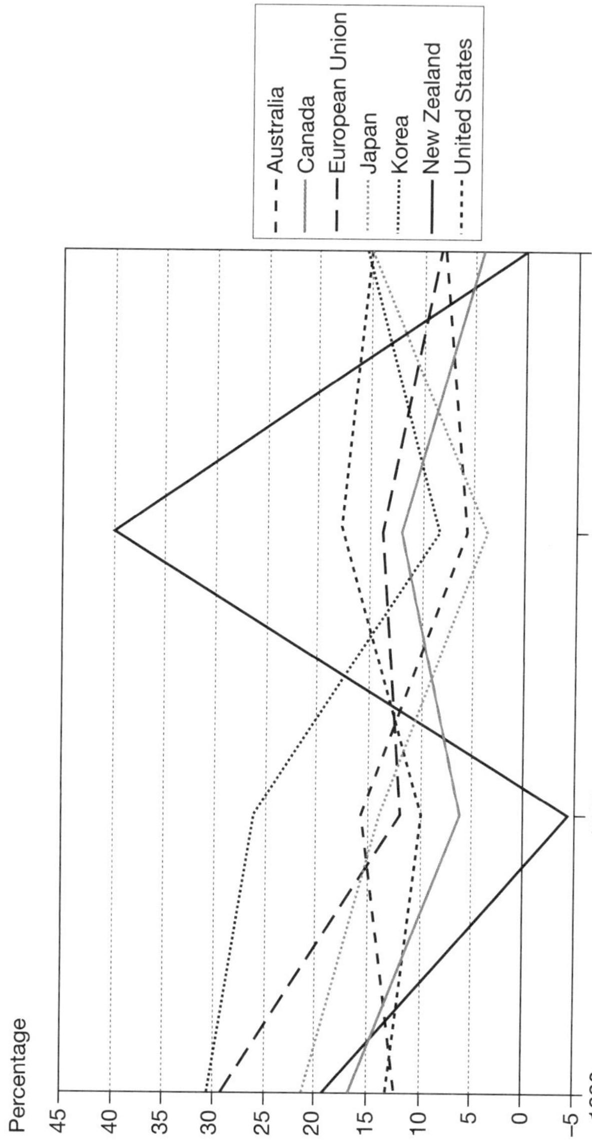

Source of basic data: International Monetary Fund, *Direction of Trade Statistics* (1994).

processing, pharmaceuticals, textiles, packaging industry, marine industries, and industrial machineries and parts manufacturing, among others. In an effort to promote ASEAN-Australia investments, ASEAN suggested that the Australian Government either co-finance or guarantee loans.

The ASEAN-Australia Economic Co-operation Programme (AAECP), which was established in 1974, is the main vehicle for Australian assistance to ASEAN. Now in its third phase (it began in 1994), the Programme aims to promote (a) intra-ASEAN regional co-operation, (b) economic, scientific, and technical co-operation and human resource development, (c) mutual understanding of benefits, and (d) the building and strengthening of ASEAN and Australian institutions. The sectors benefiting most from development assistance funds provided by Australia under the AAECP are science and technology, environment, and communications.

The AABC was formed to provide a forum for discussing trade and environmental linkages, environmental matters, and technology. Since the 12th Forum in 1989, the AABC formally participated in the dialogue process and have also participated in meetings at the working level since 1992 to prepare for Phase III of the AAECP. Private sector participation in these meetings ensures that the framework for future activities include the views of prospective participants.

B. ASEAN-Canada

Co-operation between ASEAN and Canada began formally during the first meeting of ASEAN Directors-General and Canadian officials in Manila in 1979. A Joint Co-operation Committee (JCC) was established to review the various co-operation schemes between the two. The first three JCC meetings focused on development co-operation projects. Only at the fourth JCC did discussions begin on economic and commercial matters.

ASEAN's trade with Canada grew at an average annual rate of 9.59 per cent from 1989 to 1993 (see Table 6.1). In terms of value, however, ASEAN trade with Canada remained small, at US$3.3 billion in 1993, representing only about 1 per cent of Canada's global trade. Since trade relations began, the balance of trade was always in Canada's favour. Starting in 1991, however, ASEAN exports to Canada exceeded im-

Table 6.1
Trade between ASEAN and the EU, 1989–93
(US$ million)

Year	Exports (f.o.b.)	Imports (c.i.f.)	Trade Balance
1989	17,377	16,931	446
1990	21,495	22,821	–1,326
1991	24,922	24,759	163
1992	28,818	27,738	1,080
1993	31,138	30,181	957

Source of basic data: International Monetary Fund, *Direction of Trade Statistics*.

ports by US$54 million in 1991 and US$424 million in 1992 (see Figures 6.1 and 6.2).

Non-tariff barriers remain a constraint in the promotion of ASEAN exports to Canada. Specific cases include problems arising from the proliferation of anti-dumping and countervailing measures on ASEAN products, the certification requirements of the Handicrafts Goods Order, the introduction of the Import Control List, the Packaging and Labelling Act, and the Food and Drugs Act. There were also tariff barriers such as the differential treatment on canned tuna (preserved in oil and in alternative mediums) and discriminatory tariffs on processed palm oil and palm kernel oil.

ASEAN enjoys preferential access for its exports to Canada through the General Preferential Tariff (GPT) scheme. As ASEAN exports to Canada are heavily dependent on inputs from developed countries, ASEAN requested a liberalization of this scheme with respect to Canada's global cumulative rule of origin. ASEAN also requested an expansion of the product list covered under the GPT.

Co-operation between ASEAN and Canadian private sectors are carried out through the activities of the ASEAN-Canada Business Council (ACBC), aimed at increasing the flow of information and facilitating personal contacts between the two parties. The activities of the ACBC are focused on trade and investment promotion, joint ventures, technology transfer and licensing, and human resource development. Sectors that provide investment and technology transfer opportunities include infrastructure development (particularly in the ASEAN growth areas, or through build-operate-and-transfer schemes), energy, telecommunications, fresh fruit technology, natural resource extraction, and information technology.

C. ASEAN-EU

ASEAN established dialogue relations with the EC in 1977 although it was not until 1980 that the ASEAN-EC Co-operation Agreement was signed. The Agreement established a Joint Co-operation Committee (JCC) to co-ordinate and implement various co-operation activities. In 1978, the first ASEAN-EC Ministerial Meeting (AEMM) was held, elevating the dialogue to ministerial level. Since then, the AEMM has met regularly, about once every eighteen months.

Since 1992, the ASEAN-EU economic ministers have met to address economic issues and chart new directions. During the ASEAN-EU Ministerial Meeting in 1994, both sides agreed to the formation of an Eminent Persons Group (EPG) that would recommend long-term directions for ASEAN-EU relations.

Despite differences in the level of development between ASEAN and the EU, sufficient areas of complementarity exist. In the early stages of the dialogue relationship, the primary focus was on narrower issues of functional and development co-operation to help in the social and economic development of ASEAN member countries. Since 1977, however, ASEAN-EU relations expanded in coverage and, with the growth and transformation of both regions, the agenda of the dialogue went through substantive changes.

Trade between ASEAN and the EU doubled between 1989 to 1993 from US$34.3 billion to US$61.3 billion (see Table 6.1). ASEAN exports to the EU increased from US$17.4 billion to US$31.14 billion, while ASEAN imports from the EU increased from US$16.9 billion to US$30.2 billion for the same period (see Tables 6.2 and 6.3). In 1993, the EU accounted for 20 per cent of total foreign investment inflows into ASEAN. Although ASEAN was, for a long time, a net importer of capital, its rapid economic growth in recent years transformed it to a significant investor, regionally and globally. ASEAN is thus uniquely poised to serve as a gateway for the flow of trade and investments between Europe and East Asia.

Compared with the institutional links between Asia and the Ameri-

Table 6.2
ASEAN Exports to Dialogue Partners, 1989–93
(US$ million)

Country	1989	1990	1991	1992	1993
Australia	2,767	2,706	3,305	3,627	3,726
Canada	1,118	1,248	1,435	1,712	1,961
European Union	17,377	21,495	24,922	28,818	31,138
Japan	23,194	26,921	29,807	29,651	32,233
Korea	3,734	4,794	5,796	5,771	6,553
New Zealand	316	398	324	592	566
United States	25,977	27,986	30,236	36,583	42,241

Source of basic data: International Monetary Fund, *Direction of Trade Statistics*.

Table 6.3
ASEAN Imports from Dialogue Partners, 1989–93
(US$ million)

Country	1989	1990	1991	1992	1993
Australia	3,565	4,398	4,906	5,050	5,644
Canada	1,318	1,611	1,589	1,658	1,537
European Union	16,931	22,821	24,759	27,738	30,181
Japan	29,918	37,460	43,754	46,762	55,650
Korea	3,816	5,061	6,639	7,726	9,009
New Zealand	570	658	685	819	845
United States	19,624	23,556	26,275	29,935	34,394

Source of basic data: International Monetary Fund, *Direction of Trade Statistics*.

cas that was enhanced by the establishment of APEC, the institutional links between Asia and the EU are still relatively weak although ASEAN recently initiated measures to strengthen these links. For instance, the participation of the EU in the ASEAN Regional Forum (ARF) and the Asia-Europe Meeting are important initiatives aimed at enhancing mutual understanding and co-operation between the two regions. The first Asia-Europe Meeting was held in Bangkok in 1992.

D. ASEAN-Japan

The ASEAN-Japan dialogue began in the early 1970s when ASEAN had extensive discussions with Japan on the question of synthetic rubber and its effects on ASEAN's exports of natural rubber. The dialogue gradually broadened and was formally institutionalized as the ASEAN-Japan Forum in 1977. At present, the Forum provides the venue for discussing a wide range of concerns in the areas of trade, commodities, investments, transfer of technology, and development assistance. In 1992 the first ASEAN Economic Ministers–Ministry of International Trade and Industry (AEM-MITI) meeting was held in Manila, marking the intensification of dialogue in the economic area.

ASEAN-Japan relations is marked with several notable achievements. These include (a) the establishment of the Fukuda Fund of US$1 billion to assist in the financing of AIPs; (b) the establishment of the ASEAN Promotion Centre in Tokyo in 1981 to promote ASEAN exports, Japanese investments in ASEAN, and tourism between ASEAN and Japan; and (c) the setting up of the ASEAN-Japan Development Fund in 1988, which apart from allocations to each member country, provided a regional fund of US$200 million for ASEAN joint venture projects. In non-economic areas, Japan provided ASEAN with a number of substantial financing facilities. These include (a) a seed fund of about US$20 million to support culture and information activities in ASEAN; (b) the Japan Scholarship for ASEAN Youth Programme (US$2 million per year); (c) the ASEAN-Japan Co-operation Promotion Programme; and (d) the ASEAN-Japan Exchange Programme.

Japan is a major trading partner of ASEAN. In 1993 it accounted for about 34 per cent of ASEAN's total trade, while ASEAN's share in Japan's total trade was 13 per cent in the same year. From 1989 to 1993, trade between the two sides grew by an average of 13.6 per cent although the trade balance remains in Japan's favour (see Figure 6.3).

To address its trade deficit with Japan, ASEAN urged Japan to assist in the utilization of its GSP scheme and to remove tariff and non-tariff barriers on ASEAN imports. ASEAN's requests include increasing the ceiling quota for several product groups, deepening of tariff preferences, eliminating differential treatment clauses, and deregulating import measures.

ASEAN remains an important destination for Japanese investments. In recent years, ASEAN's attractiveness as a location for Japanese investments was affected by Japan's export-substitution investment policy designed to maintain or expand market share through local production or through joint venture companies operating in the United

States and Europe — Japan's major export markets. With the implementation of AFTA, ASEAN made strong representations to Japan to consider the region an alternative production base, thus opening up new opportunities for Japan's direct investments in ASEAN. As a major supplier of inputs to ASEAN's manufacturing sector, Japan can actively pursue the promotion of backward linkages through investments in technology transfer schemes to support SMEs and other ASEAN industries. At the AEM-MITI Meeting in Singapore in 1993, ASEAN and Japan agreed on a programme of industrial co-operation in four areas, namely, the development of supporting industries, protection of IPR, industrial standardization and quality control, and industrial technology research.

Private sector participation in ASEAN-Japan co-operation is carried out through the ASEAN-Japan Economic Council. The Council's activities are guided by a Joint Work Programme directed at strengthening ASEAN-Japan business ties, providing a forum for exchange of information and ideas, identifying problems and seeking solutions, and providing inputs into the government policy-making process.

E. ASEAN–New Zealand

Dialogue relations between ASEAN and New Zealand started in 1975 and focused primarily on agriculture, forestry, health, and education. Today, it covers trade, investment promotion, tourism, science and technology, and human resource development.

The ASEAN–New Zealand Economic Co-operation Programme (ANZECP) is the main vehicle for implementing co-operation activities between the two sides. Funded by an initial pledge of NZ$12 million in 1986, the four major components of the ANZECP are the Inter-Institutional Linkages Programme (IILP), the Trade and Investment Promotion Programme (TIPP), the Natural Gas Utilization in Transport Programme (NGUT), and the Science and Technology Programme (which was added in 1994). In 1993, ASEAN and New Zealand established a Joint Management Committee (JMC) to ensure the smooth implementation of projects under these major components.

The growth of trade between ASEAN and New Zealand did not exhibit a steady trend in the last five years baring the need for continuing improvements in commercial linkages between the two sides (see

Figure 6.3). In 1993, ASEAN exports to New Zealand actually dropped by 4.4 per cent although imports registered an increase of 3.17 per cent (see Figures 6.1 and 6.2). While ASEAN recognizes that the New Zealand market on its own may not be too large, higher per capita incomes and its membership in the CER offer attractive scope for increased ASEAN exports to the region. In various dialogue meetings, ASEAN proposed improvements in its market access to New Zealand. These include the raising of bench-mark levels in the GSP Product Graduation Scheme and a three-month advance notice on products to be withdrawn from the GSP. Requests for tariff reduction on various products were also discussed.

The implementation of AFTA would further boost New Zealand's investment into the region. Similarly, the New Zealand market, as part of the CER, presents an attractive proposition to ASEAN investors, especially within the context of the deregulatory efforts of the New Zealand Government under its Asia 2000 policy.

The private sectors from both sides, through the ASEAN–New Zealand Business Council (ANZBC), have established a good working relationship. Their active involvement in the dialogue meetings and in the Trade and Investment Promotion Programme (TIPP) projects strengthened commercial ties between the two sides. ANZBC activities are guided by a work programme that is implemented largely through the TIPP and is aimed at increasing commercial linkages between partners. Conscious efforts are made to undertake TIPP activities that are complementary to public sector programmes and initiatives.

F. ASEAN–Republic of Korea

ASEAN-ROK relations was elevated to full dialogue status in 1991. With the elevation of relations to a full dialogue status, the ASEAN-ROK Joint Sectoral Co-operation Committee (JSCC) was replaced with the ASEAN-ROK Dialogue. Prior to 1991, and since 1989, country relations were on a sectoral basis, concentrating on the areas of trade, investment, and tourism. After 1991, co-operation expanded to include science and technology and human resource development. An ASEAN-ROK Joint Sectoral Co-operation Committee, established as an intergovernmental consultative body, facilitates ASEAN-ROK relations.

In 1990, ROK established a Special Co-operation Fund (SCF) by pledging US$5 million for the period 1993–98. However, as of 31 December 1995, the ROK has already contributed a total of US$9.762 million. Again, a JMC manages the Fund, which supports approved projects in various sectors of co-operation in ASEAN and the ROK.

In 1993, the ROK ranked fourth among ASEAN's dialogue partners in terms of total trade (see Table 6.1). Trade between ASEAN and the ROK grew at an annual average rate of 20.14 per cent over the last five years, outpacing the growth of ASEAN's trade with the United States, Japan, and the EU. Over the years, ASEAN's imports from the ROK were consistently higher than its exports, thus bringing the trade balance in Korea's favour.

Trade is the centrepiece of ASEAN-ROK relations since the inception of the dialogue in 1991. In recent years, ASEAN aired its concerns about market access barriers in the ROK on account of ROK quarantine measures, in particular, the introduction of the Green Card Declaration system in 1994. Other market access problems include regulations pertaining to health, phytosanitary, and technical standards, prohibitive tariffs, import bans, and import quotas. Apart from non-tariff barriers, some ASEAN exports to the ROK, in particular farm products, continue to face high tariff walls. Although the ROK adopted a liberalized policy in agricultural products trade, the accompanying requirements for import permits, among others, still constrain trade in goods.

ASEAN is the second largest destination of ROK overseas investment. As of the end of 1994, investment to ASEAN countries amounted to US$1.46 billion. Since 1992, however, some investment flows shifted to China and Vietnam, and there was an apparent shift in ROK investments in ASEAN from resource-based to high-end product manufactures. Still, ROK investment flows to ASEAN, as a percentage of its GNP, remains small (that is, 1.7 per cent), compared with 5 to 10 per cent in some developed countries. However, ROK investment in ASEAN is expected to increase with the financial liberalization measures introduced in 1994, which would induce potential ROK investors to relocate their investments overseas to circumvent domestic inflation and rising land and labour costs. AFTA, as well as the growth areas in ASEAN, could provide the inducement for ROK investors to come into the region.

G. ASEAN–United States

ASEAN-U.S. dialogue began in 1977. Early discussions centred on commodities, access to markets and capital, transfer of technology, energy, shipping, and food security. Since 1990, the agenda expanded to cover broad political and economic issues in the international and regional arenas. Other than the regular ASEAN-U.S. dialogue, which is held every eighteen months, and the annual PMC 6 + 1 sessions, the AEM and the U.S. Trade Representative (USTR) have met regularly since 1991. The latter meetings are preceded by working-level meetings of their respective senior economic officials.

The United States is ASEAN's largest export market and is the second largest source of imports after Japan. Total trade between ASEAN and the United States grew by an average of 13.89 per cent from US$45.6 billion in 1989 to US$76.64 billion in 1993. The United States accounted for approximately 18 per cent of ASEAN's global trade in 1992 while ASEAN exports to the United States grew by an average of 13 per cent from 1989 to 1993, surpassing the average growth of ASEAN exports to Japan for the same period (see Figure 6.2).

While ASEAN exports to the United States grew at a healthy pace, the increased use of non-tariff barriers for manufactured products (for example, quotas, voluntary export restraints, and orderly marketing arrangements), including subsidies, countervailing duties, and anti-dumping measures affected some sensitive categories of exports. Commercial legislation such as the Omnibus Trade and Competitiveness Act of 1988 and the heightened pressure to protect intellectual property became additional trade concerns of ASEAN.

Relatedly, ASEAN expressed its collective stand on the issue of linking a country's GSP eligibility status with its ability to safeguard workers' rights. ASEAN also opposed the linking of trade with environmental issues (for example, the U.S. Marine Mammal Protection Act and the Fishery and Conservation Amendment Act). The former allows the United States to impose trade sanctions against countries that do not prohibit imports from harvesting nations that undermine U.S. laws. The latter calls for international agreements that would impose trade sanctions against countries that do not enforce special certificates of origin in certain fish products (for example, the Pacific salmon). In addition, ASEAN expressed its concern on the smear campaign against tropical timber that could eventually become a non-tariff barrier for ASEAN exports of timber products.

The growing interdependence between the ASEAN and U.S. economies is indicated by the notable growth in investment flows. U.S. direct investments in ASEAN rose by 13.3 per cent between 1980 and 1990 and by 22 per cent between 1990 and 1992. U.S. direct investment in ASEAN is presently concentrated in petroleum and electronics. Still, the remarkable growth in the exports of services from both sides bodes well for future investment flows in the sector even while the parameters of global trade continue to evolve.

To further strengthen ASEAN-U.S. economic relations, a Memorandum of Understanding was signed in Washington in 1990 that established a Trade and Investment Co-operation Committee (TICC). The TICC is the venue for both sides to consult on trade and investment and related issues (for example, transfer of technology and human resource development). The private sector is an active participant in the TICC process. Following the fourth TICC meeting in Honolulu, ASEAN and the United States agreed to embark on action-oriented programmes, one of which paved the way for the establishment of the Alliance for Mutual Growth (AMG).

The U.S.-initiated AMG was designed to harness human and financial resources from the public and private sectors to create business opportunities between both sides and create the foundation for long-term expansion of trade and commercial ties. There are six mutual areas of co-operation under the AMG, namely, human resources, infrastructure, SMEs, standards, technology, and trade promotion. A unique feature of the programme is the differentiation between country-specific activities and ASEAN-wide activities. Again, the private sector is active in the AMG.

Until the late 1980s, U.S. development assistance to ASEAN supported projects in the areas of crop protection, forestry resources management and conservation, agricultural development planning, and non-conventional energy research. However, as the U.S. economy declined, the focus of support shifted in favour of projects that promoted trade and investment, technology transfer, environmental protection, and the participation of the private sector. The Private Investment and Trade Opportunities (PITO) Project, an umbrella project implemented from 1990 to 1995, was the vehicle for undertaking trade and investment promotion activities between the two sides. The Project is now maintained by the private sector on a self-sustaining basis. Another umbrella project, the Environmental Improvement Project (EIP), is in progress, and supports projects in waste management and environmental technology.

Private sector participation is the key feature of the ASEAN-U.S. dialogue, with its support of activities that enhance trade. For instance, a Centre for Technology Exchange, which was initiated by the private sector, assists ASEAN's small business sector in gaining access to capital markets.

H. ASEAN-UNDP

The United Nations Development Programme (UNDP) formally launched a programme of technical assistance for ASEAN in 1977 as a component of UNDP's Regional or Inter-Country Programme (ICP). The sub-regional programme was designed to assist ASEAN member countries in their various regional co-operation programmes. Through the years, the sub-regional programme grew, both in terms of funding and projects, from under US$2 million in 1977–81 (Second Cycle) to US$13 million in 1987–91 (Fourth Cycle). The allocation for 1992–96 (Fifth Cycle), however, is only US$5.8 million.

In recognition of the special technical assistance programme that the UNDP extended to ASEAN under its ICP, the UNDP was officially designated a dialogue partner of ASEAN, the only international organization accorded this status. In terms of its assistance programme for ASEAN in earlier years, most of it was geared to support capacity building and institutional development. Under the Fifth Cycle, though, funds were allocated in five areas, namely (a) liberalization of trade and investment including the implementation of AFTA, (b) science and technology, (c) trade and the environment, (d) human resource development, and (e) capacity building.

I. ASEAN-India

The ASEAN-India sectoral dialogue was established in 1993 and is being implemented through the ASEAN-India Joint Sectoral Co-operation Committee (AIJSCC). Since then, ASEAN and India made substantial progress in identifying areas of co-operation in trade and investments, focusing on liberalization, facilitation, and promotion, and infrastructure development. Other areas of co-operation include the promotion of tourist destinations, and joint workshops on science and technology development (that is, in advanced materials science, biotechnology, and information technology). India provided an initial allocation of US$158,478 to set up an ASEAN-India Fund that would finance mutually agreed programmes and projects. In addition to the Fund, India also offered to provide training modules in specific projects in designated areas of interest to ASEAN within the framework of the India Technical and Economic Co-operation (ITEC) Programme.

The first meeting of the AIJSCC featured the participation of the private sector, which adopted a framework for the establishment of an ASEAN-India Business Council (AIBC). The framework provides for private sector representatives to participate fully in the deliberations of the AIJSCC.

In the area of trade, the AIJSCC and the AIBC agreed to jointly formulate the policy framework and institutional mechanisms to remove impediments and accelerate the progress of trade co-operation. The AIBC, in its first meeting in February 1995, formulated a specific action plan for enhancing trade, investment, tourism, and other services-related activities between the two. Among them is a Roundtable Conference designed for officials and private sector representatives to exchange views on the prospects of expanding trade between ASEAN and India in the wake of the implementation of major economic reforms in India, and the full-scale implementation of AFTA.

Meanwhile, several activities are planned to promote co-operation in the tourism sector. These include a reciprocal familiarization programme for travel agents and tour operators, and the conduct of a tourism workshop to initiate dialogue between tourist partners on matters pertaining to marketing, investment, and human resource development.

In the field of science and technology, a plan of action was recently formulated in the area of advanced materials, biotechnology, and information technology. Specific project proposals will be developed during reciprocal visits of ASEAN and Indian scientists and at workshops held for the purpose. In support of these activities, the Government of India provided an additional contribution of approximately US$190,000 to the ASEAN-India Fund.

The ASEAN-India co-operation was upgraded into full dialogue partnership by a decision of ASEAN Leaders at the Fifth Summit in Bangkok in mid-December 1995.

J. ASEAN-China

The exchange of letters between the Secretary-General of ASEAN, the Chinese Deputy Premier, and Foreign Minister Qian in Bangkok in 1994 formalized the consultative relationship between ASEAN and China. Two joint committees were established — one on economic and trade co-operation and the other on scientific and technological co-operation.

The ASEAN-China Joint Science and Technology Committee met for the first time at Bandar Seri Begawan in 1995 to endorse its terms of reference and procedural guidelines. The Committee agreed to implement feasible projects as soon as possible on a cost-sharing basis as China proposed collaborative projects in remote sensing, meteorology, and the earth sciences. The Joint Committee on Economic and Trade Co-operation met, for the first time, in August 1995 in Jakarta.

ASEAN-China consultative relations were reinforced following the first series of consultations held between senior officials of ASEAN member countries and China in April 1995. Senior officials exchanged views on international and regional security issues, including rival claims over the Spratly Islands. In this forum, ASEAN expressed its concern over the intentions and policy of China in the South China Sea and advocated a peaceful solution to maintain peace and stability in the region.

K. ASEAN-Russia

Since 1991 the foreign ministers of ASEAN and the Soviet Union had several consultative meetings, which are ongoing efforts to find an appropriate modality for institutionalizing the consultative relationship. In October 1994 the Russian Federation suggested the establishment of joint committees on a number of areas of mutual interest, such as economic and trade co-operation and science and technology. Meanwhile, the ASEAN Business Forum planned a seminar between its members and their Russian counterparts in the private sector to promote awareness of trade and investment opportunities on both sides.

III. ASEAN Sectoral Dialogue Relations

In recent years, the changing content and nature of ASEAN's external relations was manifested by its efforts to expand ties with other countries in Asia and with international regional organizations. The Fourth Summit in 1992 affirmed ASEAN's intent to intensify its co-operative relationships with interested non-dialogue countries and international organizations. Presently, ASEAN has a sectoral dialogue relation with Pakistan.

A. ASEAN-Pakistan

Pakistan was accorded sectoral dialogue status in 1993. The process of consultation is ongoing to formulate appropriate modalities for conducting the ASEAN-Pakistan sectoral dialogue. As a result of exploratory consultations, Pakistan agreed to undertake an in-depth study on the state of relations between Pakistan and ASEAN member countries to serve as a basis for formulating a programme of co-operation for ASEAN-Pakistan sectoral relations. Steps were also taken to initiate contact between the private sector of ASEAN and Pakistan through an investment promotion seminar sponsored by the Pakistan Board of Investment. Its purpose was to generate awareness of the economic and investment opportunities available in Pakistan. In addition, Pakistan plans to conduct a survey of perceptions among executives on both sides to promote better understanding among the private sector.

B. Relations with Other Regional Organizations

A number of regional organizations expressed interest to establish formal ties with ASEAN. These include the ECO, SAARC, the Rio Group, and the Gulf Co-operation Council. Currently, ASEAN maintains a formal relationship with the South Pacific Forum at the Secretariat level. In 1995, the ASEAN Secretariat hosted the Second Consultative Meeting among executive heads of sub-regional organizations in Asia and the Pacific, held under the auspices of the United Nations Economic and Social Commission for Asia and the Pacific (UNESCAP).

The Meeting provided the opportunity for informal discussions on issues of mutual interest and to explore areas of possible co-operation at the inter-regional level.

IV. Changing Parameters in ASEAN's External Relations

Recent economic developments are changing the parameters of ASEAN's external environment. By the turn of the century, it is expected that most developed countries will be in the midst of their de-industrialization process. This means that manufacturing will constitute a lesser proportion of their national output. Already, ASEAN has recognized the opportunity that this development brings in terms of increasing its value-added manufactures for export. National strategies in this direction could be complemented by deepening industrial co-operation and accelerating trade liberalization in ASEAN.

The global trend towards the establishment of trade blocs will undoubtedly affect the manner in which ASEAN conducts itself in the international arena. As regional trading blocs began to crystallize in Europe and in North America, ASEAN opened itself to the possibility of linking with these trading arrangements based on the concept of open regionalism. The argument behind linking or expanding regional trading arrangements is to provide a larger framework that would enhance and facilitate flows of trade and foreign direct investment and technology, reduce uncertainty, increase market information, and increase technology transfer.

In the 12th ASEAN-U.S. dialogue in 1994, the idea of linking AFTA with NAFTA was brought up by the United States. Although the proposal did not take off, it reflected the U.S. agenda to establish a trade bloc covering the Asia-Pacific region — an agenda that it pushed in APEC. Australia proposed (with New Zealand's support) a similar initiative to link AFTA with ANZCERTA. In the first informal consultation between ASEAN and CER officials in Jakarta in 1995, mutually beneficial areas of co-operation (that is, customs matters, investment facilitation, rules of origin, industrial co-operation, human resource development, and information exchange on regional integration) were discussed. In the end, the manner and the pace by which ASEAN responds to initiatives for grouping and regrouping trade blocs in the

Asia-Pacific region, without losing sight of its regional purpose and identity, will be one of its major challenges in the twenty-first century.

ASEAN's participation in APEC brought new opportunities and concerns. The latter presents an enormous opportunity for ASEAN in terms of better international relations and economic integration as it allows ASEAN to discuss regional issues with its most important trading partners in the light of emerging rules in the global trading environment and provide a window for new avenues of co-operation (see Box 6.3 for ASEAN's view of APEC).

The greater internationalization of ASEAN economies rendered them more sensitive to changes in international economic policies and trends. Concerns about new forms of protectionism, regional trading

BOX 6.3: ON ASEAN'S VIEW OF APEC

"While there is yet no common perception of APEC amongst ASEAN member countries, APEC has moved ahead. The original premise on which ASEAN based its participation in APEC has been largely overtaken by events, with the establishment of the APEC Secretariat in Singapore, the institutionalization of the leaders' meeting in all but in name and the expanding activities of the various working groups. I believe that there is room for more consultations within ASEAN on this issue so that we can put to rest once and for all this nagging problem and make everyone feel comfortable in participating within an APEC framework. This will be to the ultimate benefit of ASEAN and APEC.

"I have often been asked by the press and the media whether there is any danger of APEC railroading ASEAN. I reject this notion. I do not think we can necessarily compare the two groupings. ASEAN has a twenty-seven-year history and a proud record of co-operation on political, security, economic, and social issues. It has been a factor for peace and stability in the region and is an organization that is respected and admired for what it has achieved by all, including members of APEC, many of whom are also its dialogue partners. I recall the former U.S. Secretary of State, Mr James Baker, saying at an ASEAN Foreign Ministers' Meeting that ASEAN was the core of APEC and that without ASEAN, there would be no APEC. Perhaps, as a reflection of this, we still have every other APEC Ministerial Meeting in an ASEAN capital."

December 1994

Dato' Ajit Singh
Secretary-General of ASEAN

blocs, the outcome of the recent Uruguay Round — all these strengthened ASEAN co-operation on international economic issues. To preserve the gains brought about by the rapid growth of ASEAN economies, ASEAN will have to increase its efforts to safeguard the institutions and principles that guided the promotion of free market principles. In the future, the challenges posed by an ever-changing global environment could prove to be the force that binds ASEAN together.

7

Prospects

I. Overall Assessment

ASEAN economic co-operation, by all accounts, stands at a crossroads. It underwent a long transition period of accumulation, both process and substance, that became the basis for subsequent transformation. The period was marked with varied degrees of commitment and coverage, from half-hearted measures to dramatic initiatives, from exemptions and exclusions to full participation, from selected and narrow scope to broad coverage.

Chapter 2 has traced ASEAN economic co-operation along several fronts and each of the six areas reviewed had underlying directions. For example, co-operation in trade aimed to push vigorous intra-ASEAN transactions; in transport, communications, and tourism, co-operation aimed to connect ASEAN; in finance and in banking, co-operation aimed to integrate financial sectors closer.

Many of the early co-operation schemes hardly made inroads into the lofty aims espoused in each sector or area. As a collective group, ASEAN experienced early fumbles in economic co-operation. From trade to industrial development, agriculture to minerals, ASEAN co-operation was characterized by fits and starts. Despite the number of economic co-operation meetings, the outputs generated were not that normally expected from a regional group. Yet, they became important strands of confidence that each of the ASEAN states had strewn towards a regional network. The numerous meetings attended by ASEAN member countries served to continue the process of building trust and familiarity, consensus building, and internalizing a regional perspective among ASEAN officials.

Whether turning the corner in ASEAN economic co-operation was long in coming or not depends on the time frame to be reckoned from the start of regional efforts. The organization began with the First ASEAN Ministerial Meeting and was marked by the signing of the ASEAN Declaration in 1967. Although this was followed by subsequent ministerial meetings, multilateral agreements, other political and organizational arrangements, the First ASEAN Economic Ministers Meeting did not take place until November 1975. Four months later, in March 1976, the Second AEM Meeting was held in Kuala Lumpur. In a seeming effort to keep pace with changing global economic developments as these affect ASEAN, three AEM meetings were held in 1979 and 1982, and four in 1987. In many of the interim and subsequent years (after 1987), at least two AEM meetings were held every year. This trend reflected the intensification of member countries' collective interest in finalizing mechanisms to promote economic co-operation.

Events since the Fourth ASEAN Summit marked ASEAN's transformation in economic co-operation. Indeed, ASEAN abandoned its lingering timidity towards the concept of a common market or free trade area that was tabled at the Third ASEAN Summit.[1] As detailed in Chapter 2, member countries agreed to undertake concrete and specific courses of action. In the traditional sectors of economic co-operation, the focus was also intensified amidst institutional consolidation and implementation of long-term programmes.

The bold initiatives, as summarized in Chapter 3, were beyond

AFTA. They cover concerns that previously were either ignored or discussed without clear directions. They are essential to ASEAN as it taps the advantages of freer trade among member states and, increasingly, with the rest of the world.

The Fifth ASEAN Summit formalized much of the new areas of economic co-operation through the Bangkok Summit Declaration and protocols signed by ASEAN leaders and appropriate ministers. These included an agreement in services, the establishment of an ASEAN investment region, the implementation of a new industrial co-operation scheme, and an action plan for SME development. These are along the lines described in Chapter 3 (see Box 7.1).

ASEAN's actions, reflected in the declarations of the Fourth and Fifth Summits, galvanized the region's full commitment to a single economy as the two summits pronounced the unrelenting pursuit of free trade. Exemptions from economic co-operation (for certain sectors or products) were officially set aside as protocols called for the reduction and eventual elimination of the exclusion list in the CEPT scheme, and the elimination of non-tariff barriers, the weak spots of the CEPT scheme.

The dramatic initiatives that ASEAN governments took in the two summits were deliberate policy moves floated as an ASEAN agenda.[2] Given the degree of protection in the region, it is understandable that these were not officially considered. Yet, member states, armed with the confidence resulting from familiarity with each other's markets, came to accept the initiatives accompanying liberalization and regional co-operation.

ASEAN economic co-operation is partly driven by market forces. The pace and amount of intra-ASEAN trade, initially slow and inconsequential, gradually became significant in the last few years, and now appear to be self-expansionary as the region becomes more integrated. There is evidence of greater vertical and horizontal transactions taking place, for instance, intra-industry, combined with the emergence of various investment schemes such as joint ventures and brand-to-brand complementation. In addition, ASEAN is host to many foreign investments and vice versa. ASEAN's economic openness and outward orientation places it within the ambit of economic dynamism in the Pacific.

The close relationship between trade and investment requires

BOX 7.1: DECISIONS FROM THE FIFTH ASEAN SUMMIT

Focusing on the theme "Greater ASEAN Economic Integration", the recently held Fifth ASEAN Summit in Bangkok resulted in (a) the acceleration and deepening of commitments made under the ASEAN Free Trade Area (AFTA), (b) expansion of ASEAN economic co-operation in new sectors, and (c) increased linkages with other countries in Southeast Asia.

To achieve the goal of AFTA by 2003, the Summit endorsed the revised ten-year tariff reduction schedule of products in the CEPT scheme. At the Summit, Vietnam acceded to the Framework Agreement on Enhancing ASEAN Economic Co-operation and the CEPT agreement. The Summit also endorsed the list of unprocessed agricultural products for inclusion into the CEPT scheme.

The Summit agreed that harmonization of tariff nomenclature at the 8-digit Harmonized System code is to be completed by 1997. It also agreed that the GATT Valuation Scheme should be put in place by 1997, well ahead of the WTO deadline of year 2000 for developing countries.

With regard to the elimination of non-tariff barriers, three important decisions were made at the recent Summit. First, member countries should aim to eliminate non-tariff barriers earlier than currently allowed for and no later than the year 2003. Second, the Summit agreed that the private sector is an important information source on trade barriers and agreed to the establishment of a mechanism for monitoring them at the National AFTA Unit and at the AFTA Unit in the ASEAN Secretariat. Finally, the Summit agreed to give priority to sectors that are widely traded in ASEAN, such as electrical appliances and machinery, base metals, plastics, and chemicals.

In other areas of economic co-operation, member countries signed a Framework Agreement on Services to enhance co-operation in the sector and begin, by January 1996, a process of preferential liberalization of trade in services. Priority sectors include financial services, air and maritime transport, telecommunications, tourism, and construction. The Summit also agreed to complete the process of negotiations in tourism, telecommunications, and financial services within eighteen months.

Member countries signed the Framework Agreement on Intellectual Property Co-operation. Also endorsed was a new industrial co-operation scheme called ASEAN Industrial Co-operation (AICO), which will replace the current Brand-to-Brand Complementation (BBC) and ASEAN Industrial Joint Ventures (AIJV) schemes.

One of the important proposals in the Summit was the creation of an ASEAN Investment Area (AIA) to encourage more investment into the region by, among others, reducing barriers to the free flow of capital and the adoption of simpler and more transparent rules.

Finally, the leaders also decided to discuss how ASEAN might participate in the development of the Mekong Basin and engage China, South Korea, and Japan in the process. ASEAN will be looking into the development of a railway running from Singapore to Kunming in southern China and gas pipelines to further stimulate growth in the entire region. The Summit also proposed greater co-operation by the region's central banks to minimize currency instability in the region.

that ASEAN raises FDI flows within itself to match the increased trade generated via the CEPT scheme and compensate for the declining share of ASEAN in global FDI flows since 1990. In this regard, the task of promoting larger FDI flows within ASEAN was one of the core activities after the Fifth ASEAN Summit. A proposal was made to establish an ASEAN Investment Area (AIA) to address this task.

Within ASEAN itself there are market ramifications. For instance, intense local transactions are taking place (for example, growth triangles) amidst a broader set of economic transactions. The private sector is more active in intra-ASEAN trade and the great number of business dealings within ASEAN (either among ASEAN or with non-ASEAN) is a clear expression of self-sustained co-operation. The profile of recent intra-ASEAN FDI reflects the fast pace and diversity of these transactions, sectorally and geographically. For example, there is significant Malaysian exposure to investments in the Philippines (from infrastructure to palm-growing) as there are Thai investments (the Shirawatra Group) in telecommunications, and Indonesian financial interests through the Salim Group and Dharmala (in the Philippines and other ASEAN states). Even more significant, however, are the alliances that ASEAN businesses are forming in response to opportunities arising from an ASEAN single market. In anticipation of providing a one-stop telecommunication service in ASEAN, telecommunications companies within ASEAN are already forming an alliance. This is an example of the initiatives prompted by market forces. Of course, all these are in addition to the expansion of traditional global firms in the region that are consolidating and modifying specializations in the context of AFTA. As other elements of economic co-operation supportive of a single ASEAN economy are put in place, one can expect a further surge of trade and investments from among member countries themselves. Without doubt, these would maintain the magnitudes of FDI in ASEAN.

Other than market forces, ASEAN economic co-operation is also partly driven by institutional factors and changes. A strengthened ASEAN Secretariat is not only a regional organization in the real sense but a credible representative in the international community. Its increased authority and responsibility are a reflection of the acquired individual and collective self-confidence that past co-operation activities had built. Although the Secretariat could use even more co-ordinating functions, in recent years, especially after the Fourth ASEAN Summit, it undoubtedly played a more substantive role than it did in the past. ASEAN's reorganization and active participation of its economic bureaus were instrumental in defining and mapping out directions in ASEAN economic co-operation.

As noted in Chapter 1, the ASEAN Secretary-General sits in ASEAN ministerial committees as well as in Senior Officials Meetings. Consequently, the ASEAN Secretariat is deeply involved in all ASEAN matters. Chapter 1 has also indicated that the Secretariat, while reporting directly to the ASEAN Standing Committee, provides consultative and servicing functions to all relevant committees. In the case of AFTA, the Secretariat has specifically dedicated a technical unit to support it.

The institutional changes in ASEAN, especially those made at the Secretariat, are a product of a changing philosophy among members of the potential strength of ASEAN as a cohesive group and a single regional economy. The changes in the Secretariat are actually hinged on this framework as it graduates from the common perception of being a "post office" to being an important figure in ASEAN co-operation deliberations. In this spirit, the regional headquarters of ASEAN carries a leadership role that, although short of the political similarity with the EC, is sufficient to keep ASEAN solidarity going. In this sense, economic co-operation is aptly supported.

ASEAN's joint economic activities with its dialogue partners are instruments in carrying out specific projects (for example, many sectoral ASEAN Centres) and of sustaining market transactions. Thus, both as an institutional machinery and as a market framework, the ASEAN dialogue process is important to the transformation of ASEAN economic co-operation.

The expansion in the number of dialogue partners, including China and India, enables ASEAN to cover more markets, and focus on areas of mutual interests and co-operation activities. In addition, UNDP's distinction as a dialogue partner assures continued support for ASEAN economic co-operation projects and programmes.

Finally, ASEAN's private sector has also shaped economic co-operation in ASEAN. From passive involvement, the ASEAN-CCI has become an active partner in formulating ASEAN's economic agenda.

More recently, other private sector groups, in particular NGOs, have evolved in ASEAN and are involved in regional co-operation activities.

Both market- and institution-driven elements combine to move ASEAN economic co-operation from a period of transition to transformation in a continuous feedback process. The integrated approach to the agenda for economic co-operation and the "ASEAN-plus" participation in global economic agreements indicate that ASEAN can confidently undertake policy changes as a collective whole without the marked reluctance of the past.

II. ASEAN Economic Co-operation: The Next Generation

Once core economic initiatives take place, the CEPT scheme is completed, and new areas of economic co-operation are implemented, the structure of the ASEAN economy will change significantly. A new generation of ASEAN people is expected, but what would the profile of economic co-operation then be?

A lot depends on the degree to which the current agenda is taken to heart in implementation, monitoring, and adjustment. Any hesitation or delay in timetable makes succeeding tasks more difficult as time and effort will have to be spent on correcting previous errors, setting in motion elements of the package that were delayed, and other remedial measures to keep economic co-operation on track.

With success in the present ASEAN economic agenda, however, the next generation of ASEAN economic co-operation activities is expected to take a different shape. ASEAN will encompass most of Southeast Asia (it already has seven members as of 1996), and will become a "single" economy by the turn of the century. This means that mobility of goods and resources will guarantee convergence of prices; progress in transport and communications will allow widespread (if not perfect) information about markets, business, and trade; and common standards will ensure the international competitiveness of ASEAN goods.

The agenda is therefore aimed along two fronts. Internally, the task entails continuing the fine-tuning of the various economic co-operation schemes laid out earlier (and summarized in the previous chapters), as mechanisms for carrying out new areas of co-operation, as ratified in the Fifth ASEAN Summit, are already in place. Initially,

ASEAN's lack of substantive experience in the new areas may subject it to "trials and errors" in the process of arriving at specific courses of action. The same will be true in areas that are subject to international discussions or negotiations (for example, services, intellectual property). ASEAN would thus need to be firm on its targets and timetables without losing the flexibility of modifying them as necessary. Both these and the directions set out for the existing economic co-operation areas give comprehensiveness to ASEAN's internal agenda. With their implementation, a single ASEAN market in goods and factors will be achieved, and subsequently a higher plane of co-operation, in the area of macroeconomic policies, could be considered. While these can be addressed at the summit level, it may be necessary to institutionalize regular macroeconomic policy consultations especially at the technical level. As the current agenda takes effect, this will have to be addressed. The success of institutionalizing free trade depends, to a large extent, on the implementation of consistent macroeconomic policies as slight disturbances in any one member country's macroeconomic parameters tend to be quickly transmitted to other members via trade transactions. Though co-ordination may be desirable, frequent consultations will suffice that can be made part of regular AEM meetings.

ASEAN, as a single economy driven by the force of trade (but still defined by sovereign national boundaries), may also consider building the capacity to concretize a collective view in such areas as product standards, competition policy, environmental standards, and related issues. Sectoral policies and programmes (for example, infrastructure) may have to be synchronized, if not co-ordinated, through a continuous dialogue process. As supporting mechanisms, ASEAN networks and fora have to be maintained and nurtured as these are vehicles for sustaining and ensuring compatibility and comparability.

Externally, as ASEAN becomes an internationally significant player in the global economy, its collective voice becomes important in the international resolution of economic problems. Thus, ASEAN will need to be in the network of international institutions and bilateral powers. This means ASEAN will have to create a feedback mechanism among its members to provide a sounding board on international economic issues. The AEM meeting's agenda regularly includes discussions on latest international economic issues where ministers come to a common understanding, if not a view, of them. Whether this is institutionally sufficient as ASEAN becomes a larger grouping depends on two factors. The first is the systemic way AEM monitors international economic issues and discern their ASEAN implications. Each country obviously follows global economic events relative to its own interests but it would be a more complicated process to deliberate on their regional context. The second is the amount of time ASEAN economic ministers can comprehensively spend on them given the expanding internal agenda for ASEAN, and the limited amount of time that individual ministers can devote to ASEAN matters. For these reasons, the ASEAN Secretariat may be tasked to be at the forefront of ASEAN external economic co-operation activities, as it can provide a regional perspective of international economic issues, spell out their impact on individual members, indicate potential economic co-operation considerations, and provide ASEAN economic ministers with clear policy options for decision. To the extent that a certain degree of political dimension is inherent in these tasks, the ASEAN Secretariat needs flexibility to accomplish these as a regional political entity.

III. ASEAN in Asia

There is no doubt that by the end of the twentieth century, ASEAN will become a group of ten members. Its population size, from its size in 1970, will double to about 450 million people. Geographically, ASEAN will encompass the whole of Southeast Asia.

In economic terms, ASEAN will be faced with a larger, more powerful market as incomes continue their upward trend following historical records. If AFTA is completed at the beginning of the twenty-first century, ASEAN will become "one region, one economy", and characterized by the free flow of goods, services and resources.

Although the geographical configuration of ASEAN as a consolidated Southeast Asia would somehow bring back memories of a landlocked region eons ago, the task for economic co-operation will continue to be formidable.

In general, the newer member states will pay particular attention to economic reconstruction while others grapple with speeding up modernization and coming to grips with competition in a global economy. Thus, even a "single economy" like ASEAN will have members that opt to place different degrees of emphasis on economic co-operation.

Economic co-operation among the ten members is likely to cover at least three directions. First, there is the need to promote support to capacity building among the newer members in terms of development planning, project preparation and development, policy analysis and monitoring, among others. As the transitional-economy members adopt market systems and institutions, their ASEAN identity requires these capacities. ASEAN, with the support of its dialogue partners, will be able to promote such capacities as the latter brings to bear their development assistance for these needs. Second, ASEAN is likely to pursue its co-operation in setting standards and quality specifications for traded products and services. As pointed out in Chapter 3, some of these new areas of economic co-operation may have to be consistent with international agreements (as in the WTO), require reciprocity of tests and other measures that newer members have to build capacity for. Thus, there may have to be "timed" stages by which ASEAN members fully conform to this co-operation modality. Finally, ASEAN may have to begin looking into resource mobility issues as these tend to be more compelling in a regional context than if it were only confined to individual countries, especially when free trade is institutionalized. For instance, some ASEAN members are labour-deficient while others are labour-abundant. If greater resource movements are to be part of a fully integrated ASEAN, it may be necessary to phase stages across member countries (analogous to AFTA) over a period of time.

For the private sector, economic co-operation derives from market signals. Even as free trade takes place in an expanded ASEAN, one can expect co-operation in at least three areas. First, there would be greater specialization among member countries as comparative advantage becomes the prime basis for trade. With the absence of distortions (caused by tariff and non-tariff barriers), resource endowments would dictate comparative advantages. Again, members may decide the degree of free trade and fashion their policies accordingly. Second, with a larger market in ASEAN, one can also expect greater alliances among business groups than would be true in other (non-ASEAN) countries. These alliances accommodate and reinforce the market specialization that eventually takes place. Finally, one can expect the emergence of more sub-regional markets and co-operation arrangements to take advantage of geographical proximity (for a limited number of countries). These sub-ASEAN areas build on the larger scope of liberalization existing among all members. The formation of alliances among these sub-ASEAN areas is another basis for greater economic transactions.

As ASEAN moves into the next century, and as it covers the whole of Southeast Asia, its economic co-operation will be dictated by the nature of regional public policies fashioned by member countries that have matured in collective interests, and by private sector initiatives that react to, and anticipate, regional economic parameters.

Individual ASEAN member countries, while increasing intra-ASEAN transactions, have historically increased trade with other Asian countries particularly those in North Asia. In recognition of the importance of these countries to ASEAN, ASEAN leaders, at the Fifth Summit, urged advancing further the East Asia Economic Caucus (EAEC). The manner in which ASEAN will relate to the EAEC and the modes of economic co-operation that will shape up remains to be seen. ASEAN's experience with the CEPT scheme for AFTA may very well be the bench-mark for future co-operative endeavours with the rest of Asia and other regional blocs.

IV. ASEAN in the Global Village

The array of international economic changes partly prodded ASEAN to pursue greater trade liberalization as its anchor of economic co-operation, although it is doubtful that this, together with the bold moves it took beginning with the Fourth ASEAN Summit, would have occurred were it not for the transitional experiences in economic co-operation.

The acceleration of economic co-operation within ASEAN did not mean the region raised its economic walls against the rest of the world. On the contrary, ASEAN continued its openness with non-member countries, and its economic distortions diminished along the path of economic co-operation.

ASEAN's global fit appears in at least two ways. The region, for one, is host to many MNCs, is active in the globalization process taking place among firms, and participates in networks and alliances with other countries. More concretely, ASEAN countries are regional headquarters for global firms. In short, the region is at the forefront of the many changes taking place in global business. For another, ASEAN countries are significant participants in global capital markets, and hosts as well as sources of FDI. The institutionalization of regional economic co-operation, notwithstanding, did not prevent ASEAN countries from optimizing their opportunities wherever they are located.

In a global economy made more manageable by advances in telecommunications and technology, ASEAN is not far behind; in fact, in some cases it is even ahead of firms in North America, Europe, or Japan. ASEAN's place in the global village is therefore aptly configured both by its economic co-operation activities and the changes taking place in the world economic environment.

Apart from these developments (and ASEAN's response to them), the global economic community reaffirmed its commitment to multilateralism with the ratification of new international trade rules. At the same time, in the Asia-Pacific region APEC was formed as an inter-governmental group with similar objectives as a multilateral body but limited to eighteen economies. In the face of these, where does ASEAN stand?

As a matter of policy, ASEAN encourages global approaches to international economic issues. It might be recalled that it called for the early harvest of the Uruguay Round, participated actively in the negotiations through the ASEAN-Geneva Committee, and were among the early ones to ratify the Uruguay Round agreements. This is not indicative of an aversion to multilateralism.[3]

ASEAN's initiatives are, in fact, additions to the objectives of a multilateral trade regime — freer trade, elimination of non-tariff barriers, and effective dispute settlement mechanisms, among others. These "AFTA-Plus" initiatives are really directions for global multilateral agreements. Indeed, if many of these are implemented in ASEAN, they would have a demonstration value for the rest of the international economic community.

ASEAN's participation in APEC (where ASEAN is often considered its core) follows the same mould at some sub-global level. ASEAN and APEC have similar goals, and even if the former's goals are subsumed in the latter's agenda, the identity remains. APEC's adherence to "open regionalism" implies that accelerated liberalization in the context of global liberalization is less trade-diverting than a closed regional grouping. This is the same philosophy in ASEAN economic co-operation. Indeed, as a regional group accounting for a significant part of world trade, ASEAN can influence the direction of multilateral trade negotiations.

ASEAN's continued progress and expansion does not necessarily mean a preference for regionalism as a code of trade conduct or its market definition. As earlier mentioned, the existence and expansion of ASEAN is not purely on economic terms. Even its regional economic co-operation arrangements are rooted on other considerations, such as political and institutional concerns.

V. Conclusions

As a regional body, ASEAN has acquired a life of its own. As the vehicle of economic co-operation, its importance will vary depending on the region's composition and its substantive agenda. Given the trend towards global liberalization and the re-emergence of multilateralism, ASEAN's economic significance may diminish over time. On the other hand, to the extent that newer members are phased into ASEAN, economic dimensions will remain important (as spelled out in Section II).

The moving force behind ASEAN's economic co-operation lies in the organization itself and its outer strength comes from its long existence. Other than the EU, it is the only regional organization that has lasted for more than two decades amidst the many regional entities that fell by the wayside after only a few years of existence. ASEAN's international credibility to address regional concerns remains intact. As in previous occasions, the most recent Post-Ministerial Conference was attended by foreign ministers of dialogue partners, which are not members of ASEAN. Drawing from its reservoir of regional confidence, knowledge, and experiences, the organization is able to address a wide range of agenda items — security, cultural, and economic issues. As ASEAN gains further experience in tackling a varied agenda, its outer strength becomes more firmly rooted and assures it a greater chance of surviving the ravages of economic dislocation.

ASEAN's inner strength derives from the ability of seven (and eventually, ten) independent and sovereign states to come together, deliberate on a wide range of concerns, promote dialogue and debate, and arrive at common solutions and directions based on regional interests. ASEAN meetings, as always, end in the spirit of solidarity. This is a product of a transition period that built trust and confidence among ASEAN officials. Decision by consensus appears to be a uniquely ASEAN way of arriving at courses of action.

ASEAN's inner and outer strength gives it a collective clout that each individual member would be unable to achieve. Such clout is increasingly becoming a force to reckon with, as is evident in the way that APEC, the EU, and the rest of the world, view ASEAN.

The strengths of ASEAN, in a way, also hide its own weaknesses. To the extent that the pace of its activities and co-operation schemes is slowed down by the reluctance or hesitation of any one member or members, ASEAN is prevented from realizing its full potential at the shortest possible time. As the organization expands to include more members, ASEAN is expected to take a longer period of time and may take a more careful, if not altogether, cautious stand on issues in which it has had no previous experience. While this is understandable due to the uneven benefits of regional efforts and the concern of member countries for individual advantages or disadvantages, it reflects a shorter horizon than what is required for collective actions to bring long-term results. In the end, differences among member countries give way to the ascension of individual country interests on certain issues. This will tend to overshadow the formation of a collective regional perspective, and will eventually dilute the credibility and clout of ASEAN in the global community.

Still, as member countries continue to put their stakes in ASEAN, the primordial mission of preserving ASEAN into succeeding generations entails being aware of the potentials that ASEAN, as an enlarged grouping of seven (eventually ten) member states, can achieve for all its members.

NOTES

1. In Hans Christoph Rieger's compilation of *ASEAN Economic Co-operation*, the chronology of main events notes a private meeting on 7 February 1987

between "President Soeharto of Indonesia and Prime Minister Lee Kuan Yew of Singapore (at which they agreed) not to discuss a common market or a free trade area at the forthcoming Summit" (Hans Christoph Rieger 1991, p. 23). Coincidentally, this was also the time that an external report for COTT was prepared by Seiji Naya (1987) on an ASEAN Free Trade Area.

2. An illustration of these can be found in the 1987 and the 1991 ASEAN Roundtables on ASEAN Economic Co-operation: Institute of Southeast Asian Studies (1987), and Institute of Policy Studies and Institute of Southeast Asian Studies (1991).
3. The expansion of ASEAN can be viewed as an expansion of regionalism or its consolidation in the context of multilateralism. See Leszck Buszynski (1996).

8 Postscript

Several changes have taken place in the area of ASEAN economic co-operation during the brief interim between the completion of this draft and its publication. ASEAN expanded its membership to include Laos and Myanmar on 23 July 1997. The macroeconomic profile of ASEAN's nine member countries is shown in Table 8.1. The ASEAN Heads of Government meet formally every three years, and in between on an informal basis. The first informal ASEAN Summit was held in Jakarta on 30 November 1996. At the informal Summit the Leaders requested the ministers to develop an ASEAN Vision towards 2020 and the possibility of ASEAN co-operation on the facilitation of goods in transit. The ASEAN Secretariat now has two Deputy Secretary-Generals, one responsible for economic co-operation and the other for other areas of co-operation.

Table 8.1
Macroeconomic Profile of ASEAN-9

Country	Population (million)	GDP (billion US$)	GDP per Capita (US$)	Export (billion US$)
Brunei	0.30	6.12	20,400	2.30
Indonesia	197.60	185.74	940	49.80
Laos	4.90	1.00	204	0.30
Malaysia	20.60	80.96	3,930	78.20
Myanmar	47.70	9.71	204	1.00
Philippines	69.30	78.31	1,130	2.50
Singapore	3.10	81.84	26,400	125.00
Thailand	61.40	164.55	2,680	56.90
Vietnam	76.30	19.08	250	5.20
ASEAN-9	481.20	627.31	1,304	339.20

I. AFTA

The year 1997 marks the fifth year of the implementation of the CEPT scheme for AFTA. Although member countries are only halfway to the deadline of 2003 for realizing AFTA, nearly 42,253 tariff lines (about 90.6 per cent of all tariff lines in ASEAN) have already been included in the CEPT scheme. Average tariff rates for products in the Inclusion List have now fallen to 6.38 per cent from 12.76 per cent in 1993. With the participation of Laos and Myanmar, the Inclusion List under the CEPT scheme will increase from 42,253 to about 45,119 tariff lines, or about 81 per cent of the total tariff lines in ASEAN.

Progress has also been achieved in other areas of implementing AFTA. Firstly, member countries have agreed to issue one legal enactment in 1997 which would cover the whole period of tariff reduction. The previous practice of issuing legislation at the beginning of each year to enact tariff reduction mandated by the CEPT scheme prevented some exporters from immediately enjoying the lower tariffs when the legal enactments were delayed.

Secondly, a great deal of progress was made in eliminating non-tariff barriers in the past year. ASEAN removed all customs surcharges on CEPT products at the end of 1996. In the area of technical barriers to trade (TBTs), a list of twenty priority product groups for standards harmonization has been identified. In addition, some member countries are concluding mutual recognition agreements on a bilateral basis.

Thirdly, in the area of customs co-operation, ASEAN agreed on the harmonization of tariff nomenclature at the Harmonized System (HS) 8-digit level, the adoption of the GATT Valuation Agreement, and the harmonization of customs procedures. This commitment was further strengthened with the signing of the ASEAN Agreement on Customs on 1 March 1997 at the first ASEAN Finance Ministers Meeting. The Agreement provides a legal framework by which co-operative activities in this area will be governed.

Finally, as part of the effort to facilitate the cross-border flow of goods within ASEAN, the Green Lane System for CEPT products was launched in 1996. A review of the System during its first year of implementation showed that it improved the average clearing time of CEPT products in Malaysia and Thailand by 5 and 2 hours, respectively.

As a result of the above measures, intra-ASEAN trade continued to grow in 1996 in spite of the slowdown in export growth experienced by some member countries. For the first half of 1996 (January–June), intra-ASEAN exports of all products reached $36.28 billion. This was 11.7 per cent higher than the $32.47 billion of intra-ASEAN exports during the same period in 1995.

ASEAN is facilitating trade not only among its member countries but also with groups of countries that share the principle of open regionalism and a rules-based multilateral trading system. Following ASEAN's establishment of regional links with the Australia–New Zealand Closer Economic Relations Trade Agreement (ANZCERTA or CER) in September 1995, a Memorandum of Understanding on Standards and Conformance was signed between the ministers of ASEAN and CER in September 1996. Efforts were also made to develop linkages with other regional groupings such as NAFTA, the Mercado Comun del Sur (MERCOSUR), the European Free Trade Association (EFTA), and the Southern African Development Community (SADC).

II. Services

ASEAN has also made progress in liberalizing its trade in services.

Along the lines of the ASEAN Framework Agreement on Services, a Co-ordinating Committee on Services (CCS) was set up in January 1996 with seven sectoral negotiating groups corresponding to the seven priority sectors identified by the Fifth ASEAN Summit. The Committee is now in the process of finalizing an initial package of commitments by the 29th AEM. This initial package is expected to contain market access openings in air transport, business services, maritime transport, telecommunications, and tourism and will be implemented no later than 31 March 1998.

III. Industry

In the area of industry, the Basic Agreement on ASEAN Industrial Co-operation (AICO) scheme was signed on 26 April 1996 during the AEM Retreat in Singapore and became operational on 1 November 1996. Twenty AICO arrangement applications from automotive and automotive component companies, consumer electronics, and chemical companies have been submitted and are being considered by member countries. In order to promote AICO, the ASEAN Secretariat has published leaflets and organized an AICO scheme workshop in Jakarta with the financial assistance of ASEAN Promotion Centre, Tokyo, on 29–30 April 1997.

IV. Investment

Following the directive of the fifth meeting of the ASEAN Heads of Government in 1995, ASEAN is currently formulating measures to establish an ASEAN Investment Area (AIA) to further enhance the region's competitiveness and conduciveness for attracting higher and sustainable levels of FDI flows. The AIA is also expected to give impetus to investors to think ASEAN and adopt a regional business strategy and network of operations on the basis of the complementary advantages of ASEAN economies. While a framework agreement on AIA is currently being drafted and will be completed in 1998, ASEAN has already been implementing various investment co-operation and facilitation and promotion and awareness programmes of activities. The implementation of these activities will provide a strong foundation to effectively implement further measures to realize AIA expeditiously and at the same time execute the Plan of Action on Co-operation and Promotion of Foreign Direct Investment and Intra-ASEAN Investment adopted by the Fifth ASEAN Summit.

V. Finance

Co-operation in the field of finance has made notable progress with the implementation of the Ministerial Understanding (MU) on Finance Co-operation and the ASEAN Agreement on Customs signed early in 1997. The MU provides a framework for enhancing co-operation in banking, financial and capital markets development, customs matters, insurance matters, taxation and public finance matters, monetary policy co-operation, and human resource development in the area of finance. In addition, the ASEAN Agreement on Customs will enhance ASEAN co-operation in customs activities and will help facilitate greater intra-regional trade and investment flow. Concomitantly, these two finance agreements will help ASEAN expedite its integration process and support the early realization of the various existing regional arrangements such as AFTA, AIA, and AICO.

VI. Food, Agriculture, and Forestry

In the area of food security, with Laos and Myanmar becoming members of ASEAN, the total earmarked quantity for the ASEAN Emergency Rice Reserve (AERR) now stands at 84,000 metric tons. In the area of food handling, member countries have finalized the General ASEAN Guidelines on the Preparation and Handling of Halal Food for endorsement by the 19th Meeting of the ASEAN Ministers of Agriculture and Forestry (AMAF) in Bangkok on 11–12 September 1997. A project on "Quality Assurance Systems for ASEAN Fruits Fresh and Minimally Processed" and a seminar on food irradiation technology were also organized.

In the area of agriculture, activities pursued included a model system for the harmonization of phytosanitary measures for rice and mango and establishing harmonized maximum residue levels (MRLs) of pesticides in vegetables. A project on strengthening technical co-operation in corn and soybean production was also implemented.

For the livestock sector, member countries are in the process of drafting the criteria for accreditation of livestock establishments and the criteria for accreditation of livestock products establishments in an effort to enhance international trade in livestock and livestock products.

In the fisheries sector, the Manual on Good Shrimp Farm Management Practices has been completed and will be published by the ASEAN Secretariat. The ASEAN Network of Fisheries Post-Harvest Technology Centres Electronic Information System will be maintained to serve as a linkage between fisheries post-harvest technology centres in the region.

In agricultural training and extension, the co-operation activities under the project on Promotion and Intensification of Application of Integrated Pest Management (IPM) in Fruits and Vegetables are proceeding as planned. The IPM Training Programme in Vegetables has been developed and a regional training has been planned for the fourth quarter of this year in Indonesia. To further strengthen regional co-operation in this area, member countries are planning to establish an ASEAN IPM Knowledge Network.

Regional co-operation in the forestry sector has also taken an expanded dimension. In the implementation of United Nations Conference on Environment and Development (UNCED) Decisions on Forestry and Attainment of International Tropical Timber Organization (ITTO) Objective Year 2000, member countries have agreed to establish the Regional Criteria and Indicators (C&I) for Sustainable Forest Management (SFM).

Co-operation has extended to trade of agricultural and forest products. A total of 1,385 unprocessed agricultural products (UAP) have been included in the CEPT scheme for AFTA, while 377 are in the Temporary Exclusion List and 287 in the Sensitive List. At the same time trade strategies for most of the eleven commodities that have been identified for promotion under the ASEAN Co-operation and Joint Approaches in Agriculture and Forest Products Promotion Scheme, namely, carrageenan, cocoa and cocoa products, frozen chicken, frozen shrimps, canned tuna, canned pineapples, tapioca, and forest products, continued to be discussed by the respective National Focal Points Working Groups and Industry Clubs.

In considering ASEAN co-operation and joint approaches in international issues, member countries have also identified new tariff and non-tariff barriers imposed by some of ASEAN's trading partners which affect trade of ASEAN products, especially frozen chicken meat, frozen shrimp, and canned tuna. In addition, there are also other environmental issues relating to ASEAN's agriculture and forestry in general.

VII. Transport and Communications

ASEAN member countries are implementing the ASEAN Plan of Action in Transport and Communications through the Integrated Implementation Programme, involving forty-five projects and activities in the following co-operative areas: multimodal transport; interconnectivity in telecommunications; harmonization of road transport laws, rules, and regulations; airspace management; maritime safety and pollution; human resources; and air services liberalization. Feasibility study for the Singapore-Kunming (China) Rail Link Project and the development of the ASEAN Framework Agreement on the Facilitation of Goods in Transit will also be undertaken. Future collaborative efforts to keep pace with the increasing demand for improved infrastructure and communications will be towards the development of an integrated and harmonized trans-ASEAN transportation network and the harnessing of technology advances in telecommunications and information technology especially in linking the information highways/multimedia corridors in ASEAN, promoting open sky policy, developing multimodal transport, facilitating goods in transit, developing regional shipping policy, and integrating further telecommunications networks.

VIII. Energy

In line with the Agreement on ASEAN Energy Co-operation of 1986, the Medium-Term Programme of Action on Energy Co-operation (1995–99) is vigorously implemented in the following sectors: electricity, oil and gas, coal, new and renewable sources of energy, energy efficiency and conservation, energy and environment, and energy policy and planning. An ASEAN emergency petroleum sharing scheme is likewise in place. Co-operative efforts will focus on the realization of regional interconnecting arrangements for electricity and natural gas, through the ASEAN Power Grid and Trans-ASEAN Gas Pipeline

Projects. The ASEAN-EC Energy Management Training and Research Centre (AEEMTRC) will be eventually transformed into the ASEAN Energy Centre.

IX. Tourism

ASEAN co-operation in tourism will develop and promote ASEAN as a single tourism destination product with world-class attractions, standards and facilities, achieve facilitation of intra-ASEAN travel and freer trade in tourism services, and promote sustainable tourism development. Joint efforts of member countries will entail policy co-ordination and/or harmonization in areas such as investment policy, tourism development planning, human resources, and environmental and cultural preservation. The tourism ministers will henceforth convene formal meetings to pave the way for developing co-ordinated and concrete strategies for tourism development and co-operation in ASEAN. The formation of the ASEAN Crises Team for Tourism (ACTT) has also been launched by the ASEAN National Tourism Organizations (NTOs).

X. Minerals

The first ASEAN Senior Officials Meeting on Minerals (ASOMM) was held on 22–24 October 1996 in Bali. ASOMM has agreed to implement the three activities identified in the Programme of Action on Minerals Co-operation:

1. the development of a database on mineral resources, supply, demand, and trade of ASEAN member countries;
2. the exchange of information on minerals and environmental legislation;
3. the establishment of a directory of research and development (R&D) training facilities, expertise, and investment opportunities in ASEAN member countries.

XI. Intellectual Property

A Working Group on Intellectual Property Co-operation (WGIPC) has been established to implement the ASEAN Framework Agreement on

Intellectual Property Co-operation and to serve as a forum for regular consultations to monitor regional and international developments on intellectual property. For the period under review, the WGIPC met four times. The Working Group has formulated its Programme of Action (1996–98) to implement the activities contained in the Framework Agreement.

Among the activities agreed to in the Programme were measures to enhance and strengthen intellectual property enforcement, protection, administration, legislation, and activities to promote public awareness, as well as private sector participation. Recognizing the different degrees of intellectual property rights (IPRs) development in ASEAN, the member countries agreed that the programme to explore the possibility of the setting up of an ASEAN Patent and Trademark System will be a long-term objective and that it can extend beyond 1998. The participation of member countries in this programme is on a voluntary basis.

XII. Small and Medium Enterprises

In line with the ASEAN Plan of Action for SME Co-operation, ASEAN implemented and formulated several projects to assist SMEs in the region. The ASEAN-EU Partenariat Project jointly financed by ASEAN and the EU will focus on matching the SME companies of the two regions. The Partenariat is scheduled to be held in Singapore in November 1997. A training programme for ASEAN SME entrepreneurs was conducted in the Philippines in July 1997. This project is funded by the UNDP ASP-5 Programme. There are also several SME-related projects proposed under the ASEAN-Korea Dialogue. Another SME project scheduled for implementation is the ASEAN Small and Medium Industries Business Forum which will be held in Kuala Lumpur in August 1997. The Partenariat and the SMI Business Forum are oriented towards the promotion of joint ventures/investment rather than the traditional self-improvement activities for SMEs.

XIII. Private Sector Participation

The ASEAN-CCI representation during the SEOM and AEM meetings has been extended to the working group level. The ASEAN-CCI is invited to all meetings of the SEOM and WGIC. Whenever necessary, ASEAN-CCI has also been invited to the AEM. The Permanent ASEAN-CCI Secretariat has been established at the premises of the ASEAN Secretariat in Jakarta. It was officially inaugurated on 9 April 1996 during the 50th ASEAN-CCI Council Meeting. The First ASEAN Business Summit held in Jakarta in March 1997 was organized by the ASEAN-CCI and drew some 600 participants from all over the world.

XIV. ASEAN-Mekong Basin

The ASEAN-Mekong Basin Development Co-operation (AMBDC) initiative was discussed and agreed upon at the Fifth ASEAN Summit in Bangkok in 1995. Malaysia chaired the Ministerial Meeting on AMBDC in Kuala Lumpur on 17 June 1997. The Meeting adopted the Basic Framework of the AMBDC, which aims to support and complement national development plans of countries in the Mekong Basin and mobilize the participation of the private sector in the implementation of projects and activities deemed to be of paramount importance.

Two working groups were formed. The Working Group on Rail Link met on 2–3 December 1996 to discuss the proposed Trans-Asia Rail Link to connect Kunming in China with Singapore. Malaysia pledged RM2 million for the feasibility study for which consultants have been appointed. The Working Group on Finance at its meeting on 11–12 November 1996 suggested that ASEAN could set up an ASEAN-Mekong Feasibility Study fund and two possible mechanisms for managing the fund:

1. multilaterally through the ASEAN Secretariat or other appropriate bodies;
2. nationally or through the national window.

XV. Regional Linkages

At the second AEM-CER Consultation held on 13 September 1996 in Jakarta, the AEM and CER ministers signed a Memorandum of Understanding to further enhance regional co-operation in the area of standards and conformance. The AEM has also sought to develop linkages with other regional groupings such as the North American Free Trade Agreement (NAFTA), the Mercado Comun del Sur (MERCOSUR), the

European Free Trade Association (EFTA), and the Southern African Development Community (SADC). The AEM met with NAFTA ministers on 23 November 1996 in Manila, and with ministers from the MERCOSUR, SADC, and EFTA countries during the World Trade Organization Ministerial Conference in Singapore. During the consultations with EFTA, MERCOSUR, and SADC in Singapore, the ministers agreed on the need to promote greater trade and investment flows to exchange views on international trade issues and to bring the private sectors of ASEAN and the other regional groupings together.

In view of the above developments, ASEAN is poised to deepen and widen its economic co-operation in the coming decade and ultimately realize its objective of becoming one of the world's most competitive regions.

Appendix A: Basic Data

Table A1
Mid-Year Population, 1994
(Million)

Country	Population
Brunei	0.3
Indonesia	193.7
Malaysia	19.5
Philippines	67.1
Singapore	2.9
Thailand	59.1
Vietnam	72.5

Source: Asian Development Bank.

Table A2
Annual Growth Rates of Gross Domestic Product, 1985–89
(Percentages)

Country	Base Year	Average, 1971–80	Average, 1981–90	1988	1989	1990	1991	1992	1993	1994
Brunei		n.a.	n.a.	n.a.	n.a.	n.a.	4	–1.1	0.5	1.8
Singapore	1985	7.9	6.3	11.1	9.2	8.8	6.7	6.0	9.9	10.0
Indonesia	1983	7.7	5.5	5.8	7.5	7.2	7.0	6.5	6.5	6.9
Malaysia	1978	7.8	5.2	8.9	9.2	9.7	8.7	7.8	8.3	8.5
Philippines	1985	6.0	1.0	6.3	6.1	2.7	–0.4	0.6	2.1	4.3
Thailand	1988	7.9	7.9	13.3	12.2	11.6	8.4	7.9	8.2	8.5
Vietnam	1989	n.a.	7.1	5.0	7.8	4.9	6.0	8.6	8.1	8.8

n.a. = Not available.

Source: Asian Development Bank.

Table A3
Annual Changes in Consumer Prices, 1971–94
(Percentages)

Country	Average, 1971–80	Average, 1981–90	1988	1989	1990	1991	1992	1993	1994
Brunei	n.a.	n.a.	n.a.	n.a.	2	1.8	2	2.1	4
Singapore	7.4	2.5	1.5	2.4	3.4	3.4	2.3	2.4	3.8
Indonesia	17.5	8.5	8.0	6.4	7.8	9.4	7.6	9.2	9.2
Malaysia	6.0	3.6	2.6	2.7	2.7	4.4	4.7	3.6	3.8
Philippines	14.8	13.4	8.7	12.2	14.2	18.7	8.9	7.6	9.0
Thailand	10.0	4.4	3.8	5.4	5.9	5.7	4.2	3.5	5.0
Vietnam	n.a.	194.6	310.9	95.8	36.4	83.1	37.6	8.5	9.9

n.a. = Not available.

Source: Asian Development Bank.

Table A4
Merchandise Exports, 1988–94
(US$ million, f.o.b.)

Country	1988	1989	1990	1991	1992	1993	1994
Singapore	37,993.0	43,572.0	51,095.0	57,156.0	62,068.0	71,959.0	89,229.2
Indonesia	19,509.0	22,974.0	26,807.0	29,635.0	33,796.0	36,607.0	39,497.0
Malaysia	20,852.0	24,633.0	28,636.0	33,534.0	39,613.0	45,912.0	57,035.6
Philippines	7,074.0	7,821.0	8,186.0	8,840.0	9,824.0	11,375.0	13,423.0
Thailand	15,781.1	19,834.0	22,811.0	28,232.0	32,100.0	36,410.0	42,792.7
Vietnam	1,038.4	1,320.0	1,731.0	2,042.0	2,475.0	2,850.0	3,437.1

Source: Asian Development Bank.

Table A5
Merchandise Imports, 1988–94
(US$ million, f.o.b.)

Country	1988	1989	1990	1991	1992	1993	1994
Singapore	–40,338	–45,687	–55,812	–60,948	–67,850	–80,025	–99,231
Indonesia	–13,831	–16,310	–21,455	–24,834	–26,774	–28,376	–31,654
Malaysia	–15,306	–20,251	–26,014	–33,007	–36,238	–42,503	–57,798
Philippines	–8,159	–10,419	–12,206	–12,051	–14,519	–17,597	–21,644
Thailand	–17,856	–22,750	–29,561	–34,222	–36,261	–40,556	–47,195
Vietnam	–2,619	–1,670	–1,772	–2,105	–2,535	–3,505	–4,020

Source: Asian Development Bank.

Table A6
Annual Growth Rates of Value-Added in Agriculture, 1971–94
(Percentages)

Country	Average, 1971–80	Average, 1981–90	1988	1989	1990	1991	1992	1993	1994
Singapore	1.1	–6.8	–12.2	–6.9	–7.6	–9.4	1.1	0.1	0.2
Indonesia	3.6	3.2	4.9	3.3	2.0	1.6	6.6	1.4	1.6
Malaysia	4.9	3.9	5.4	6.0	0.4	0.0	4.3	3.9	0.5
Philippines	3.9	1.1	3.2	3.0	0.5	1.4	0.4	2.1	2.4
Thailand	3.1	3.9	10.5	9.6	–3.7	5.9	4.2	–1.7	2.9
Vietnam	n.a.	5.3	4.0	6.9	1.5	2.2	7.2	3.8	3.6

n.a. = Not available.

Source: Asian Development Bank.

Table A7
Annual Growth Rates of Value-Added in Industry, 1971–94
(Percentages)

Country	Average, 1971–80	Average, 1981–90	1988	1989	1990	1991	1992	1993	1994
Singapore	8.1	5.2	13.2	8.3	9.1	7.8	5.4	9.3	12.8
Indonesia	11.3	5.9	5.2	7.8	9.9	10.4	5.6	7.3	9.5
Malaysia	9.6	7.4	12.7	12.4	13.2	11.2	8.9	10.0	11.4
Philippines	8.2	–0.8	7.6	8.2	2.6	–3.6	–0.5	1.6	6.1
Thailand	12.1	10.4	16.4	17.5	16.3	12.5	10.0	10.8	12.0
Vietnam	n.a.	6.5	2.3	–4.6	1.1	8.3	13.5	12.8	13.6

n.a. = Not available.

Source: Asian Development Bank.

Table A8
Share of Industry in Value-Added, 1970–95

Year	Singapore	Indonesia	Malaysia	Philippines	Thailand	Vietnam
1970	36.4	28.0	n.a.	33.7	25.7	n.a.
1980	38.8	41.3	35.8	40.5	30.1	26.3
1995	37.6	43.4	46.3	35.5	43.5	25.3

n.a. = Not available.

Source: Asian Development Bank.

Table A9
ASEAN Exports to Dialogue Partners, 1989–93
(Million US$)

Country	1989	1990	1991	1992	1993
Australia	2,767	2,706	3,305	3,627	3,726
Canada	1,118	1,248	1,435	1,712	1,961
European Union	17,377	21,495	24,922	28,818	31,138
Japan	23,194	26,921	29,807	29,651	32,233
Korea	3,734	4,794	5,796	5,771	6,553
New Zealand	316	398	324	592	566
United States	25,977	27,986	30,236	36,583	42,241

Source of basic data: International Monetary Fund, *Direction of Trade Statistics*.

Table A10
ASEAN Imports from Dialogue Partners, 1989–93
(Million US$)

Country	1989	1990	1991	1992	1993
Australia	3,565	4,398	4,906	5,050	5,644
Canada	1,318	1,611	1,589	1,658	1,537
European Union	16,931	22,821	24,759	27,738	30,181
Japan	29,918	37,460	43,754	46,762	55,650
Korea	3,816	5,061	6,639	7,726	9,009
New Zealand	570	658	685	819	845
United States	19,624	23,556	26,275	29,935	34,394

Source of basic data: International Monetary Fund, *Direction of Trade Statistics*.

Table A11
Growth Rates of ASEAN's Total Trade with Dialogue Partners, 1990–93
(Percentages)

Country	1990	1991	1992	1993
Australia	12.19	15.58	5.68	7.99
Canada	17.36	5.77	11.44	3.8
European Union	29.17	12.11	13.84	8.42
Japan	21.22	14.25	3.88	15.01
Korea	30.53	26.18	8.54	15.3
New Zealand	19.19	–4.45	39.84	0
United States	13.03	9.64	17.71	15.21

Source of basic data: International Monetary Fund, *Direction of Trade Statistics*.

Appendix B: Abbreviations

AAA	ASEAN International Airports Association
AABC	ASEAN-Australia Business Council
AAECP	ASEAN-Australia Economic Co-operation Programme
ABA	ASEAN Bankers Association
ABC	ASEAN Banking Council
ACBC	ASEAN-Canada Business Council
ACCSQ	ASEAN Consultative Committee for Standards and Quality
ACTS	ASEAN Cargo Transport Study
ACTT	ASEAN Crises Team for Tourism
ADB	Asian Development Bank
AEEMTRC	ASEAN-EC Energy Management Training and Research Centre

AEM	ASEAN Economic Ministers
AEM-MITI	AEM-Ministry of International Trade and Industry (Japan)
AEMEC	ASEAN Economic Ministers on Energy Co-operation
AEMM	ASEAN-EC/EU Ministerial Meeting
AERR	ASEAN Emergency Rice Reserve
AFC	ASEAN Finance Corporation
AFF	ASEAN Fisheries Federation
AFHB	ASEAN Food Handling Bureau
AFSRB	ASEAN Food Security Reserve Board
AFTA	ASEAN Free Trade Area
AIA	ASEAN Investment Area
AIBC	ASEAN-India Business Council
AIC	ASEAN Industrial Complementation
AICO	ASEAN Industrial Co-operation (scheme)
AIFM	ASEAN Institute of Forest Management
AIJSCC	ASEAN-India Joint Sectoral Co-operation Committee
AIJV	ASEAN Industrial Joint Venture
AIP	ASEAN Industrial Projects
AJBC	ASEAN-Japan Business Council
AMAF	ASEAN Ministers of Agriculture and Forestry
AMBDC	ASEAN-Mekong Basin Development Co-operation
AMG	Alliance for Mutual Growth
AMM	ASEAN Ministerial Meeting
ANZBC	ASEAN–New Zealand Business Council
ANZCER	Australia–New Zealand Closer Economic Relations
ANZCERTA	Australia–New Zealand Closer Economic Relations Trade Agreement
ANZECP	ASEAN–New Zealand Economic Co-operation Programme
ANZUK	Australia–New Zealand–United Kingdom
APAA	ASEAN Ports Authorities Association
APEC	Asia-Pacific Economic Co-operation
ASA	Association of Southeast Asia
ASC	ASEAN Standing Committee

ASCOPE	ASEAN Council on Petroleum
ASEAN	Association of Southeast Asian Nations
ASEAN-CCI	ASEAN Chambers of Commerce and Industry
ASOMM	ASEAN Senior Officials Meeting on Minerals
ASPAC	Asian and Pacific Council
BBC	Brand-to-Brand Complementation
BEC	Bureau of Economic Co-operation
C&I	Criteria and Indicators
CCS	Co-ordinating Committee on Services
CEPT	Common Effective Preferential Tariff
CITES	Convention on International Trade in Endangered Species
COFAB	Committee on Finance and Banking
COFAF	Committee on Food, Agriculture, and Forestry
COIME	Committee on Industry, Minerals, and Energy
COTT	Committee on Trade and Tourism
EAEC	East Asia Economic Caucus
EAGA	East ASEAN Growth Area
EC	European Community
ECO	Economic Co-operation Organization
EEZ(s)	Exclusive Economic Zone(s)
EFTA	European Free Trade Association
EIP	Environmental Improvement Project
EMS	Express Mail Service
EU	European Union
FASA	Federation of ASEAN Shipowners' Association
FASC	Federation of ASEAN Shippers' Council
FDI	foreign direct investment
G-14	Group of Fourteen
GATS	General Agreement on Trade in Services
GATT	General Agreement on Tariffs and Trade
GDP	gross domestic product
GNP	gross national product
GPT	General Preferential Tariff
GSP	Generalized System of Preferences
HRD	human resource development
HS	Harmonized System

ICP	Inter-Country Programme
IMT-GT	Indonesia-Malaysia-Thailand-Growth Triangle
IPM	Integrated Pest Management
IPR(s)	intellectual property right(s)
ISO	International Standardization Organization
ISQAP	Industrial Standards and Quality Assurance Programme
ITEC	India Technical and Economic Co-operation
ITTO	International Tropical Timber Organization
JCC	Joint Co-operation Committee
JMC	Joint Management Committee
JMM	Joint Ministerial Meeting
MAPHILINDO	Malaysia, Philippines, and Indonesia
MERCOSUR	Mercado Comun del Sur
MITI	Ministry of International Trade and Industry
MNC(s)	multinational corporation(s)
MOP(s)	Margin of Preference/Margins of Preferences
MOU	Memorandum of Understanding
MRL(s)	maximum residue level(s)
MU	Ministerial Understanding
NAFTA	North American Free Trade Agreement
NCC(s)	national commodity club(s)
NGO(s)	non-governmental organization(s)
NIC(s)	national industry club(s)
NIEs	newly industrializing economies
NRSE	New and Renewable Sources of Energy
NTO(s)	National Tourism Organization(s)
PITO	Private Investment and Trade Opportunities
PMC(s)	Post-Ministerial Conference(s)
PTA	Preferential Trading Arrangement
RCC(s)	Regional Commodity Club(s)
RICs(s)	Regional Industry Club(s)
SAARC	South Asian Association for Regional Co-operation
SADC	Southern African Development Community
SEATO	Southeast Asia Treaty Organization
SEOM	Senior Economic Officials Meeting
SFM	Sustainable Forest Management

SIJORI	Singapore-Johor-Riau
SME(s)	small and medium enterprise(s)
SOM	Senior Officials Meeting
TBT(s)	technical barrier(s) to trade
TICC	Trade-Investment Co-operation Committee
TIPP	Trade and Investment Promotion Programme
TRIMS	trade-related investment measures
TRIPS	trade-related aspects of intellectual property
TWGs	technical working groups
UAP	unprocessed agricultural products
UNCED	United Nations Conference on Environment and Development
UNCTAD	United Nations Conference on Trade and Development
UNDP	United Nations Development Programme
WGIPC	Working Group on Intellectual Property Co-operation
WIPO	World Intellectual Property Organization
WTO	World Trade Organization
ZOPFAN	Zone of Peace, Freedom, and Neutrality in Southeast Asia

Appendix C: ASEAN-Affiliated Non-Governmental Organizations, by Sector

A. Finance, Trade, and Industry Group

ASEAN Banking Council (ABC)
ASEAN Chambers of Commerce and Industry (ASEAN-CCI)
ASEAN Confederation of Employers (ACE)
ASEAN Constructors Federation (ACF)
ASEAN Federation of Accountants (AFA)
ASEAN Federation of Forwarders Association (AFFA)
ASEAN Fisheries Federation (AFF)
ASEAN Federation of Furniture Manufacturers Association (AFFMA)
ASEAN Handicraft Promotion and Development Association (AHPADA)
ASEAN Insurance Council (AIC)
ASEAN Music Industry Association (AMIA)

ASEAN Vegetable Oils Club (AVOC)
Federation of ASEAN Shipowners Association (FASA)

B. Engineering Group

ASEAN Federation of Electrical Engineering Contractors (AFFEC)
ASEAN Federation of Engineering Organization (AFEO)
ASEAN Federation of Mining Association (AFMA)
Federation of ASEAN Consulting Engineers (FACE)
Southeast Asia Association of Seismology and Earthquake Engineering (SEASEE)

C. Medical Group

ASEAN Association of Medical Laboratory Technologists (AAMLT)
ASEAN Association of Radiology (AAR)
ASEAN Federation for Psychiatric and Mental Health (AFPMH)
ASEAN Neurosurgical Society (ANS)
ASEAN Orthopaedic Association (AOA)
ASEAN Paediatric Federation (APF)
Medical Association of Southeast Asian Nations (MASEAN)
Rheumatism Association of ASEAN (RAA)

D. Services Group

ASEAN Association for Planning and Housing (AAPH)
ASEAN Association of Maritime Education and Training Institutions (AAMETI)
ASEAN Law Association (ALA)
ASEAN Law Students Association (ALSA)
ASEAN Port Authorities Association (APAA)
ASEAN Valuers Association (AVA)
Federation of ASEAN Economic Association (FAEA)
Federation of ASEAN Public Relations Organization (FAPRO)
Veterans Confederation of ASEAN Countries (VECONAC)

E. Youth, Sports, and Co-operative Group

ASEAN Confederation of Women Organization (ACWO)
ASEAN Co-operative Organization (ACO)

ASEAN Council of Teachers (ACT)
ASEAN Football Federation (AFF)
ASEAN NGOs for the Prevention of Drug and Substance Abuse
ASEAN University Sports Council (AUSC)
Committee for ASEAN Youth Co-operation (CAYC)

Appendix D: Current Publications by the ASEAN Secretariat

27th Meeting of the ASEAN Economic Ministers, 7–9 September 1995, Bandar Seri Begawan: A compilation of speeches and joint press statements of meetings and sessions.

28th ASEAN Ministerial Meeting and Post Ministerial Conferences with Dialogue Partners, and Second ASEAN Regional Forum, 29 July to 3 August 1995, Bandar Seri Begawan: A compilation of statements, speeches, and joint communiqués of meetings and sessions.

AFTA Reader Volume I: A specialized publication on latest developments on AFTA. The first issue of the publication provides answers to basic questions on the CEPT for AFTA and the Products and Programmes of Tariff Reduction under the CEPT scheme. It also includes the basic documents, CEPT Agreement, the Interpretative Notes, the Operational Procedures, and the Rules of Origin.

AFTA Reader Volume II: The second issue of this specialized publication on latest developments on AFTA focuses on more detailed analysis of the CEPT Product Lists and the trade values involved in the CEPT products.

AFTA Reader Volume III: A specialized publication on latest developments on AFTA. The third volume of the publication focuses on the decision of the 26th ASEAN Economic Ministers (AEM) Meeting held in September 1994 in Thailand, namely, the new time frame in the acceleration of tariff reduction. It also includes among others: harmonization of tariff nomenclature, customs valuation and procedures, and co-operation in services.

Annual Report of the 1994/1995 ASEAN Standing Committee: Progress report on political and security co-operation, economic co-operation, functional co-operation, and external relations.

ASEAN Economic Info View, vol. 2, no. 3/4, September/December 1995: A quarterly publication that provides an update on the implementation and developments of AFTA as well as other economic activities.

ASEAN Macroeconomic Outlook 1995: This is the second publication arising from the ASEAN Macroeconomic Outlook project of the ASEAN Secretariat. The publication presents results of the country researchers' discussions on their individual country predictions for 1995–96, which turn out to be both insightful and provoking. Tables and figures augment the text.

ASEAN Plan of Action on Culture and Information, October 1994: This publication provides background and basic information concerning the ASEAN Plan of Action on Culture and Information for the period 1994–97. It includes the Joint Declaration of the Third Conference of the ASEAN Ministers Responsible for Information, Global Thrusts and Priorities of COCI for 1994–97.

ASEAN Plan of Action on Drug Abuse Control, January 1995: This publication provides background and basic information concerning the ASEAN Three-Year Plan of Action on Drug Abuse Control. It also includes the ASEAN Declaration of Principles to Combat the Abuse of Narcotic Drugs of 1976, the ASEAN Foreign Ministers Joint Statement on the International Problem of Drug Abuse and Trafficking of 1985.

ASEAN Plan of Action on Science and Technology, July 1994: This publication provides information on the updated 1994 ASEAN Plan of Action on Science and Technology, which represents the strategic blueprint for the implementation of ASEAN Science and Technology co-operative programmes that will support national and regional economic and social development initiatives into the next century.

ASEAN Plan of Action on Social Development, April 1995: This publication provides background and basic information concerning the ASEAN Plan ofaction on Social Development for the period 1994–98. Included in the publication are the related ASEAN Documents on Social Development.

ASEAN Regional Programme on HIV/AIDS Prevention and Control 1995–2000: This publication contains the ASEAN Regional Programme on AIDS Prevention and Control as adopted by the ASEAN Task Force on AIDS, Committee on Social Development, and ASEAN Standing Committee.

ASEAN Strategic Plan of Action on the Environment, July 1994: This publication provides information on ASEAN Strategic Plan of Action on the Environment, 1994–98, including Ministerial Resolutions, Post–UNCED issues, that is, ASEAN's priorities and responses, ASEAN harmonized environmental quality standards.

ASEAN University Networking: This publication contains the Charter and Agreement on the Establishment of ASEAN University Network Study, as approved by the relevant bodies.

ASEAN Update, January/February 1996: A bimonthly publication reporting on current activities of ASEAN. The January/February 1996 issue focuses on the 5th ASEAN Summit, Bangkok, 14–15 December 1995 and its major decisions.

ASEAN Update, May/June 1996: The ASEAN Update is a bimonthly publication which reports on current activities of ASEAN. The May/June 1996 issue focuses on the 29th ASEAN Ministerial Meeting and Post Ministerial Conferences with Dialogue Partners (AMM/PMC) 20–25 July 1996.

ASEAN Workshops Report: Trade and the Environment: Issues and Opportunities: A publication which summarizes the reports of the ASEAN workshops on trade and the environment held in May 1995 in Manila, Bangkok, Kuala Lumpur, and Jakarta.

ASEAN: An Overview, 1995: This publication covers general information on ASEAN, including the history and background of the Association, the organizational structure, political and security, economic, and functional co-operation as well as external relations, country profiles, and important basic documents.

ASEAN: From Strength to Strength: A publication concerning the review of all areas of the ASEAN functional co-operation reviewed in the past twenty-five years. It also indicates some of the possible future directions and thrusts of ASEAN functional co-operation.

CEPT Product List (supplemented with "Index of CEPT Products at HS4-Digit level"): A compilation of CEPT Product Lists and their tariff reduction schedules approved by the AFTA Council in October 1993.

Co-operation Plan on Transboundary Pollution: This publication contains the ASEAN Co-operation Plan on Transboundary Pollution as adopted by the ASEAN Ministers on the Environment during the Informal Ministerial Meeting held in Kuching, Malaysia, 21 October 1994.

Fifth ASEAN Summit: This is a compilation of statements, speeches of meetings and sessions. This also includes the Bangkok Declaration of 1995 and nine other important ASEAN Documents signed during the Summit meeting.

Handbook on ASEAN Protocol and Practices: The handbook is a reference guide on the preparations and arrangements for ASEAN meetings. It provides information on the current protocol and physical arrangements practised by the various ASEAN bodies such as the ASEAN Summit, ASEAN Ministerial Meetings, the ASEAN Standing Committee, the ASEAN Senior Officials' Meeting, ASEAN Sub-Committees, and Working Groups.

Medium-Term Programme for ASEAN Science and Technology Development (1996–2000): A publication intended to increase the focus on programmes that promote technology transfer and comercialization, networking of centres of excellence, and science and technology awareness.

Medium-Term Programme on Drug Abuse Control (1996–98): Work Programme to Operationalize the ASEAN Three-Year Plan of Action on Drug Abuse Control: This publication contains the ASEAN Regional Programme on AIDS Prevention and Control as adopted by the Task Force on AIDS, COSD, and ASC.

Appendix E: References

1995 Report on the APEC Regional Economy. Singapore: Asia Pacific Economic Co-operation Secretariat.

Abonyi, George. "Growth Triangles in Southeast Asia: Strategies for Development". Paper presented at the Fourth Southeast Asia Roundtable on Economic Co-operation, 27–28 June 1994, Kuala Lumpur.

Alburo, Florian A. "The ASEAN Summit and ASEAN Economic Co-operation". In *Economic Development in East and Southeast Asia: Essays in Honor of Professor Shinichi Ichimura*, edited by S. Naya and A. Takayama, pp. 299–306. Singapore: Institute of Southeast Asian Studies, and Honolulu: East-West Center, 1990.

Asian Development Bank (ADB). *Key Indicators of Developing Member Countries*. Manila, various years.

Buszynski, Leszck. "Trends, Developments and Challenges in Southeast Asia". In *Southeast Asian Affairs 1996*. Singapore: Institute of Southeast Asian Studies, 1996.

Cabanilla, L.S. "ASEAN Cooperation in Food, Agriculture, and Forestry". First published 1988. Reprinted in abridged form in *The ASEAN Reader*, compiled by K.S. Sandhu et al., pp. 254–59. Singapore: Institute of Southeast Asian Studies, 1992.

Chee Peng Lim. "Small Enterprises in ASEAN: Need for Regional Cooperation". *ASEAN Economic Bulletin* 1, no. 2 (November 1984): 89–114.

Chee Peng Lim and Jang-Won Suh. "ASEAN Industrial Cooperation". First published 1988. Reprinted in *The ASEAN Reader*, compiled by K.S. Sandhu et al., pp. 242–47. Singapore: Institute of Southeast Asian Studies, 1992.

Chia Siow Yue, ed. *ASEAN Economic Cooperation*. Singapore: Institute of Southeast Asian Studies, 1980.

Chng Meng Kng. "ASEAN Economic Cooperation: The Current Status". In *Southeast Asian Affairs 1985*. Singapore: Institute of Southeast Asian Studies, 1985.

Drysdale, Peter and Ross Garnaut. "The Pacific: An Application of the General Theory of Economic Integration". In *Pacific Dynamism and the International Economic System*, edited by C.F. Bergsten and M. Noland. Washington, D.C.: Institute for International Economics, 1993.

Economic and Social Commission for Asia and the Pacific (ESCAP). *Statistical Yearbook for Asia and the Pacific*. Bangkok, Thailand: ESCAP, various years.

Hagiwara, Yoshiyuki. "The Formation of ASEAN". First published 1973. Reprinted in abridged form in *The ASEAN Reader*, compiled by K.S. Sandhu et al., pp. 35–37. Singapore: Institute of Southeast Asian Studies, 1992.

Hill, Hal. "Challenges in ASEAN Economic Cooperation: An Outsider's Perspective". In *ASEAN at the Crossroads: Obstacles, Options and Opportunities in Economic Co-operation*. Kuala Lumpur: Institute of Strategic and International Studies, 1987.

Imada, Pearl, Manuel Montes, and Seiji Naya. *A Free Trade Area: Implications forASEAN*. Singapore: Institute of Southeast Asian Studies, 1991.

Indorf, Hans. "ASEAN: Problems and Prospects". Occasional Paper no. 38. Singapore: Institute of Southeast Asian Studies, 1975.

Institute of Policy Studies and Institute of Southeast Asian Studies. "Resume of Major Themes of Discussion at the Joint IPS-ISEAS Roundtable on ASEAN Economic Cooperation in the 1990s, 27–28 June 1991, Singapore.

Institute of Southeast Asian Studies. *ASEAN: The Tasks Ahead*. Singapore, 1987.

International Monetary Fund (IMF). *Direction of Trade Statistics*. Washington, D.C., various years.

———. *International Financial Statistics*. Washington, D.C., various years.

Khaw Guat Hoon. "The Evolution of ASEAN, 1967–75". First published 1984. Reprinted in abridged form in *The ASEAN Reader*, compiled by K.S. Sandhu et al., pp. 38–42. Singapore: Institute of Southeast Asian Studies, 1992.

Lee Tsao Yuan, ed. *Growth Triangles: The Johor-Singapore-Riau Experience*. Singapore: Institute of Southeast Asian Studies, 1991.

Lyon, Peter. "Post-War Regional Co-operation". First published 1973. Reprinted in abridged form in *The ASEAN Reader*, compiled by K.S. Sandhu et al., pp. 25–26. Singapore: Institute of Southeast Asian Studies, 1992.

Naidu, G. "ASEAN Co-operation in Transport". First published 1988. Reprinted in abridged form in *The ASEAN Reader*, compiled by K.S. Sandhu et al., pp. 277–80. Singapore: Institute of Southeast Asian Studies, 1992.

Narongchai Akrasanee et al. *ASEAN and the Pacific Community*. Jakarta: Center for Strategic and International Studies, 1981.

Naya, Seiji. "Towards the Establishment of an ASEAN Trade Area". Report prepared for the ASEAN Committee on Trade and Tourism (COTT), East West Center, 1987.

Naya, Seiji and Michael Plummer. "ASEAN Economic Co-operation in the New International Economic Environment". *ASEAN Economic Bulletin* 7, no. 3 (March 1991): 261–76.

Noordin Sopiee, Chew Lay See, and Lim Siang Jin, eds. *ASEAN at the Crossroads: Obstacles, Options and Opportunities in Economic Cooperation*. Kuala Lumpur: Institute of Strategic and International Studies, 1987.

Palmer, Norman D. "SEATO, ASA, Maphilindo and ASPAC". First published 1991. Reprinted in abridged form in *The ASEAN Reader*, compiled by K.S. Sandhu et al., pp. 27–29. Singapore: Institute of Southeast Asian Studies, 1992.

Pangestu, Mari, Hadi Soesastro and Mubariq Ahmad. "A New Look at Intra-ASEAN Economic Cooperation". *ASEAN Economic Bulletin* 8, no. 3 (March 1992): 333–52.

Rieger, Hans Christoph, comp. *ASEAN Economic Cooperation: A Handbook*. Singapore: Institute of Southeast Asian Studies, 1991.

Sandhu, Kernial S. et al., comps. *The ASEAN Reader*. Singapore: Institute of Southeast Asian Studies, 1992.

Tan, Gerald. *Trade Liberalization in ASEAN: An Empirical Study of the Preferential Trading Arrangements*. Singapore: Institute of Southeast Asian Studies, 1982.

Tan Ming Tang and Myo Thant. *Growth Triangles: Conceptual Issues and Operational Problems*. Manila: Asian Development Bank, 1994.

Teh, Robert, Jr. "ASEAN Cooperation in Services". Paper presented at the ASEAN Roundtable 1995, Singapore, 30–31 August 1995.

The Group of Fourteen of ASEAN-CCI. *ASEAN: The Way Forward.*

Kuala Lumpur: Institute of Strategic and International Studies, 1987.

United Nations. *Human Development Report, 1995*. New York: Oxford University Press.

Index